THE FENWAY PROJECT

June 28, 2002

A Project of the
Society for American Baseball Research
and SABR Boston

Edited by
Bill Nowlin
and
Cecilia Tan

Rounder Books
Cambridge, MA

The Fenway Project

First Printing March 2004

Designed by Cecilia Tan
Indexed by Bill Nowlin

CONTENTS

Photographs:

WHAT IS THE FENWAY PROJECT?

Bill Nowlin

Everyone who sees a ballgame inevitably sees it differently, because we each have our own unique experiences and perceptions. A baseball game as seen and reported by six hundred fans? That was the goal of The Fenway Project. Maybe six hundred was a little extravagant. We do have contributions by more than fifty fans, though, and The Fenway Project presents the most mutlifaceted view of a single baseball game ever published.

The direct inspiration for the Project was a publication put together by San Diego's Ted Williams chapter of SABR (the Society for American Baseball Research.) The January 1999 publication was entitled Facets of the Diamond. Eight chapter members attended the May 13, 1998 baseball game between the San Diego Padres and the New York Mets (final score: Mets 4, Padres 3.) They all sat together but, being distinct individuals, each viewed the game from different angles.

Facets of the Diamond was the brain child of Tom Larwin and Andy Strasberg. Their report was created with offerings and appreciations by: Dan Boyle, Bob Boynton, Tom Larwin, Frank Myers, Anna Newton, Ron Roberts, Andy Strasberg, G. Jay Walker and editor Carlos Bauer.

I read about Facets of the Diamond in a SABR newsletter and purchased a copy. One hundred copies were produced, and it came nicely presented with spiral binding. I really enjoyed their report. Andy was a Padres employee at the time and they were thus able to include even photocopies of the "incident reports" on individuals detained by Padres security during the course of the game. Of course, most authors focused on the game. I thought it would be wonderful to attempt a similar look at a ballgame in Boston—Facets of Fenway? And then an idea struck me.

I was actively involved with the local Greater Boston

chapter of SABR in hosting SABR's 32nd annual convention in Boston in late June 2002. On Friday evening June 28, 2002 some six hundred members of SABR attended the scheduled Red Sox-Atlanta Braves game at Boston's Fenway Park as a highlight of the Boston convention. What an opportunity—maybe we could develop a report on a ballgame as written by hundreds of people, all offering their own perspectives.

Building on *Facets of the Diamond*, we have in *The Fenway Project* an excellent example of one research idea fostering another. The local Boston chapter liked the idea, and the project was added to the list of convention activities. Each and every member of SABR was encouraged to attend the game—with scorecard, notebook and perhaps cassette recorder at the ready. They were encouraged to enjoy the game, yes, and share with us their thoughts and observations on the game. We never thought that all six hundred people would contribute. We're gratified at how many people did offer their thoughts, 64 in total.

To keep the book of manageable size, there are elements we did not include, such as transcripts of the five radio and television broadcasts (Boston radio and TV, Atlanta radio and TV, and the Spanish language broadcast of the Boston-based *Spanish Beisbol Network*.) In the latter case, though, we did benefit from Anthony Salazar's presence in the broadcast booth observing the Spanish language broadcasters call the game.

Because we wanted to provide as many perspectives as possible, I asked several SABR members to cover certain areas. In addition to Anthony, there were several volunteers who contributed key pieces. The Boston Red Sox supplied special credentials for these volunteers. Co-editor Cecilia Tan covered the press box, watching the working press at work. My frequent co-author Jim Prime visited the Red Sox locker room before and after the game, including the postgame press conference. I'd met Stew Thornley on a baseball tour of Cuba; Stew's beat was the Braves clubhouse. While in Cuba, Eric Enders and I both visited inside the manual scoreboard during a game at Estadio Capitan San Luis in Pinar del Rio, so Eric was the logical choice to observe from the

very special vantage point inside Fenway's old manual scoreboard. F. X. Flinn worked where the computers are, noting how the electronic message board and other communications tools help present the ball game to the 33,137 officially in attendance during the three hour and ten minute long game.

For some, it was their first visit to Fenway Park. We have the perspective of a grandmother and seven-year-old Ryan Saccoman. There were those who were unable to attend the convention in Boston, so they followed the game in other ways. Some listened to the radio in Atlanta. Others watched it on TV. Ken Carpenter and Zack Triscuit followed the game via the Internet. There was even Denis Repp who went to Fenway Park—but never entered. He watched the game in barrooms around Fenway, moving from one locale to another as the game progressed.

THE JUNE 28TH GAME

It matched up as a very important contest near the midpoint of the 2002 season. The host team Boston Red Sox had been in first place in the American League East from April 15 until June 23, when they fell a half-game behind the Yankees. The 26th, with a Red Sox win and a Yankee loss, put the Sox back on top by a half game. But on the 27th, the Sox-Indians game was postponed by torrential rains, while the Yankees eked out a 3-2 win over Baltimore. Before the game on June 28, the Red Sox were just percentage points ahead of their AL East (and long-time) rivals, .622 to .615. Boston was 46-28 and NY was 48-30.

The Atlanta Braves were much more comfortably placed in the National League. The Braves were also leading the East, with a 48-30 record. They had a night off, too, their game with the Mets having been postponed. But the Braves had won seven of their last eight, and held a seven game lead in their division.

What had loomed as a classic pitching matchup between Derek Lowe (11-3) and the Braves' Greg Maddux (7-2) was altered by the postponements. Although Braves manager Bobby Cox stuck with Maddux, Sox manager Grady Little slotted John Burkett to pitch, holding his place in the rotation with just one more day's rest. Lowe was pushed back to the Saturday game. Burkett, interestingly, had been on the Braves staff just the year before.

Burkett had already faced the Braves back on June 15, at Turner Field in Atlanta, and lost to Greg Maddux. This had dropped Burkett to a 7-2 record and raised Maddux to 7-2. Boston had lost the first two of the three games in Atlanta in mid-June, salvaging a win only on the final game, with Derek Lowe beating Tom Glavine (who grew up just outside Boston) 6-1.

The Red Sox lost the June 28 game, 4-2, on the strength of a two-run Braves rally in the top of the ninth. The game looked like an exciting one—on paper. Fan Danny Szecskas termed it the "boringest game" he'd seen in years.

The Braves scored first with a run in the top of the third on a walk to Darren Bragg, a single that moved the runner to third and then a double play ball which brought Bragg in.

Bragg, who had been with Sox 1996 through 1998, now was a Brave and played a big part in their win, going 2-for-2 and walking 3 times. He scored two of Atlanta's four runs.

Boston rebounded with a run of its own, tying the score 1-1 in the bottom of the third. Again, the first batter walked. Jose Offerman, given the free pass, then stole second. He took third on a Johnny Damon grounder to second, then scored when Castilla muffed Garciaparra's ball hit to third.

In the top of the fifth, Atlanta scored once more. Bragg again led off, and he beat out an infield hit to second base, taking third on Baerga's error. He scored two batters later when Lockhart singled to center.

The score stood at 2-1 until the bottom of the seventh, when the Bosox tied it again. Varitek stroked a single to left off Chris Hammond, moving up a base when Offerman drew a walk on a 3-2 count. With two outs, Baerga doubled in Varitek.

After eight, the score was tied 2-2. As I said, on paper this looked like a really exciting game. In reality, it felt exceptionally dull, neither a true pitcher's duel, nor a

heated offensive battle. The weather induced a feeling of torpor, and Boston fans may have felt a not-atypical fatalism. (Atlanta fans might feel differently, though.) In the top of the ninth, Sheffield doubled to lead off. Two fly outs followed, but then Castilla singled in Sheffield. Bragg walked, advancing Castilla who then scored on Blanco's double to right field. The Braves held Boston scoreless, and won the game 4-2.

Burkett had a no-decision, having left after seven. Tim Wakefield took the loss; he'd only pitched the ninth but was responsible for both runs. Mike Remlinger ran his record to 4-0, pitching the eighth, and John Smoltz racked up his 26th save with a flawless ten-pitch bottom of the ninth.

Rickey Henderson set a world's record with his 2,158th bases on ball in the June 28 game. He walked, pinch-hitting for Brian Daubach in the eighth inning. Walk #2,158 eclipsed the old mark (also held by Rickey Henderson) set just five days earlier on June 23. The new world's record lasted only four days this time—until the July 2 game against Toronto, the second game of a day-night doubleheader when Mr. Henderson set a new world's record with his 2,159th career walk.

Game over, the Red Sox lost the next two to the Braves as well, while the Yankees built up a 2 game lead in the AL East. Swept by Atlanta, Boston was 5-13 in interleague play in 2002.

After the Braves left town, and the Sox returned to facing American League opponents, they promptly won their next five games, all against the Toronto Blue Jays. By the time the season was over, though, there sat the Braves in first place atop the NL East, a full 19 games ahead of the second place Expos. The Red Sox finished second in the AL East, 10.5 games behind the Yankees. The Giants knocked out the Braves in the Division Series and the Angels knocked out the Yankees at the same stage of the post-season. Most Braves and Sox players watched the World Series on TV.

INTERLEAGUE PLAY
Interleague play between the Braves and the Red Sox began on August 29, 1997 and in their first four games,

the Braves extracted a measure of revenge against their former American League rivals. It's not like they'd ever played each other, other than in exhibition games such as the old City Series. But there is no question that the teams were rivals for the attention of New England fandom for the first half of the twentieth century—and the Red Sox drove the Braves out of Beantown.

Charter members of the National League, the Boston Braves (they sported other names in earlier years) left town just before the start of the 1953 season. They'd been skunked by the Sox at the gate, almost from the launch of the AL franchise team in 1901. When Ban Johnson put together the upstart American League, and decided to go head-to-head with the National League in Boston, he helped orchestrate a successful debut. Johnson (and his designated owner Charles Somers) tried two time-tested techniques: they enticed the best players away from Boston's NL team by offering them substantially more money than the cartel that was the National League permitted, and they offered the public ticket prices that were half what they were on the other side of the tracks (the two Boston teams initially played on rival grounds that were separated only by railroad tracks.) It worked. The "Nationals" drew 146,502 in 1901 but the American League entry drew 289,448—almost double. Even when the Braves won the pennant in 1914, the Red Sox out-drew them by nearly 100,000 fans. The same was true in 1948—when the Braves won the pennant again, but the Sox outdrew the Braves by around 100,000.

The Braves' draw rarely matched that of the Red Sox. Had the Sox won the playoff game against Cleveland in 1948, there would have been a "streetcar" series between the two teams—Braves Field was only 1.3 miles from Fenway Park. Might that have inspired a Braves renaissance? We'll never know. Denny Galehouse lost the game for the Sox, and the Braves lost a hard-fought World Series against the Indians (a Native American matchup in name only.) The 1949 Braves finished in fourth place, 22 games out of first; the Red Sox went right down to the final inning of the season once more. It was kind of downhill from that point forward.

Braves' attendance grew steadily in the three post-war years, peaking at 1,455,439 in 1948. There followed a dramatic decline, with the club only drawing 281,278 in 1952.

On April 1—and this is no joke—Braves groundskeeper Al Oliver burned all of the pre-printed 1953 Boston Braves tickets, as Lou Perini moved the team to Milwaukee and started a new era for the franchise. The announcement of the move had been made just two weeks earlier. Everyone was taken by surprise, including star pitcher Warren Spahn, who had a new restaurant bearing his name opening right across from Braves Field. "The restaurant opened in Boston. The Braves opened in Milwaukee," Spahn noted wryly.

Though 13 games behind the Dodgers, the Milwaukee Braves took second place in 1953. And they drew fans—1,826,397 the first year, despite the short notice of their arrival. The four years after that, attendance exceeded two million per year. They missed by just one game in 1956, then won the pennant (and the World Series) in 1957. They won the pennant again in 1958 and only lost the Series in the eighth inning of Game Seven. Given how bad the Red Sox had become by this time, Richard Johnson indicates that some fans felt the "wrong team departed Boston." The Braves were contenders more often than the Red Sox in the years that followed, though they moved to Atlanta in 1966 (attendance in Milwaukee had dropped to 555,584 in 1965) and the Sox surprisingly won the pennant in '67. The 1967 Impossible Dream season reignited a fervor at Fenway that has never abated, with the Red Sox drawing consistently large crowds ever since.

In more recent times, too, the Atlanta Braves have been one of the most reliably successful teams in major league baseball. Between 1991 and 2002, the Braves have been to the post-season every single year (except for the shameful season of 1994 when there was no post-season.) Not even the vaunted New York Yankees can claim a record twelve straight playoff appearances. The Red Sox record has certainly been spottier, though hope springs eternal (tempered by some serious skepticism) in "Red Sox nation."

Was there any lingering wish to get back at the Bosox, the team that remained in Beantown while the Braves made their way west to Milwaukee? With the institution of interleague play, the opportunity arose for the Braves to come back "home"—over forty years later—and beat the Red Sox on the field of play. In 1997, the Braves swept the Sox—in Boston—winning all three games 9-1, 15-2 and 7-3. In 1998, they won the first one, but then dropped two. (The winner in that first game was Alan Embree, who surfaced with the Sox in 2002.) Stephen Brooks investigates the history of the "natural rivals" in his entry on interleague play between the two teams. These modern Braves probably did not feel much in the way of sweet revenge on their old rivals, but the fact still stands that overall the Braves have outplayed the Red Sox in interleague play by a wide margin, and swept all six games from the Sox in 2002.

The Sox' interleague play may have cost them a bid at the 2002 postseason. Take away their dismal interleague record (5-13), and the Anaheim Angels' decent one (11-7), and the two teams would have finished in a dead heat for the American League Wild Card. Six games was the difference.

We'll never know what might have been if the Braves had not dominated the Sox as they did. Instead we can remember the history of the rivalry and look back on this one night when two great teams met.

Without further ado, let's see how 64 SABR members viewed the ballgame between the Braves and the Red Sox.

Bill Nowlin
Cambridge, MA

PART ONE:
SOX VS. BRAVES HISTORY

BOSTON RED SOX - Friday, June 28, 2002

Red Sox vs. Atlanta

UMPIRES: HP Tim Timmons, 1B Paul Emmel, 2B Gary Darling, 3B Rob Drake

OFFICIAL SCORER: Bruce Guindon

		POS	1	2	3	4	5	6	7	8	9	10	AB	R	H	RBI
1	1 Rafael Furcal	SS	P5		4-3		-3	4-3		8B						
2	23 Julio Franco	1B	SK			-8	-7		4-3	4-3						
3	11 Gary Sheffield	DH	SK			L5	7		SB BB		(3-7					
4	10 Chipper Jones	LF		SK		SK	7		8		L8					
5	25 Andruw Jones	CF		9		BB		E6 -8	4-3		8					
6	19 Vinny Castilla	3B		13		8		L9	6-3	(3-8			4-11-1-14			
7	28 Darren Bragg	RF			8-BB		E4 24	E6 -9	FC BB	BB						
8	20 Henry Blanco	C			4-3 -9		6-3	9	FC BB	=9						
9	7 Keith Lockhart	2B			DP 4-6-3		-8	E6	1-3	cK						
18 (4) 2 GRCIA																
TOTALS		R/H	0/0	0/0	1/1	0/1	1/4	0/2	0/0	0/0	2/3	1				

PITCHERS	IP	H	R	ER	BB	SO	W/L			
31 RHP Greg Maddux	5	3	1	0	1	4		1	3	2
49 GRYBOSKI (6)	1	0	0	0	2	0				
36 HAMMOND (7)	0.2	2	1	1	2	1				
40 HOLMES (7)	0.1	0	0	0	0	0				
37 REMLINGER (8)	1.0	0	0	0	1	1				
29 SMOLTZ (9)	1.0	0	0	0	0	1				
	9	5	2	1	6	7				

M.L. Staff

6 Cox, Bobby - Manager
5 Yost, Ned - Coach   33
9 Pendleton, Terry - Coach
17 Hubbard, Glenn - Coach   13
39 Corrales, Pat - Coach
52 Dews, Bobby - Coach
54 Mazzone, Leo - Coach

706
10 LS
310

1 Furcal, Rafael - INF
2 Garcia, Jesse - INF
4 Franco, Matt - INF
7 Lockhart, Keith - INF
8 Lopez, Javy - C
10 Jones, Chipper - OF
11 Sheffield, Gary - OF
18 Helms, Wes - INF
19 Castilla, Vinny - INF

20 Blanco, Henry - C
23 Franco, Julio - INF
25 Jones, Andruw - OF
27 Moss, Damian - LHP
28 Bragg, Darren - OF
29 Smoltz, John - RHP
31 Maddux, Greg - RHP
34 Millwood, Kevin - RHP
36 Hammond, Chris - LHP

37 Remlinger, Mike - LHP
38 Marquis, Jason - RHP
40 Holmes, Darren - RHP
43 Spooneyberger, Tim - RHP
46 Ligtenberg, Kerry - RHP
47 Glavine, Tom - LHP
49 Gryboski, Kevin - RHP

D.L.
Lopez, A.
DeRosa, M.
Giles, M.

33,137

RED SOX	POS	1	2	3	4	5	6	7	8	9	10	AB	R	H	RBI
1	18 Johnny Damon	CF	4-3		4-3		cK	FP5			SK					
2	10 Carlos Baerga	2B	-4 -7		SK			4-3	=7							
3	5 Nomar Garciaparra	SS	5-4 -7		SB E3			6-3	13B							
4	24 Manny Ramirez	LF			4-3		5U	7								

Public Address Announcer Ed Brickley's scorecard

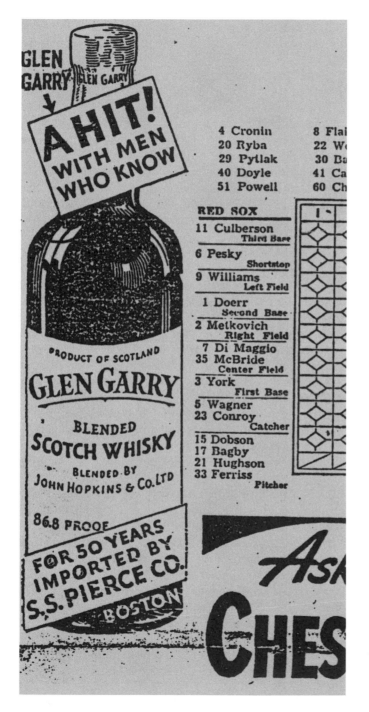

4 Cronin	8 Flai
20 Ryba	22 W
29 Pytlak	30 Ba
40 Doyle	41 Ca
51 Powell	60 Ch

RED SOX

11 Culberson	
Third Base	
6 Pesky	
Shortstop	
9 Williams	
Left Field	
1 Doerr	
Second Base	
2 Metkovich	
Right Field	
7 Di Maggio	
35 McBride	
Center Field	
3 York	
First Base	
5 Wagner	
23 Conroy	
Catcher	
15 Dobson	
17 Bagby	
21 Hughson	
33 Ferriss	
Pitcher	

A TALE OF ONE CITY
BOSTON'S CITY SERIES

Phil Bergen

When Aaron Sele and John Smoltz hooked up at the end of August 1997, it was trumpeted in the Boston media as the "return of the Braves." Nostalgia reigned. The Braves' regular uniforms are retro-themed to begin with, but nostalgia was in evidence both on the field and in the stands when the two teams met in Interleague play. Both teams sported retro uniforms— the Braves wore "Boston" on their chests—and in the stands, older Boston Braves fans were finally able to see their team once more, albeit 45 years after their final game in town.

Nomar Garciaparra's batting streak came to an end that weekend, but the consensus was that it was great to finally see the two teams play games that mattered. Major League Baseball bought into this idea as well, declaring the Braves and Red Sox "natural rivals," and matching them for twice-yearly interleague series, a la the Yankees-Mets and Cubs-White Sox. As rivals for the Boston baseball scene for half a century, the Sox and Braves in their various incarnations bounced up and down (mostly down) as their fortunes waxed and waned; moving in parallel tracks separated by a mile of Commonwealth Avenue.

One place where these tracks would briefly intersect was the Boston City Series, a yearly exhibition show-down that took place immediately preceding the season, and which ran pretty much consecutively from 1925-1953. The City Series was a long time in coming and the two teams spent most of the early years of the century studiously avoiding each other in Boston competition, going so far as to play college nines rather than with each other.

Technically, the father of the City Series was played in 1905, when the American and National League teams played each other in a seven-game series following the season, in direct competition with the World Series. While the Giants and Athletics fought it out for world supremacy, the American Leaguers nearly ran the table, taking six of seven games. The seventh-place (51-103, 54 games behind) National League "Beaneaters" featured—if that word can be applied—four 20-game losers, and form was followed. Bouncing back from a 5-2 National League victory in the opener, the Americans swept six in a row, culminating with a double-header double-dip. Bob Unglaub homered twice in the Series, the first long balls hit in the competition (after hitting none in the 1905 regular season), and "Old" Cy Young bested Irving "Young Cy" Young in game two, allowing but two hits while striking out fifteen.

Crowds were fairly consistent, considering that all games were played at the Huntington Avenue Grounds largely on weekday afternoons, and the players received half of the net proceeds. Similar city series were being held at the same time in Chicago and St. Louis, but this would be the first year of post-season play in Boston. Two years later they did it again with even more decisive results, the Americans taking six of seven games from the NL "Doves," with the final game a 10-inning tie. [Early team nicknames were often changed. —Eds.]

The unequal level of play was responsible for the eighteen-year hiatus during the period of the Red Sox's strongest teams and Boston's unlikeliest championship team, the 1914 Braves. (1948 nearly brought about a real post-season Series, but Messrs. Boudreau and Bearden had other ideas.) The Red Sox christened Fenway Park in 1912 against Harvard, winning 2-0, while the National Leaguers practiced two miles away at their South End Grounds. The defending World Champion 1915 Braves, one year removed from their Miracle, played Harvard, and later Brown, at Fenway Park, leaving their landlords out on the road. The following year, the Crimson upset the Champion Sox 1-0, the day following Tris Speaker's controversial trade to Cleveland.

It would not be until the 1920s, with both teams securely in the basement during the worse decade in

Boston baseball history, that the two teams would begin to play exhibitions against one another on a regular basis.

Some years the clash came in the final encounters in a series that would start in Florida during the Grapefruit League. Some years the series was strictly the games played in Boston. Occasionally exhibitions would be played in nearby minor league cities like Hartford and Springfield against the local team, and draw a big gate. Ted Williams hit three homers against the Braves in a 1949 exhibition played in Hartford, a 10-10 tie that temporarily deflected rumors of Brave dissension and mutiny against manager Billy Southworth. For the purposes of this article, I've arbitrarily considered the City Series to be strictly those pre- and post-season games played in Boston itself.

The City Series made for good publicity. Although Boston's baseball fans were generally not as partisan as Chicago's, where Cubs fans rejoice in White Sox misfortune, or New York, where Yankee, Dodger, and Giant fans kept their allegiances separate, Braves fans would at least tolerate Red Soxers, even while rooting for their respective teams. Perhaps it was the close proximity of the two ballparks that made a difference, perhaps the fact that seldom were both teams contenders at the same time (it is difficult to really get angry at a seventh-place team).

Whatever the reason, one team's winning the Series from the other produced little in the way of bragging rights. Having the two teams square off against each other meant mostly that opening day was a bit closer, the heroes of the diamond were back in town, and newcomers and rookies could get their feet wet in their new town. For the players, the Series was a time to get settled in for the upcoming year, play a couple of exhibitions at their home field, and have a respite from the daily barnstorming grind that would bring them north each year from Florida. Baseball junkies who had gone six months without a fix could be relied on to fill the seats. Yet, columnist Bill Cunningham in the *Boston Herald* called the games "good, clean, fun" and the mythical title of supremacy "as phony as a $3 bill." It was accepted that the games were dress rehearsals for the main event.

Playing at the start of the season, instead of afterwards, as the White Sox and Cubs tended to do, was not without its problems. As we've learned in recent years, with major league seasons that start earlier than ever, mid-April weather in Boston can vary wildly. This resulted in a good number of postponements and dreadful games over the years, in which the players built fires to keep warm in the dugout and bullpen and fans shivered through nine innings. Certainly the fluctuation in attendance over the years may be as much due to the weather as anything else. Ranging from a few thousand on chilly days, to sellouts in the late 1940s, the Series would usually bring in enough revenue to out-draw gates in Greenville, Memphis, and Baltimore.

Exhibitions of long ago were different from today. Generally, regulars started the games and often played the whole nine innings. Complete games from pitchers were not uncommon, although to a lesser extent than regular season games from the period. By the time the teams had arrived in Boston, most fringe players had been cut and the regular season roster was intact, although occasionally a scrub or two would be retained for use. A late 1952 roster change for the Braves would portend better times in the future—Ed Mathews, Gene Conley and George Crowe remaining with the big club, with Bill Bruton and Leo Righetti going down. (Leo's big league connection would stem mostly from his son, Dave.)

In the 1920s, neither Boston team was much of a draw on the road, and their owners agreed that an exhibition series at home might provide needed income, as well as publicity for what would be a tough sell at the box office. The homestanding Braves won the inaugural game, 4-3, in front of a rabid crowd of 12,000 on April 11, 1925, Johnny Cooney besting spitballing Jack Quinn. In what would be a traditional hazard for the Series, the second game was cancelled due to cold weather. The first Sunday ball game in Boston was held in the 1929 Series, and was considered a success, as 5,000 fans turned out despite weather so inclement that oil stoves were used in the dugout. In one of the last cities with Blue laws, the arrival of Sunday ball would prove profitable at a time when fans were few and far between.

With a single exception, 1928, the pre-season format would continue until 1953, extending through World War II (when both teams practiced nearby anyway), the rise of the House of Yawkey, and the Three Little Steamshovels. Heroics would come from star players, unlikely sources, and cup-of-coffee nonentities. The first decade saw both teams evenly matched in ineptitude, while subsequent seasons generally handed the Red Sox superiority in talent and money—a high hurdle for the Braves and Bees to overcome. Some games were classic, and would go down in Series annals. The third game of the 1947 series, played before a full house at Fenway Park (newspaper accounts had 20,000 fans remaining till the bitter end) ended in a 16-inning 7-7 tie. Starters Boo Ferriss and Warren Spahn were long gone at the end of a game which featured five hits from Earl Torgeson, and back-to-the-wall relief pitching from Braves hurler Walt Lanfranconi, who twice pitched out of bases-loaded, no-out jams in extra innings. "This clinched his spot with the Braves," reported the Herald.

Vermont native Lanfranconi would go 4-4 during the season (2.95 ERA), in what would be the high-water mark of his career.

Although the games were exhibitions, emotions would sometimes run high. During a 19-6 Red Sox rout in the first game of the 1948 Series, tempers got the better of two players. Not surprisingly, the Brave in question was Torgeson, who was regularly led off the field, eyeglasses askew, after a donnybrook. His opponent this time was future Braves manager Billy Hitchcock, who tangled with Torgy after a tag play at first base. Bad blood stemming from a Florida game incident was reported as the cause, which left both players ejected and Hitchcock riding a taxi back to Fenway Park to pick up his belongings. The 24-hit Sox attack featured a home run from Ted Williams.

Ah, the Thumper. This .344 lifetime hitter swatted even higher in the City Series, accounting for nine home runs and an average of .366 from 1939 to 1952. Williams had two-home run games in 1946 and 1952

('46 was a grand slam) and was held hitless in only five games. Ted's first Boston appearance, in 1939, saw him play right field and bat sixth in a 7-1 loss to the Bees. Fellow Hall of Famer Jimmie Foxx provided the Hose with their only run, off of Lou Fette. Babe Ruth's first appearance in Boston as a National Leaguer also occurred in the City Series, where he played first base, went hitless, and made an error in the only 1935 game to get played. His appearance at Fenway drew 11,000 to the game, which was won by Ben Cantwell and the Braves, 3-2. They would have been advised to save it for the regular season, winning only 35 games in that year (Cantwell went 4-25).

Williams was the focus of an odd 1952 game. During the Grapefruit League season the Braves had touted their up-and-coming rookies, which in truth were plentiful. An off-season barnstorming press junket touted their young blood, some of whom would indeed form the nucleus of the World Champions of 1957, and would hopefully draw attention away from the regulars who were aging and destined to finish seventh. The *Herald*, perhaps looking for a promotional hook, suggested that one of the Series games that year be an all-rookie affair, showcasing each team's future. Surprisingly, it was the Red Sox who took up the offer, and played the second game of the '52 Series with Ted surrounded by eight rookies, while the Braves went with their regular lineup. Amidst the Red Sox youngsters was a mixture of future regulars (Jimmy Piersall, Sammy White, and Dick Gernert) and the not so fortunate (Hal Bevan, Faye Throneberry). Williams prevailed, hitting two home runs as the Sox and Bill Henry beat the Braves and Vern Bickford, 12-7, in front of over 8,000 curious fans at Fenway. While the (nearly) all-rookie game had merit, this was the only year it was tried.

Other good players would enjoy forgettable days in the Series. Rookie Johnny Pesky's first game in Boston saw him commit four errors, replacing Manager Joe Cronin at shortstop; and usually reliable Warren Spahn was touched for eight runs in just over two innings in a 1951 game that saw Williams drive in six runs. Surprises also popped up in Series history. The only player to hit home runs in all three Series games in one year was Red Sox outfielder Carl Reynolds in 1934. He would hit only four during the regular season. One Woody Rich pitched a five-hit shutout for the Sox in 1939. Names long-forgotten appear in the home runs and pitchers of record—Fabian Gaffke, Lou Tost, Rex Cecil, Gordon Rhodes ("The Utah Daddy"), and George Estock. What -might-have-beens abound: a 1946 rumor about Bing Crosby buying the Braves (could they have moved to the West Coast seven years later?); a short article a year earlier headlined "Negro Players To Have Tryout at Yawkey Yard," (with a follow-up note a day later quoting Hugh Duffy that he saw "pretty good ballplayers." One "pretty good ballplayer," Sam Jethroe, would get four hits (one a home run) in the final game of the 1950 City Series, while another, an infielder, would help draw 25,211 people to an exhibition game in Atlanta four years later. "13,885 were Negroes," the *Herald* helpfully reported.

Without a doubt, the oddest City Series was the final one in 1953, the Braves having made the decision to move to Milwaukee that spring. The first game was played in Milwaukee, the first appearance of the Braves in their new wigwam. Reverting to true Boston form, the game was rained out after two innings, the Sox ahead, 3-0.

Then the Braves flew to Boston (as did the Sox) from the upper Midwest. "What Does the M Stand For?" was the sardonic photo caption in the *Boston Post*, as local players Chet Nichols and Dick Donovan checked their newly-issued caps, and a wit remarked as the Milwaukee Braves plane touched down at Logan Airport, "Make 'em go through customs."

In an act of bravery or foolishness, Braves owner Lou Perini took his place in a Fenway Park box, and weathered the fans' reception. Not surprisingly, the visiting Braves received the largest round of applause from the crowd of 9,000. "Those still faithful to the Braves raised louder applause than did the supporters of the winning Sox," reported the *Post* (itself to fold within the next five years), though the *Herald's* Bill Cunningham scornfully noted, "Milwaukee, or anybody else, is welcome to our

casualties.... By disdaining to stage any angry scenes, those who braved the elements really contributed to the status of this Citadel of Culture, as a poised and civilized community that can take something or see it go without becoming hysterical."

The final official City Series contest was held April 12, 1953. Fittingly, the departing Braves won 4-1, with veterans Andy Pafko and Walker Cooper homering for the victors. Despite Lou Perini's hopeful comments that the Series could be continued, it was not to be. A sobered crowd finally realized that the two-team city was no more. "The game seemed to have a very great and terrifying significance as though the events of the past month could not be considered a bad dream and the time had come to face an awesome reality," reported the *Boston Globe*.

In a final blow to the Braves' faithful, Lolly Hopkins, the Braves' most publicized fan, was struck in the mouth by a foul ball of Sox catcher Gus Niarhos and was taken from the park. Had the Braves managed to stay in Boston a few more years, the seeds of the future championship clubs that had been planted might have blossomed. The Braves of Ebba St. Claire, Vern Bickford, and Sibby Sisti were morphing into the Braves of Aaron, Mathews, Adcock, and Burdette. Whether their success was tied to the fanatical reception the team received in Milwaukee, or if young players would have withered in a second-rate franchise like Boston's is a matter for conjecture. Perhaps a successful Braves team, coupled with lackluster Red Sox teams of the 1950s ("Ted Williams and the Seven Dwarfs" according to some), could have tipped the balance of power to the point that the Red Sox might have been the team to move. But that is tinkering with the facts, and creating virtual history.

The Red Sox and Braves played a preseason series in Milwaukee in 1954, splitting two games. A small note in Boston papers that same weekend announced the name change of Braves Field to Boston University Field, cutting a final tie of the team with the city. The Sox would play an exhibition game with the New York Giants that year for the Jimmy Fund, a children's cancer research foundation sponsored initially by the Braves, and passed along to the Red Sox for safekeeping. The Braves and Sox would continue to play an occasional mid-season charity game in Boston, when schedules would allow, but it was not the same. Gerry Hearn of the *Post*, had summed it up best in 1953: "When the Braves come to Boston for the weekend games it should be remembered by the fans that the players didn't make the decision to move to Milwaukee. They only go where they are sent."

SPAHN, SAIN, AND SIBBY GET THE LAST LAUGH

Saul Wisnia

When Sebastian "Sibby" Sisti made his way to the Fenway mound on June 28, 2002 to throw out the ceremonial first pitch, there were undoubtedly tens of thousands of fans on hand who were hearing his name for the first time. Lifetime .244 hitters whose careers ended nearly a half century ago don't normally come up in daily conversation or barroom debates, but there was a smattering of mostly older folks in the crowd for whom Sibby's appearance prompted smiles.

You can spot these patrons at every Red Sox home game, but their numbers increased dramatically on those nights in recent years when a certain National League team occupied the visitors' dugout at Fenway. Mostly men in their 60s and 70s with graying hair and scorebooks in their laps, they sport blue and red caps emblazoned with a simple white "B" that are easy to distinguish from the solid blue versions worn by the majority of fans and the home team. And while they may root for the Sox the rest of the year, on this night their hearts are with the opposition: a club the city once called its own.

Atlanta may now be known as "America's team," but for 81 years Boston was the home of the Braves.

With ties dating back to the original Cincinnati Red Stockings—baseball's first acknowledged professional team—the Braves represented New England on the diamond each summer between 1871 and 1952. Now relocated to Georgia by way of Milwaukee, the squad is the only surviving entrant from the National League's debut season of 1876 still in existence. Most of the Braves' glory days in the east (including eight NL pennants) came before 1900, but well-seasoned fans still remember the final Boston years when utilityman Sisti and his mates battled the Red Sox for city bragging rights at ballparks separated by less than a mile of trolley track.

At one time, this had been a fairly even fight. Both teams reached championship heights during the teens, the Red Sox with World Series victories in 1912-15-16-18 and the "Miracle Braves" of 1914 by means of a legendary last-to-first streak over the season's final two months punctuated by a Series sweep of Connie Mack's mighty Athletics. When bad luck and bad trades doomed the years that followed, Boston endured an extended stay at or near the bottom of the National and American Leagues through the 1920s and early '30s. Then, in 1933, the tide seemed to turn; multi-millionaire "sportsman" Tom Yawkey celebrated his 30th birthday and the hefty inheritance that came with it by purchasing the Red Sox, and the Braves stayed in the pennant hunt most of the season before fading to fourth—their best standing in 12 years. Boston's baseball future looked bright.

But while Yawkey was soon restocking the Sox with the greatest stars money could buy—including future Hall of Famers Jimmie Foxx, Lefty Grove, and Joe Cronin—Braves owners with far smaller pockets could only acquire such luminaries well past their primes. The classic example was none other than Babe Ruth, who, after two record-breaking decades with the Sox and Yankees, ended his career with a .181 average for the cellar-dwelling Braves of '35. Yawkey turned around his club's farm system as well, the high point coming when a 1936 scouting trip to California by Sox general manager Eddie Collins yielded two teenagers with Cooperstown in their future: Ted Williams and Bobby Doerr. Once this duo reached the big leagues, only World War II could temporarily stall a 15-year run by the Sox as annual threats to Yankee American League dominance. The Braves, meanwhile, would remain second-class citizens in the senior circuit for most of the same span.

The competition for fans and glory between the two squads played out much like the rivalry waged in New York by the Dodgers and Yankees. Like their Brooklyn counterparts, the Braves played the underdogs in this battle, attracting a mostly working-class, urban crowd with a lovable (if not often successful) team of low-budget ballplayers. The Red Sox drew a far tonier crowd, including visiting businessmen yearning to witness the skills of Williams, Doerr, and fellow young all-stars such as Dom DiMaggio and Tex Hughson. The eleven home games the Sox played annually against the mighty Yankees alone drew more fans to Fenway Park than Braves Field saw in half a season, and the added revenue generated from such crowds assured that Red Sox players would always be well compensated even if the team finished behind New York in the standings—which it usually did.

Money was seldom a concern for Yawkey no matter what his team's record, but a succession of Braves owners seemed always to be one step away from bankruptcy. A young standout like pitchers Warren Spahn and John Sain or outfielder Tommy Holmes occasionally appeared on the Braves roster, but normally there was no cash to go after established stars who could generate the level of electricity at Braves Field that Williams and Co. were displaying down the road at Fenway. This fact further endeared blue-collar fans to Braves players, who were among the poorest-paid in the majors. At the same time, it also assured the Red Sox would be the home team drawing most of the headlines in Boston's seven daily newspapers. Sportswriters of the era received their meal and travel money from the teams they covered rather than from their publishers, and while riding by train from town to town, they routinely dined and played cards with those very players. Yawkey always made sure his athletes—and "his" writers—traveled first class, with plenty of food and booze for all. Things were not usually as posh for the Braves press corps, and a "rich boy"/"poor boy" feeling between the clubs often worked its way into print—and into the consciousness of Boston's sports fans.

The Braves' financial straits improved considerably when Boston-bred contractor Louis Perini and two partners took over the team in the mid-1940s, and top-notch talent such as Bob Elliott, Al Dark, and manager Billy Southworth (a three-time pennant winner) was brought in. The result was the wild summer of 1948, when the Braves and Red Sox were both in the title hunt all season and nearly faced each other in a "streetcar" World Series. The clubs combined to draw more than 3 million fans—including a record 1.45 million by the Braves—but the Cleveland Indians topped first the Sox in a one-game AL playoff and then the Braves in a six-game Fall Classic. No NL club in Boston would reach such heights again, and fan fallout of epic proportions soon had Perini's investment back in the red. In reality, post-season success had little bearing on the situation.

Although the Red Sox contended far more often, each of Boston's teams won just one pennant and no World Series titles during the final 35 years of their co-existence. Yet in the minds of fans and sportswriters, the Red Sox were clearly the top dogs in town. When the teams met each spring for an annual "City Series" just before the start of the regular season, Braves players and supporters viewed the exhibition contests as an opportunity to prove their mettle against Yawkey's "Gold Sox." These supposedly meaningless games, played in usually chilly conditions at Fenway Park and Braves Field, received extensive press coverage, and both teams played to win. Beanballs and even fistfights occasionally occurred, and once again it was the Red Sox who most often claimed victory.

Although very close in proximity, the venues where these clubs played further mirrored their differences. Fenway, a red-bricked beauty opened in 1912, gave the Red Sox a cozy, hitter-friendly home where they could thrill crowds seated close to the action with their fence-busting displays of power. Massive Braves Field, heralded as "the world's biggest ballpark" when unveiled just three years later, was designed for the hit-and-run, "inside" style of baseball soon to fall out of favor. It had deep fences—the original dimensions included a ridiculous 550 feet to center—and vast expanses of foul territory that distanced fans from the field, and it was the setting for far more 2-1 games than slugfests. It took nearly a decade for anyone to hit a ball out of this con-

crete edifice, and after Babe Ruth emerged as a supreme slugger in 1920, it was home runs that sold tickets.

Fenway was well-suited for this new trend; Braves Field was not. Smack dab in the middle of bustling Kenmore Square, a short distance from several colleges, restaurants, and top hotels (visiting ballplayers and reporters were a five-minute walk from work), Fenway was also well-located.

Braves Field was near no major social spots, but it did have both the Charles River and Boston-Albany railroad line situated just beyond its outfield fences. The resulting cold air and soot that blew into the stands did little to help make this a more fan-friendly park; when the team began televising its games heavily around 1950, many folks decided it was more comfortable to simply watch the Braves from home.

The result of all these factors was a terrific disparity in attendance between the teams. With the exception of a five-year span from 1946-50, the Red Sox consistently topped the Braves by a wide margin at the gate. The incongruity reached its apex in 1952. The Sox were a sixth-place club with Ted Williams back in the Marines, yet they still drew a very respectable 1.1 million fans to Fenway Park. The Braves were not much worse on the field—they finished seventh—but their park was little more than a smoky, windy ghost town that summer. Just over 281,000 fans showed up at Braves Field during the course of the season, a figure that translated into 3,600-odd patrons per game in a 40,000-seat venue.

Ever playing the role of Avis to the Red Sox Hertz, the Braves kept seeking ways to keep up. Rookie of the Year Sam Jethroe broke the color line for the team in 1950, just three years after Jackie Robinson's debut with the Dodgers and nine years before the Sox became the last ML squad to integrate. Braves Field was home to a huge electronic scoreboard, fried clams at the concession stand, and fir trees lining the outfield. Team public relations man (and future New England Patriots owner) Billy Sullivan came out with baseball's first yearbooks, and a plane dubbed "the Rookie Rocket" jetted sportswriters around the country for interviews with the team's newest young signees. Kids who were members of the "Knot Hole Gang" with 25 cents to spare could get a pass good for every Braves home game; no such offers were necessary (or made) at Fenway.

But even fir trees could not cover Perini's mounting financial losses, and on March 18, 1953 he received permission to transplant the Braves to Milwaukee. The writing had been on the wall, but New Englanders were still shocked by the move. In a rapidly changing world, the major leagues had long been a source of stability. The same 16 teams had played in the same 11 cities for half a century, and no club had ever been situated west of the Mississippi except for St. Louis. Perini said he had no desire to break this tradition, yet he also claimed he had no choice. Boston fans had simply not stuck with the Braves in rough times, and Lou knew Wisconsin was hungry for a ML team. The immediate, dramatic success of baseball's first franchise shift in 50 years—including a first-year attendance figure of 1.8 million—validated Perini's decision and signaled the start of a western exodus that would reach California by 1958.

Some diehard Braves loyalists, jilted by the decision that cost them the chance to see Henry Aaron in a Boston uniform, pledged never to switch their allegiances to the Red Sox, and they continued cheering the Braves from afar—even after the team moved yet again (to Atlanta) in 1966. Just how devoted were these fans? In 1988, some 35 years after their heroes had skipped town, thousands of rooters attended a 40th reunion of the last Boston Braves pennant winners. An exhibit on the team, put together that same summer by the New England Sports Museum, attracted 135,000 viewers, and during 1991 a Boston Braves Historical Association (BBHA) was formed to keep alive memories of the city's National League era. The group began hosting annual dinners for former Braves players, personnel, and fans, and even started a "Hall of Fame" to honor men who, in most cases, had credentials far too modest for Cooperstown. Within a few years BBHA membership had reached to all 50 states and Europe, and when the now-Atlanta Braves faced the Red Sox in first interleague match-up in 1997, the Fenway bleachers were jammed with hundreds of club members who cheered the homecoming of "their" team and the three-game sweep that ensued. Sisti and Holmes lamented that if fans had only shown this much support when they were playing, the exodus might never have happened. Yet behind the laughs, former Braves were clearly moved by the outpouring of support. While Williams, Doerr, and other Red Sox oldtimers were still regularly in the public eye, many of the most popular Braves reunion attendees were mediocre ballplayers who had spent the intervening decades living in relative obscurity—their modest deeds long forgotten outside this circle.

Today there are only a few reminders of the team for which Cy Young earned his final four victories, Babe Ruth hit his final six homers, and Hall-of-Famers Casey Stengel, Ernie Lombardi, Warren Spahn, the Waner brothers, and Rabbit Maranville all toiled. Portions of Braves Field (now owned by Boston University) still stand, and the "Jimmy Fund" charity the team helped start up in 1948—now the official cause of the Red Sox—is still raising millions annually for Boston-based Dana-Farber Cancer Institute. The battle cry of "Spahn and Sain and Pray for Rain" heralding the pitcher aces of the '48 pennant winners has endured as one of baseball's most familiar phrases, but many modern fans have no idea to whom it refers.

Each year claims more players who represented the Braves in Boston, but if the schedule-makers ever see fit to sending Atlanta back to Fenway Park, you can be sure the stalwarts in their 1950-era caps will be back rooting for yet another one-sided series. When Bob Hohler of the *Boston Globe* suggested in his coverage of the June 28, 2002 game that the "Curse of Sibby Sisti" may be the cause of Atlanta's dominance over Boston during six years of interleague play, the 82-year-old first-pitch honoree couldn't help but chuckle. In Sibby's opinion, it was about time his club got the best of the battle.

1997 AT BOSTON
  August 29 Atlanta 9 - Boston 1
  August 30 Atlanta 15 - Boston 2
  August 31 Atlanta 7 - Boston 3
1998 AT ATLANTA
  June 8 Atlanta 7 - Boston 6
  June 9 Boston 9 - Atlanta 3
  June 10 Boston 10 - Atlanta 6 (a 10-6 score on 6-10!)
1999 AT BOSTON
  June 4 Boston 5 - Atlanta 1
  June 5 Atlanta 6 - Boston 5
  June 6 Atlanta 3 - Boston 2 (11 innings)
1999: AT ATLANTA
  July 9 Boston 5 - Atlanta 4
  July 10 Atlanta 2 - Boston 1 (11 innings)
  July 11 Atlanta 8 - Boston 1
2000: AT ATLANTA
  June 9 Atlanta 6 - Boston 4
  June 10 Atlanta 6 - Boston 0
  June 11 Boston 5 - Atlanta 3
2000: AT BOSTON
  July 7 Atlanta 5 - Boston 3
  July 8 Atlanta 5 - Boston 1
  July 9 Boston 7 - Atlanta 2
2001: AT ATLANTA
  June 15 Boston9 - Atlanta 5 (10 innings)
  June 10 Atlanta 8 - Boston 0
  June 11 Boston 4 - Atlanta 3
2001: AT BOSTON
  July 6 Atlanta 6 - Boston 5 (11 innings)
  July 7 Boston 3 - Atlanta 1
  July 8 Atlanta 8 - Boston 0
2002: AT ATLANTA
  June 14 Atlanta 2 - Boston 1
  June 15 Atlanta 4 - Boston 2
  June 16 Boston 6 - Atlanta 1
2002: AT BOSTON
  June 28 Atlanta 4 - Boston 2
  June 29 Atlanta 2 - Boston 1
  June 30 Atlanta 7 - Boston 3 (10 innings)

NATURAL RIVALS

Steven Wolfgang Brooks

When Francis T. "Fay" Vincent resigned as Commissioner of Baseball on September 7, 1992, Major League Baseball looked to establish a new form of governing body to watch over their game. According to the Major League agreement the Major League Executive Council was granted the rights to rule over baseball in the absence of a commissioner. This Executive Council was comprised of each baseball club owner. Instead of one commissioner, each owner would have a say as to which decisions needed to be made. But every organization needs a leader. The owners voted to elect a chairman of their Council, one who would become the "central figure." The owners chose the owner of the Milwaukee Brewers. He had been very active in the governance of Major League Baseball, and had built a reputation as "the right man for the job." Allan H. Selig was selected as chairman to the Executive Council on September 9, 1992. Selig quickly introduced changes to the way the game was played and to the way the fans watched the game.

In 1997 "Bud" Selig, as he was known, introduced something new. No longer would American League teams only face National League teams in the World Series. No, instead there would be a set of games during the regular season in which American League teams would face off against National League teams. The team that won would get a win in their win column, and the team that lost would get a loss in their loss column. The records counted. To fans, and owners alike (for financial reasons), it was great. Fans came out in droves to see players they could only see if they lived in another city. Interleague play was a success.

Then came the decision to make interleague play more exciting. Each team had a rival, such as the Seattle

Mariners and Oakland Athletics. But how about a rivalry consisting of teams in opposite leagues? Some were obvious. New York Yankees vs. New York Mets. Oakland Athletics vs. San Francisco Giants. And so on. Each of these pairings were deemed "Natural Rivals."

The Boston Red Sox were to play the Atlanta Braves, and nothing seemed more fitting.

The Atlanta Braves franchise played in Boston beginning in 1876, when they were called the Red Caps. They had a number of nicknames over the years, from the Beaneaters to the Doves in the first part of the twentieth century.

The way they went through team nicknames you might have thought they were escaped convicts running from the Boston Police. They were the Rustlers in 1909 and 1910. They became the Boston Braves in 1911, which would hold until 1935. They changed in 1936, this time to the Boston Bees. But the Braves seemed a better fit for the team, so they reverted to that come 1941. They played through the 1952 season as the Braves, but the American League's Boston Red Sox had proven to be the more powerful drawing card and economics forced the Boston Braves to relocate (they left for Milwaukee, where they enjoyed a number of very successful years, before moving once again to their now familiar home in Atlanta). This set the stage for Boston and Atlanta to be dubbed "natural rivals" by the powers that be.

INTERLEAGUE PLAY IN 1997

On August 29, 1997 the Braves made their return to Boston for the first time in forty-five years. 32,577 crammed their way into Fenway Park to see this historical match-up. John Smoltz was the starting pitcher for the Braves that day and he was going for his lucky thirteenth victory. Aaron Sele, who also had twelve wins to his credit, would be the starter for the Sox. Nomar Garciaparra, Boston's rookie, came to the plate four times in this game and tallied two hits that extended his American League rookie hitting streak to thirty games. But those hits went for naught when the Red Sox ran into the roadblock called Smoltz. Smoltz pitched strong

for seven innings, surrendering only four hits and striking out nine. Boston couldn't score a run against him. It was too bad Aaron Sele couldn't say the same for the Braves hitters, who got to him early. Sele was only able to last five and one-third innings giving up four earned runs on six hits. Boston's bullpen couldn't hold the Braves back either, allowing five runs in their four and two-thirds innings pitched. Boston was able to prevent the shutout however, when Reggie Jefferson hit a home run in the bottom of the ninth inning. When it was all over Atlanta had beat the team that chased them out of town.

The next day a slightly larger crowd turned out to see Tim Wakefield of the Bostons square off against Kevin Millwood of Atlanta. Coming into the game, Wakefield had already gotten fourteen losses to his credit with only nine victories. The Braves took advantage.

Once again it was another short outing for a Boston starter. Wakefield couldn't get the third out of the fourth inning. The knuckleballer gave up eight hits and seven runs, all earned, and Boston manager Jimy Williams had no choice but to take him out of the game. John Wasdin took Wakefield's place and had just as little success, surrendering six runs on seven hits in three and one-third innings. By the end of the fourth inning the Braves already had a nine-run lead.

Hoping to extend his rookie hitting streak, Nomar Garciaparra came to bat four times and tallied a run batted in on a sacrifice fly and zero hits. His batting average dropped two points from .318 to .316 and his hitting streak came to an end, failing to break Benito Santiago's major league rookie hitting streak record of thirty-four games. But that was the least of Boston's troubles, as Kevin Millwood pitched seven innings for the Braves and gave up only two runs.

The visiting Braves had already clinched the first ever interleague series between them and the Sox, and things looked to get worst for their hosts in the third and final game.

Tom Glavine was pitching. Glavine was coming into the game with eleven victories and an earned run average below 3.10. Opposite Glavine was Steve Avery whose ERA just wasn't quite that low (above 6.50). Glavine got immediate help from his hitters when, in the second inning, Andruw Jones helped the Braves set a National League record. Keith Lockhart, Tony Graffanino, and Kenny Lofton were on base when Jones came to the plate. With that grand slam home run the Braves had set a National League record by hitting their tenth grand slam of the season.

From the second inning to the eighth inning, Glavine retired eighteen consecutive batters until Mo Vaughn hit his second home run of the night (the other was back in the first inning) in the eighth. The Braves won the third and final game of the series, 7-3. Over the course of the series the Braves had outscored the Red Sox 31-6, and out-hit them 48-21. Another interesting note, 98,589 fans came to the 1997 three game set. In all of 1952, only 280,000 fans attended Braves Field—the reason it was the Braves' last year in Boston.) In a single weekend, they had drawn more than one-third the 1952 total.

REMATCH IN 1998

Interleague play was such a success that it became an annual event, and each team would play their natural rivals each year. In 1998 the Braves-Red Sox series moved from Fenway to Turner Field. In the first game the Braves beat the Red Sox by only one run (7-6) by far the closest margin of victory in the rivalry yet. The game also proved to be the most exciting, as the Braves had to rally for six runs in the bottom of the ninth inning to ensure victory. Glavine pitched in this game, but didn't fare nearly as well as he had the previous year in Boston. He lasted six innings and gave up four runs on eight hits. Derek Lowe for Boston, on the other hand, pitched six innings as well but only allowed one run on five hits. "You can't explain it," said Braves third basemen Chipper Jones of the ninth-inning rally. "I'm at a loss for words."

The Red Sox decided enough was enough. For the second game of the series, the president of Nicaragua, Arnoldo Aleman, was in attendance to cheer on Atlanta's starting pitcher, Dennis Martinez. Aleman left disap-

pointed, because in the fourth inning the Red Sox broke a 1-1 tie by scoring five runs to ensure victory, 9-3. The Red Sox had gotten their first win against the Braves.

The third game was what everybody had been talking about. Pedro Martinez would square off for the first time against the Braves in a Red Sox uniform. Denny Neagle was going against Martinez, and that was considered a pitchers' duel; both had ERA's below 3.50. John Valentin, the third baseman for the Sox, hit two home runs in a game for the third time that season, and the Red Sox were able to get to Neagle early by scoring four runs by the end of the third inning. But Martinez wasn't sharp either, giving up three runs through six and imploding by allowing another three runs in the seventh before he was lifted. "I did everything I could. I was strong, I threw the ball hard and I was on top of everybody," Martinez would say after the game. He ended up getting the victory anyway as the Red Sox scored ten runs to Atlanta's six.

THE 1999 SEASON

Interleague rules changed a bit in 1999. Instead of the accustomed three games, the Natural Rivals would now play six games in two sets of three. I'm sure this didn't bother the fans, as each town (in this case, Boston and Atlanta) would now get to see these rivals at work during the same year. The first series of 1999 opened up at Fenway Park with the pitching match-up of a lifetime: Tom Glavine vs. Pedro Martinez. One future Hall of Famer vs. another. Glavine lasted seven innings, giving up four runs and striking out four, but Martinez stole the show on this night. He struck out a career high sixteen batters and reached double digits in strikeouts for the eighth time that season. Braves batters could only muster three hits (one of them a Ryan Klesko home run in the seventh) that night and the Red Sox won easily by a score of 5-1. "I felt I could throw it by anybody, and I did," Martinez said. Boston pitching coach Joe Kerrigan said, "I've never seen anyone locked in like he is."

The Braves would rather have not seen it at all.

The next game looked like an uneven match. For the first time in history, Greg Maddux would don his spikes to take the mound against Boston. His opponent was Brian Rose, a pitcher who had never won more than seven games in a season. Maddux lasted eight innings, but barely. He gave up eleven hits with four runs. Rose struggled, only able to go five innings he gave up four runs. With two outs and two on base in the fifth, Rose pitched to Brian Jordan, the Braves' right fielder. A three-run home run brought the Braves back into the game from down by one to up by two. The Red Sox came back by scoring two in the bottom of the sixth and one more in the eighth. It was now Tom "Flash" Gordon's game to close, which he couldn't quite do. He gave up two earned runs in the top of the ninth and the Red Sox went on to lose again by a score of 6-5.

The final game of the series went into extra innings. In the seventh Pat Rapp, the Boston starter, hit the Braves' catcher, Javy Lopez, in the helmet with a pitch. That would prove to be haunting. Kevin Millwood pitched brilliantly for the Braves, allowing only two runs in eight innings on two hits. In the top of the tenth inning Javy Lopez delivered the winning RBI single to put Atlanta ahead 3-2. John Rocker, the controversial pitcher, struck out the three batters he faced in the bottom of the tenth to give Atlanta the series victory.

The rivalry moved to Atlanta later in the year, during July, and the Red Sox hoped to put an end to their losing ways against Atlanta. That didn't look like it was going to happen as soon as Atlanta opened up the first two innings with three runs. But Boston had an answer this time, scoring five in the three innings after Atlanta's outburst. That proved to be all they would need as the Red Sox cruised to a 5-4 win. But if you look deeper into the box score perhaps you'll see that Atlanta still had the upper hand. The Braves out-hit Boston 8-5, and Boston committed three errors in this single game.

The second game lasted eleven innings. Tom Glavine, pitching on three days of rest, went the regulation nine innings and allowed only one run on six hits while striking out six. Boston's starter, Mark Portugal, went six innings also allowing only one run, this one coming by way of an Andruw Jones home run. 44,871 fans were on hand in Atlanta witnessing perhaps the most exciting

ending to Boston-Atlanta game yet. In the bottom of the eleventh Brian Hunter dropped a sacrifice bunt with Andruw Jones on first base. John Wasdin, the Boston pitcher, grabbed the ball and threw it to first. It sailed over first baseman Mike Stanley's head and Jones was able to score all the way from first base to give Atlanta the victory. Boston again committed three errors, with this last one proving fatal.

The third and final Atlanta-Boston game of 1999 was nowhere near as exciting. Greg Maddux simply dominated the opposition, going eight innings and allowing only one run. The victory gave him his fourth straight. "Maddux was awesome," said Atlanta manager Bobby Cox. Ryan Klesko helped Maddux's cause by homering two times. The final game of the 1999 series was won easily by Atlanta, 8-1.

THE 2000 SEASON

Entering the series in 2000 in Atlanta, Maddux (we sure hear a lot about him, don't we?) had been unbeaten in his previous six starts. Maddux obviously didn't have his best stuff for this game, giving up seven hits and four runs in just under seven innings. But that was of no concern to the Braves, after all, they were playing the Red Sox, a team they seemingly had no difficulty with. Atlanta was able to score six runs to Boston's four and earn yet another victory.

In the second game Boston's Peter Alan Schourek would go against Atlanta's Terry Mulholland. At 31 years old, Schourek had played for four different cities before coming to Boston in 2000 (he played ten games with Boston in 1998 before heading for Pittsburgh). Entering the game Schourek hadn't been having much success in the season sporting a record of 2-5, while Mulholland wasn't too successful either, going 5-5 up until this game. But records didn't matter anymore after the first three and two-thirds innings. Schourek allowed five runs on seven hits in that time frame, and the Red Sox had still managed to not score. The Red Sox bullpen fared well, giving up only one run and two hits over the last four and one-third innings. But the Braves' bullpen fared even better. Mulholland lasted five innings pitching shutout ball and Kerry Ligtenberg, Rudy Seanez, Don Wengert, and Mike Remlinger combined for four and one-third shutout innings in relief. The Braves had won again, this time 6-0.

In the eighth inning of the third game in the series, Boston's Jose Offerman broke open the game. It was a tie game, 2-2, and Offerman lined a shot to Turner Field's center area, where Andruw Jones played flawless defense. The ball went over his head and was a sure fire double. Nothing more. Nothing less. But as Jones went to pick it up he kicked the ball (scored as an error, his first of the season), and being an alert baserunner, Offerman kept running at full tilt. Jones got the throw in to the relay man and he threw it home. But it was too late. Offerman slid across home plate and put the Red Sox ahead 3-2. "It was too hot to be running like that," said Offerman. Earlier in the game Offerman had scored from first base on a Nomar Garciaparra double. The Red Sox overcame strong pitching by Tom Glavine (seven innings, two runs, five hits) to beat the Braves for only the fifth time in series history (final score, 5-3).

The 2000 series then headed back to Beantown on July 7. Tom Glavine was pitching again, only the Red Sox didn't have a Pedro Martinez countering this time. Instead, they had the journeyman Schourek against one of the best pitchers of the era in Glavine. Schourek couldn't get past the second inning, lasting only one and two-thirds and giving up seven hits and five runs. The Red Sox hitters couldn't do much with what Glavine handed them either, scoring only three runs in the eighth inning. Jose Offerman continued to have some success against the Braves by getting three hits, but it wasn't enough as the Red Sox once again fell victim to the Braves, 5-3.

The next day the Braves once again stifled the Red Sox by out-pitching and out-hitting them. Javy Lopez, the Braves' catcher, drove in three runs while the Braves' pitcher, Terry Mulholland, pitched eight innings and gave up only one run. Mulholland entered the game leading the National League with the fewest walks per nine innings (1.9) and showed the Red Sox how, not walking anybody in his eight innings. The Braves again pulled out another easy victory, beating the Red Sox 5-1.

Nomar Garciaparra wanted to stop the bleeding. It was getting to be too much for him. He wanted to win, and if his team couldn't beat the Braves... well, just who could they beat? Boston was on a five-game losing streak heading into this game with Atlanta and Kevin Millwood would pitch against Tim Wakefield. Millwood was only able to last four innings and he gave up two home runs to Garciaparra. The first home run came in the third inning as a solo shot which gave the Red Sox a 2-1 lead. His second came in the fifth right after Brian Daubach hit a triple that gave Boston a 6-2 lead. The Red Sox were finally able to beat the Braves in a good way, winning by a 7-2 score. Boston tallied fourteen hits, an extraordinary number considering how the other games in this rivalry had gone up to that point.

The 2001 Season

Turner Field was the host for the first Braves-Red Sox series in 2001. Greg Maddux pitched against the Sox, and he had one more bit of help: thousands of swarming moths. Moths were flying all over the playing field (and the grandstands) and getting into the players' line of vision. Boston overcame the odds, though, as Boston was losing 5-4 heading into the top of the ninth inning. Trot Nixon, the Red Sox's right fielder, hit a sacrifice fly to tie the game and send it into extra innings. In the tenth inning Nixon hit an RBI single to give Boston the lead 6-5, and Boston would go on to score three more runs and ultimately win the game 9-5.

Two series wins in a row was too much for the Braves to take. John Burkett pitched for the Braves and lasted eight innings, strong ones at that, giving up only two hits and no runs. Burkett struck out eight Red Sox batters, while for the Red Sox Hideo Nomo pitched six and a third innings and gave up six runs (four earned) on seven hits. 50,544 packed into a sold out Turner Field to watch the Braves unleash their fury upon the Red Sox. The Braves scored and scored a lot: eight runs to the Red Sox zero.

But the Red Sox weren't quite ready to play the part of the "Dead Sox," as the saying goes. In the third and final game they managed to squeeze out another victory to take the series. Slugger Manny Ramirez broke out of a 3-for-38 slump with an RBI double, which at the time was only his third RBI in nine games. Frank Castillo, the Boston starting pitcher that day, held the Braves scoreless until the sixth inning when he gave up two runs. The Red Sox won 4-3, taking a rare series victory from the Braves.

The action returned to Fenway for another thriller. The Red Sox were ahead going into the eighth inning by a score of 3-2 but Chipper Jones hit a home run to tie the game. The Braves quickly scored two runs in the ninth inning, but the Red Sox weren't ready to roll over just yet. Trot Nixon and Manny Ramirez hit back-to-back home runs in the bottom of the ninth inning to send it to the tenth. But the Braves are the Braves, and that means they beat the Red Sox. Atlanta loaded the bases in the top of the tenth and Brian Jordan came to bat. The single that he hit scored one and gave the Braves a 6-5 lead, the final score of the game.

Hideo Nomo went six innings and gave up five hits and only one run with five strike outs in the second game of the series. Sox manager Jimy Williams came out to the mound in the seventh inning after a leadoff single. When Nomo saw Williams make his way out he slammed the ball into his glove, turned his back to Williams and looked out into left field. The move didn't cost the Red Sox anything as they won 3-1. Jimy Williams became the sixth manager in Red Sox history to win at least 400 games with the Red Sox, and the first since Don Zimmer from 1976-1980. Boston had previously lost six of its last eight home games.

In the final meeting of the teams in 2001, Tom Glavine pitched against Tomokazu Ohka. Glavine went seven innings giving up three hits and zero runs. After a first inning walk to Jose Offerman and a single to Trot Nixon, Glavine retired sixteen of the next seventeen batters he faced. Nothing much else happened in this game except for the fact that Glavine passed Rick Reuschel on the all-time wins list (75th place). The Braves cruised to victory by scoring eight runs and preventing the Red Sox from scoring any.

THE 2002 SEASON

Pedro Martinez was scheduled to pitch the 2002 series opener at Turner Field. His opponent would be Kevin Millwood, who had become a more established pitcher. But Martinez, in the minds of sportswriters and fans, had the upper hand. After all, this was Pedro Martinez, a three-time Cy Young award winner (he's finished in the top ten five times, never placing lower than number two). But Millwood was ready for the match-up. Millwood went seven innings while Martinez went eight. Millwood gave up one run on three hits and left after the seventh with a no-decision, the game tied at 1-1. Martinez had pitched solidly in his eight innings, giving up two runs on eight hits with five strikeouts. He recorded the loss, but it was no fault of his. The Red Sox just couldn't hit against the Braves. Chris Hammond pitched a scoreless eighth inning to earn the win for the Braves and John Smoltz earned his twentieth save of the year.

In the second game John Burkett would be pitching again. But this time it wasn't for the Braves; instead, he'd be pitching against his former team. Both starters went six innings and both gave up seven hits, but the one small difference was the one that mattered the most. Maddux allowed two runs, Burkett allowed three. Those three runs proved to be all the Braves needed as the Red Sox weren't able to score against Chris Hammond, Kevin Gryboski, or John Smoltz. The Braves would go on to score one more off knuckleballer Tim Wakefield to win the game 4-2 and hand Burkett his second loss of the season.

Derek Lowe had thrown a no-hitter earlier in the year against the Tampa Bay Devil Rays, and he was proving to be the Red Sox's best starter of the season. He had eleven wins (only two losses), so who else would you want standing on the mound in Turner Field with a series-sweep on the line? Lowe showed the Braves why he had been drawing Cy Young Award debates so early in the season by dazzling the hitters with off-speed pitches and breaking balls. Lowe went seven innings and allowed the only Braves run of the day. For the Braves, however, Glavine didn't fare as well. He allowed five runs, only three of them earned. The Red Sox ended up with six runs and a victory as the Braves' bats were quieted for at least one day.

Just over a week later the series moved to Fenway Park. In the first game John Burkett would be squaring off against old teammate Greg Maddux once again. In the fifth inning Maddux's duty was cut short. In the first inning Carlos Baerga, the Sox's second basemen, lined a Maddux pitch right back to the pitchers' mound and hit Maddux above the right ankle. In the fifth inning, after giving up three total hits and one unearned run, the ankle started to bother him and he was forced to come out of the game. Burkett pitched solidly as well, giving up only two runs in seven innings, but it wasn't good enough to get the win as the Braves got to Tim Wakefield for two runs and the victory, 4-2.

In the second game Derek Lowe would once again go against Atlanta's Kevin Millwood. Lowe pitched about as well as he could against a team like the Braves: seven innings surrendering just two runs on six hits. The only mark against him that seemed to matter was his pitch to Gary Sheffield in the third inning with one runner on. Sheffield proceeded to hit a two-run home run with two outs, which would prove to be the difference in the game. Nomar Garciaparra hit a double and Manny Ramirez drove him in sixth inning to get their only run against Millwood that day. Millwood lasted five and two-thirds innings giving up only four hits and that lone run. Atlanta gave the game to their bullpen, which had been so successful throughout the year. That same thought would hold true as the relievers didn't allow more than two hits and John Smoltz pitched a perfect ninth inning to earn his twenty-seventh save of the season.

In the final game of series Frank Castillo was set to pitch for the Red Sox.

It was the same story all over again. Boston's pitchers pitched well, but not well enough for the win.

Castillo went six innings giving up three runs, but Atlanta's starter, Jason Marquis, one-upped him by lasting six and two-thirds and giving up only two runs. The game went into the tenth inning with the score tied at

three. But Atlanta was Atlanta, and somehow they always proved to be the better team in this Natural Rivalry.

Atlanta rallied for four runs in the top of the tenth, from which Boston could never recover and went quietly into the last of the tenth. Atlanta had won again, this time 7-3.

For one reason or another the "Powers That Be" have decided that in 2003 the Red Sox and Atlanta Braves will not play each other. Perhaps the series will start up again in 2004. Or, perhaps, the fans will have to wait for these two team to play each other in a World Series.

Red Sox fans just hope that series doesn't start where it left off.

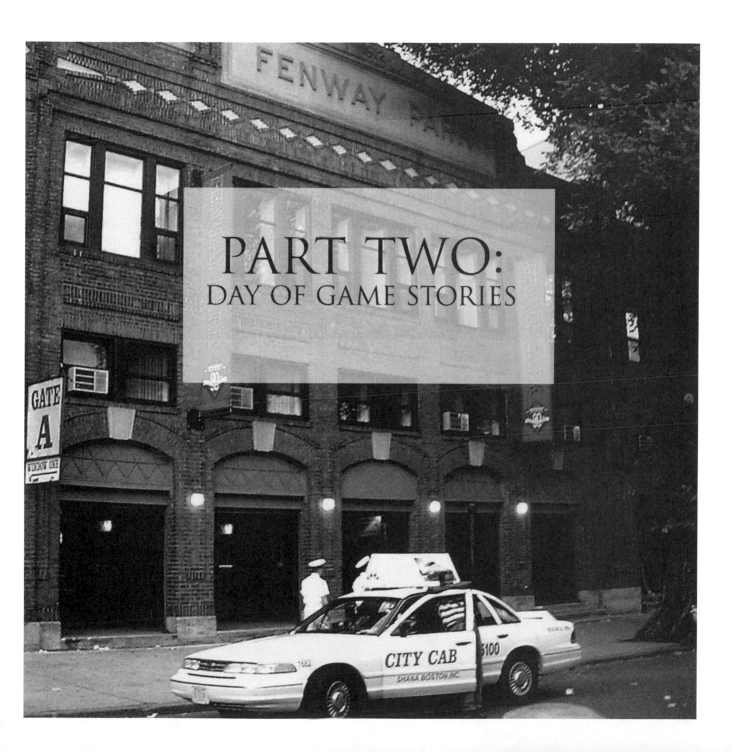

PART TWO:
DAY OF GAME STORIES

Roster lists:

1 Furcal, Rafael - INF
2 Garcia, Jesse - INF
4 Franco, Matt - INF
7 Lockhart, Keith - INF
8 Lopez, Javy - C
10 Jones, Chipper - OF
11 Sheffield, Gary - OF
18 Helms, Wes - INF
19 Castilla, Vinny - INF

20 Blanco, Henry - C
23 Franco, Julio - INF
25 Jones, Andruw - OF
27 Moss, Damian - LHP
28 Bragg, Darren - OF
29 Smoltz, John - RHP
31 Maddux, Greg - RHP
34 Millwood, Kevin - RHP
36 Hammond, Chris - LHP

37 Remlinger, Mike - LHP
38 Marquis, Jason - RHP
40 Holmes, Darren - RHP
43 Spooneyberger, Tim - RHP
46 Ligtenberg, Kerry - RHP
47 Glavine, Tom - LHP
49 Gryboski, Kevin - RHP

D.L.
Lopez, A.
DeRosa, M.
Giles, M.

33137

RED SOX	POS	1	2	3	4	5	6	7	8	9	10	AB	R	H	RBI
1	18 Johnny Damon	CF	4·3		4·3		cK	FPS			SK					
2	10 Carlos Baerga	2B	1-4 -7	SK				4·3	=7							
3	5 Nomar Garciaparra	SS	5·4 -7		SB E3			6·3	IBB							
4	24 Manny Ramirez	LF	FC	4·3			SU BB	7								
5	23 Brian Daubach	1B		6·3	4·3		BB		BB							
35 (22) CLARK																
6	29 Shea Hillenbrand	3B		=7	4·3		FC	cK		2-5-2-8						
7	33 Jason Varitek	C	cK	4·3		(x)7 DP 6·3										
8	7 Trot Nixon	RF	4·3		4·3	SK	6·3									
9	30 Jose Offerman	DH	SB E43B	cK	BB	4·3										
TOTALS	R/H	0 2	0 1	1 0	0 0	0 0	0 0	1 2	0 0	0 0	1					
		1	1	0	0	0	2	3	0	0						

PITCHERS	IP	H	R	ER	BB	SO	W/L
19 RHP John Burkett	7	8	2	2	3	4	
43 EMBREE	0.1	0	0	0	2	0	
34 GARCES	0.2	0	0	0	1	0	
49 WAKEFIELD	1.0	3	2	2	1	1	
	9.0	11	4	4	7	5	

M.L. Staff
3 Little, Grady - Manager
16 Kipper, Bob - Coach
20 Stanley, Mike - Coach
25 Evans, Dwight - Coach
39 Cubbage, Mike - Coach 3B
40 Cloninger, Tony - Coach
51 Harper, Tommy - Coach 1B

5 Garciaparra, Nomar - INF
7 Nixon, Trot - OF
10 Baerga, Carlos - INF
17 Banks, Willie - RHP
18 Damon, Johnny - OF
19 Burkett, John - RHP
22 Clark, Tony - INF
23 Daubach, Brian - INF
24 Ramirez, Manny - OF

26 Merloni, Lou - INF
28 Mirabelli, Doug - C
29 Hillenbrand, Shea - INF
30 Offerman, Jose - INF
32 Lowe, Derek - RHP
33 Varitek, Jason - C
34 Garces, Rich - RHP
35 Henderson, Rickey - OF
37 Castillo, Frank - RHP

41 Urbina, Ugueth - RHP
43 Embree, Alan - LHP
45 Martinez, Pedro - RHP
47 Kim, Sunny - RHP
49 Wakefield, Tim - RHP
56 Haney, Chris - LHP
58 Nelson, Bryant - INF/OF

D.L.
Hermanson, D.
Sanchez, R.
Pickering, C.
Arrojo, R.

Susan Riggs

I attended my first major league game at Fenway Park in the summer of 1968, between my junior and senior years in college. I sat out in the bleachers in right field as I did again tonight. I had not attended a Fenway game in the intervening thirty-four years so I was quite excited to be returning. Unfortunately, I didn't fit as comfortably in the seat now as I did then.

I remember watching others keep score that summer and trying to learn how. Everyone was friendly out there.

Tonight I had brought a Walkman-type Sony radio which really helped since it was very hard to see the ball and the plays against the background of fans. A frightening moment was the ball hit off Greg Maddux's leg.

I noticed tonight the vendors in their yellow Aramark shirts, the popcorn and cotton candy on sticks, the big Cherry Coke bottles on the lights, "the green monster," some creepy Bleacher Creatures and what looked to be hot dogs but apparently were ice cream treats. I enjoyed my Fenway Frank.

What was neat about our seats was that they were only two rows back of the bullpen, and we watched the game with baseballs sailing in front of our eyes from warming up pitchers to their catchers.

I wasn't fond of the crush of people on the subway but the "T" employees were efficient and helpful.

It was great to revisit historic Fenway again. It's a ballpark with a grand tradition. I hope it can be saved but it needs more legroom under seats!

MISERY LOVES COMPANY

Will Christensen

Being a Boston Red Sox fan is misery. And misery loves company. Generations of Red Sox fans are defined by their pain. It's what binds them. Children of today are told horror stories about Bucky "Bleeping" Dent by fathers who talked about Johnny Pesky holding the ball and who in turn were taught about selling Babe Ruth to finance *No No Nanette*.

Yet baseball fans everywhere have benefited from Sox fans' anguish. Think about it. How much richer is the history of baseball because of what New Englanders have had to endure?

Put another way, how many stories do you know about the New York Yankees? Stories, not legends. Twenty-six world championships, and if it weren't for *Ball Four* would any be part of our oral traditions? For every story you know about the Yankees, I can tell you a dozen about the Sox, and I grew up in Ohio.

Then there's the drunk who once said to no one in particular, "Why the Hell did they pull Willoughby?" and passed out on the bar, months after that fateful 1975 World Series game.

... And then there's the guy who backed up traffic for hours because he refused to drive into the Sumner Tunnel until Reggie Smith batted with bases loaded in a key game during the Sox's improbable pennant run in 1967.

... And then there's the driver who got so incensed at the sight of Bob Stanley in a car the next lane over, he pulled up beside him, rolled down his window so he could berate the hapless reliever and plowed into a parked car.

That's great stuff.

One of the two best endings to any nonfiction book was the paperback version of *The Curse of the Bambino* by

Dan Shaughnessy, who wrote in the new finale how he met Stephen King and when King found out that Shaughnessy was a baseball writer, said, "I've never written a horror story about baseball," whereupon Shaughnessy replied, "I have."

Of course, the Red Sox play in one of baseball's most storied stadiums—Fenway Park. Fenway is hallowed ground to a baseball fan. Babe Ruth played there. Ty Cobb. Ted Williams. Joe DiMaggio. It's a playground of the Gods.

Thanks to the SABR convention being in Boston, I got a chance to return to Fenway. I've seen two games there. The first one was probably the best ballgame I ever saw in person. In 1991, I saw Frank Thomas, one of my favorite players, hit a monster shot over the Green Monster off Roger Clemens. Robin Ventura hit two homers, including a two-out, two-run job in the top of the ninth inning off Jeff Reardon to tie the game. The game went 14 innings and the White Sox finally won 14-8 as Melido Perez pitched six innings of one-hit relief. There were several great defensive plays and the game even was delayed briefly in the first inning when Busty Hart bounced out on the field to buss Clemens before earning a police escort off the field.

The second game was the Futures Game at the 1999 All-Star break, when a nobody by the name of Alfonso Soriano slayed the Monster with two blasts.

So I was looking forward to seeing the Braves "come home" to Boston and play the Red Sox. My seats were out in the right-field bleachers. I took my mitt, just in case.

As the grounds crew raked the infield after batting practice, a highlight video played on the scoreboard. It was of the 1986 Red Sox.

I dined on Fenway Franks as the all-too familiar images flashed across the screen. There was the team's romp through the division and its improbable victory over the Angels in the League Championship Series, a result that led to the eventual suicide of California reliever Donnie Moore, who couldn't cope with the thought he blew the pennant when his team was one strike away from winning and going to the World Series.

But because this is Boston, the video did not stop with the pennant celebration. The video kept going, through the World Series and an interview with Bill Buckner where he said he had a nightmare that he would miss a ground ball that would cost the team the series.

The Bambino must have taken notice, because as we all know that's exactly what happened. And when the ball rolled between Buckner's legs—again—a groan filled Fenway. Three rows behind me, a young guy cringed like he had been slugged in the gut and then began to laugh. "I've seen that play 200 times, and every time I watch, I think it's going to be different."

Did I mention that Red Sox fans love their misery?

After finishing my ballpark meal, I went to find my seat, and it wasn't long before I realized my mitt would be as useless to me as Buckner's had been to him. I was in the Uecker seats, the very last row, right under the first "U" in the Dunkin' Donuts sign. If I had been any farther away from home plate, I'd have been in Pedro's ride in the players' parking lot. There would be no home-run ball for me.

It was a beautiful night. The sun was setting behind the third-base stands, throwing colors across the summer sky, and the temperature was shorts-cool. At Veterans Stadium, it would've been a great night to be at the yard. At Fenway, it was perfect.

I started talking with a gentleman in the next seat. His name was Glenn Merkel—"e-l, not l-e like the baseball player"—and he was a genial New Englander who grew up in and still lived near Worcester, Mass. Glenn was a big-time Red Sox fan and knew his history, though he is not a member of SABR.

We talked about Lee Richmond, who threw Major League Baseball's first perfect game for the Worcester Brown Stockings in 1880, and he regaled me with stories about the Royal Rooters, a band of fans who used to sit in the Fenway Park bleachers, who were so noted that sometimes the games wouldn't start until they had arrived. Glenn told me they were led by "Nuf Ced" McGreevey, who always would settle arguments the Rooters had at a bar across the street before the games.

The row would be going full tilt, and McGreevey finally would slam his fist down on the bar and say "'Nuff said," and that would be that, Glenn said. Time to head to the game.

He also gave me the perfect trivia question: Who was the only man to play for the Red Sox, Celtics and Bruins? Yep. It's a trick question. The answer is John Kiley, who played organ for the Sox and the two Boston Garden dwellers.

And he told me about Ted Williams. Williams had been four years into retirement by the time I was born, so I never got a chance to see him play except via videotape. Glenn practically grew up with the Splinter.

"What was it like to watch Ted Williams play?" I asked.

"It was electric. The entire ballpark would come alive as soon as he walked to the plate."

I volunteered that perhaps it was like with Mark McGwire in 1998 when people would leave the john, the concession-stand lines, whatever, just to see him hit and then immediately return to what they were doing. Glenn said it was like that.

"Well, he was John Wayne with a bat," Glenn said, a week before everyone was using that phrase on the news after Williams had died. They were both heroes. Except that John Wayne was an actor; Teddy Ballgame was 100 percent real, at all times.

I asked Glenn if any of the current Sox players generated the same current at the park, and without hesitating, he said, "Nomar. Nomar Garciaparra is like that."

Good choice. Boston fans can pick them. But then they have a reputation of being intelligent fans, even if they like to flog themselves a bit too much.

So, with the setting as good as it was, the game didn't need to be anything more than adequate. It was actually pretty good, the second best I've seen at Fenway. Greg Maddux started for the Braves but only went five innings before leaving with a 2-1 lead. In the first inning, he gave up back-to-back hits to Carlos Baerga and Nomar, who did in fact have the crowd buzzing with every at bat. With one out and Manny Ramirez at the plate, Maddux was in early trouble.

Or so we thought.

Instead he whipped around a pickoff toss to second and completely hung Baerga out to dry. End of threat.

On the other side, there was John Burkett, which was interesting because he had been with the Braves the year before and was a protégé of Maddux. Now the student would get to face the master, like in *Star Wars*. The student did pretty well for himself, leaving a tie game in the seventh.

The Braves got on the board first when Darren Bragg walked, moved to third on a single and scored on a double play. The Sox got the run back in their half of the third.

Bragg then scored the go-ahead run in the fifth, but the Braves blew a chance to blow the game open when Gary Sheffield and Chipper Jones left the bases loaded with two cans of corn to Ramirez in left.

Bragg was the game's MVP. With a large SABR contingent in attendance, it made sense. Bragg's game was a sabermetrician's dream. He went two-for-two, with three walks—a perfect five-for-five on-base game—and two runs.

The Sox tied the game in the seventh but, like the Braves had earlier, they missed a big opportunity when Jones caught Ramirez's bases-loaded drive with his back to the Monster.

Not that a lot of fans noticed. Bleacher bums had been trying

Michael Freiman

As I was walking toward the gate to enter Fenway Park, I heard some audio snippets from old Red Sox games, which the Sox seem to have been playing as background noise outside the stadium. Maybe this was somewhat subtle; others I talked to during and after the game did not seem to have noticed it. It seemed odd, though, that the call I picked up on was not of some "great" moment in Red Sox history, but rather of the most infamous event in the recent history of the team, Bill Buckner's error.

to get a wave started since the sixth inning and finally had succeeded, and yes, this was with the Red Sox trying to rally down one run. Maybe Sox fans aren't so bright after all.

The Sox got out of a bases-loaded jam in the eighth, but the Braves finally broke through with two out in the ninth, when Vinny Castilla singled in Sheffield. Castilla would score an insurance run.

Whereupon the Sox faithful began heading for the exits. With John Smoltz warming up, perhaps it was just as well, but I never leave a game early because you never know.

Sox fans know; they've known for decades. Sure enough, Smoltz took the Sox out one-two-three, and the Braves had a 4-2 victory.

As we began filing out of Fenway, a fan asked if anyone had heard if the Yankees had won that night. When told they had, his face fell. With a New York victory, the Sox, who had been in front nearly the whole season, had fallen behind their nemesis.

A sense of inevitable gloom descended over the crowd as they silently made their way to the T stop, their cars or the nearby drinking establishments already swelled to overflowing. The feeling dissipated quickly. When you live and die and die and die with the Red Sox, it becomes a part of you.

And as we all went our separate ways into the cool New England night, there was but one thought shared by the denizens of Red Sox Nation:

Yankees suck.

Andy Moye

To paraphrase Faulkner, the past at Boston's Fenway Park isn't dead, it isn't even past. Rising out of the dankness under the stands to the field, one can easily imagine being transported to the 1920s. As viewed from the bleachers in right center, the fans in the distance might well be wearing fedoras and wide brimmed hats with ribbons-friendly, joyous ghosts of baseball's past. Fenway's past, however, isn't just a gossamer breeze lifting fans' spirits. It's also a fearsome specter lurking in every shadow.

Before the game, they will once again replay Bill Buckner's monumental gaffe on the screen behind us, as if whistling past the graveyard. After the game, the sportswriters will blame the ghosts of the Boston Braves. The weight of the past presses down on Fenway and the Red Sox. Indeed, writing 150 years before, Boston's Nathaniel Hawthorne described it perfectly:

"Shall we never get rid of this Past? It lies upon the present like a giant's dead body! In fact, the case is just as if a young giant were compelled to waste all his strength in carrying about the corpse of the old giant who only needs to be decently buried."

How to bury the Bambino and lift the curse? Perhaps Boston's past could be turned on itself. Around the corner from Fenway, in the Governor's office, sits an old Bible—unseen by anyone save the state's Governor for 200 years. In it, each Governor on leaving office has written his worst mistakes for the next Governor to take warning.

Had the Sox kept such a document, perhaps some-one would have warned Harry Frazee not to sell a player who had just led the league in slugging, home runs, RBIs and runs while going 9 and 5 on the mound. Were they keeping it today, Tim Wakefield would write that hanging a curve to Gary Sheffield should be avoided. John Burkett might caution to never throw perfect strikes on an 0-2 count. And Grady Little might advise that testing Chipper Jones' arm was a better bet than testing Greg Maddux's.

Fenway's attraction is in its past, but one must learn from history or be buried by it. Selling the Bambino was a mistake. Not getting in front of a grounder in the 6th game of the World Series was a mistake. But neither Frazee nor Buckner served up a double to Sheffield, or gave Lockhart an 0-2 strike, or gave up a chance for the lead because of fear of one of the league's weakest left fielders. In a way, this game is a microcosm of the Sox's fail-ure to advance—basic mistakes blamed on the Babe. The Sox need to give the Babe a decent bur-ial and remember the mistakes.

GRAND TOUR

Bob Brady

It began with a note posted on a message board by the SABR 32 registration desk. The notice invited con-vention attendees to partake in a Friday morning trek of historic ballpark sites in Boston, culminating in an on-the-field afternoon tour of Fenway Park. As a native Bostonian, I've "been there and done that" but each subsequent visit seems to reveal something new or prompts the recollection of a long-forgotten, cherished memory of the Hub's 90-year-old heirloom. The tour also offered me the unique opportunity to gain a fresh perspective by observing first-time visitors' reactions to "Friendly Fenway's" hallowed ground.

Despite the prospect of having to miss conflicting and equally desirable panels and research presentations, I opted for the tour and marched with a group of over thirty SABR ballpark aficionados from the convention site to the South End Grounds, to the Huntington Avenue Grounds, to Braves Field and, finally, to Fenway Park. The group "paid its dues" in order to reach the trip's grand finale. Boston was unseasonably hot and humid that day, not optimum conditions for these out-door activities. In addition, my fellow travelers received their transit baptism on Boston's famed MBTA and shared an experience similar to "Charlie" who many years ago had difficulty trying to get off the predecessor MTA.

Just before the appointed hour of one p.m., the assembled multitude was rousted from its makeshift concrete stoop seating along Yawkey Way and led into Fenway Park via Gate E. The tour guide, along with two moonlighting "ball girls," directed the SABRites into a section of the left field loge. Our hosts valiantly tried to corral the group into the seats and fend off the urge of many of their guests to immediately commence exploring and/or photographing the numerous historically significant nooks and crannies of the ballpark. Once some semblance of order was established, our guide commenced his presentation and coupled it with trivia questions. Obviously, he was not familiar with SABR and quickly had the tables turned on him as he was peppered with trivia questions on a par with those offered during our convention contests.

Sensing that he was outmatched, our guide commenced the on-field portion of the tour.

The first stop, the home team dugout, was declared "off limits" due to the aftermath of flooding from the previous day's thunderstorm. Several of our colleagues, unwilling to forego a once-in-a-lifetime opportunity, chose to ignore the edict and proceeded to place their backsides squarely where Nomar, Manny, Pedro, Rickey, Derek, Jason, Shea, Trot and other Bosox would be perched that evening. What they discovered was that these were by far not the best seats in the house. In fact, the view was fairly limited unless one perched on the dugout's outer lip. These guerrilla actions brought about a much sterner warning from our guide regarding treading on the Fenway turf. We could tell that he meant business this time and only an occasional toe meekly intruded upon the periphery of the greenery.

Our circumnavigation of the ballpark led us next to "Pesky's Pole" and the right field box seats that are strangely angled so as not to face home plate. Above the right field grandstand is a roof adorned with the retired uniform numbers of five Sox greats as well as the immortal Jackie Robinson's numeral—and a huge jug of milk! Our guide informed us that the initial sequence of the original four retired Bosox uniform numbers, "9-4-1-8," was rearranged because it served as a sad reminder of the last, distant time that the home team claimed a World Series championship, September 4, 1918.

All along the route, we were regaled with other tales, some true and some apocryphal, about happenings on and off this illustrious diamond. From our position on the outfield warning track, we were instructed to look far up into the bleachers' sea of green chairs and locate a solitary red-backed seat in right centerfield that forever commemorates a Ted Williams record clout of yore. We passed "Williamsburg," the Spartan bullpens constructed to shorten the distance required for Splendid Splinter home runs. Reminding us of the area's ties to the Revolutionary War, John Hancock's distinct signature crowns the park's giant centerfield video scoreboard. Originally intended as a bold gesture in support of independence from an imperious king, Hancock's signature, now a corporate logo, is as close as the Red Sox have come to date toward selling the naming rights to Fenway Park.

Our next stop was to the field's crown jewel—the fabled "Green Monster." The wall cast its spell on tour members. Before us lay a symbolic barrier that kept the real world on its other side from intruding into our "field of dreams." An urge to embrace its huge emerald pockmarked façade swept through the assemblage. What had been so distant before could now be poked, prodded and peered into. Through bunker-like slits in the scoreboard, the secrets of the Monster's innards were exposed. A baseball emerged from someone's pocket and was promptly commandeered for feeble attempts at reenacting the fielding prowess of Messrs. Williams and Yastrzemski. While the ownership regime had recently changed, a vestige of the Yawkey era remained—the Morse Coded initials of Jean Yawkey, still imprinted within the striping of the scoreboard. Straining our necks upward, we could make out the painted-over outline of last year's "100 Red Sox Seasons" commemorative logo, replaced by the current celebratory graphic denoting Fenway's 90th anniversary.

Looking further upward beyond the wall's netting, acting as a companion bookend to the right field milk jug, were giant Coca Cola bottles, initially maligned by some as a desecration of this temple of baseball. The tonic (New England parlance for "soda pop") bottles had recently been retouched to reflect the marketing of a new flavor—Vanilla Coke.

Before exiting the field, we briefly stopped at the yellow left field foul line demarcation. You couldn't help but mentally replay Carlton Fisk's memorable body-English-influenced Game Six homer in the 1975 World

Series. And, you had to wonder, was this section of the wall really at least 310 feet in distance from the plate as the white numerals by the foul line declared? Painted over but still visible under the footage sign was the former companion measurement in meters. At least in this one instance, baseball tradition has prevailed and this alien dimension has been banished. Leaving the field and walking back into the left field grandstand, we could see a "second" Green Monster that emerged from the roof of a building on Landsdowne Street/Ted Williams Way. On a huge billboard, a local bank has created a replica of the wall together with a 514-foot distance notation.

We continued our uphill jaunt, having been directed to a walkway leading up to the 600 Club that resides high atop the home plate area of the park. [The 600 Club was renamed the .406 Club after Ted Williams' death the week following the June 28th ballgame. –Eds.] Upon entering the facility, one was immediately struck by the artificiality of its environment—from its cool conditioned air to the framed jersey of fictional Cheers bartender and ex-Red Sox pitcher Sam Malone on the wall. The theater-style seats seemed appropriate as the chairs faced a Cinerama-like "screen" comprised of an unbreakable mosaic of glass panels. In fact, according to the guide, field microphones are needed to pipe game-action sound into this hermetically sealed amphitheater. We were told that the Club's construction, which allegedly altered wind currents favorable to batters, was particularly disliked by former Red Sox infielder Jody Reed. Reed purportedly spent much of his pregame practice time during the season directing a barrage of hard-hit fungoes against the glass. As a reward for his politically incorrect behavior, Mr. Reed was supposedly shipped out of town.

Our tour completed, we were ushered out onto the street for our inevitable return to reality. A three stop trolley ride on the MBTA Green Line brought us back to SABR 32 in time for a rich sampling of research presentations prior to a return to the venerable ballpark for the evening's interleague contest between the Red Sox and Braves.

A SYSTEMATIC STROLL TOWARDS FENWAY PARK

Jeff Twiss

I have walked through residential neighborhoods, ethnic enclaves, and factory districts to get to baseball games. I have walked under train trestles and over interstate highways. Today I will walk through one of the most architecturally distinguished urban centers in the country.

I join a crowd of SABRites and plunge through the lobby of the Boston Park Plaza Hotel and onto Arlington Street. We cross to the other side as a roller-blader weaves in and out of our group. I can already feel the adrenaline rush of approaching the ballpark. It's only a fifteen-minute walk, Seamus Kearney had said during Wednesday's plenary session.

But there's a glorious greensward appearing before my eyes already: The Public Garden. I recognize the familiar surprise at seeing a fragment of nature clasped in a setting of concrete and steel. I pass a statue of William Ellery Channing... who's that?

It's Friday afternoon, the weekend is here; a million people are happy and about 30,000 of them will be at the game. Burkett vs. Maddux, a good match-up. I wonder if fans will be going straight from offices to the game in their suits.

I head down Newbury, past Emmanuel Episcopal Church. What a music schedule! I will have to see about coming back here on Sunday at 10 AM. Is it okay if I'm more interested in the music than the service?

I continue on down Newbury Street (am I going down or up?) and it's like I'm on Fifth Avenue, without naming any names. I see a stately building, probably hundreds of years old, that was saved by turning it into a bistro and shopping center. Looming above it are the towers that replaced the presumably less stately buildings.

I have the option to find my own way, so I turn right and head roughly north on Clarendon, towards Commonwealth. I consider the likely fate of Fenway's Green Monster: a carefully preserved relic in a corner of the new Stadium/Shopping/Entertainment Complex. Instead of the Fifth Avenue shops, I find before me a store with almost as many phonetic symbols as letters in its name. It's a pleasing effect, like a pictogram.

I arrive at Commonwealth Avenue and find that it's a boulevard with a beautiful, wide, tree-lined mall—a designated Boston landmark. Uh-oh, it appears to have a statue every block—can I note them all? Damn, it's already 6:23 and I've advanced about three blocks towards my intended destination. But Seamus said I could get there in fifteen minutes. Tonight's game should be a good match-up: Maddux is having another good year, but a note in today's paper seems to suggest he's still having problems with that butt muscle. And Burkett—the subject of some amusing repartee during today's journalist's panel, started out great but may have gone into a slide recently.

Patrick Andrew Collins, a talented, generous, kind man, is the first of those I see to be enshrined on the Commonwealth Avenue Mall. Maybe I'll get a complete lineup if I persevere.

William Lloyd Garrison, now him I've heard of. Tall slender guy, Mark Belanger type. He's my shortstop.

Samuel Eliot Morison, great name—you gotta love that single 'l' single 'r' look. Nice cap, too. Since he's clutching a pair of binoculars instead of a stopwatch, we'll make him a scout. Plus he looks real comfortable sitting down—could be a bench coach or an eye in the sky. If pressed into action he'd be a decent but light-hitting second baseman. "To my readers, young and old:"

A FLOWNE SHEATE
A FAIRE WINDE
A BOUNE VOYAGE

Yeah, we're rolling now!

One thing I really like about this mall—you can tell they're planning for the long term. They've got a good mix of young, veteran, and ancient trees. That's the sign of a dynasty like the Atlanta Braves: success over several generations. It's a nice, residential, street, lots of brownstones, good people. I wonder if it's rental or condominia? Hey look—there's a couple with a brace of cocker spaniels! Beautiful!

Whoa... here's a closer... look at this guy looking at you. He's sawed off a few bats with some inside heat. Domingo F. Sarmiento, el presidente (of Argentina)... the Argentine Machine...

Now at intersection of Hereford and Commonwealth, 6:57, eight minutes to first pitch. I really wanted to see Claudia Perry throw out the first ball. What a great, energetic President of our organization!

It looks like we're coming to a transition. Street signs are giving way to highway signs, the walkway has terminated and I am confronted with a marvel of highway engineering—some kind of underpass. And I've got only four guys on my team—five if I go back and pick up Channing for one of the power slots in the outfield.

The whole game has undergone a sea-change as I cross Massachusetts Avenue, but at least I can see where the Commonwealth Mall does attempt to resume and run its course. And, yes, there's another bronzed stalwart down at the next intersection. A brave and heroic center fielder capable of running down all fly balls and delivering the occasional clutch hit from the number seven spot in the order. And wouldn't that name look great in a boxscore in Norse runes?

But we could call him the center-fielder formerly known as Leif Ericson. We'd have to play something by Led Zeppelin when he comes up to bat.

You know, the magnitude of everything has changed at this end of the mall—instead of three story brownstones we now have six-story limestones.

I probably lost one, maybe two players to that monstrous overpass back there.

As I cross Charlesgate East, I look up over the Expressway and there it is—the Citgo Sign! I'm there, that's gotta be it.

7:23 PM. Not bad... maybe I just missed the first inning or two.

Afterword: by back-tracking to the starting point of Commonwealth Mall at the Public Garden, I was able to find a couple more players: defensive replacement/utility man John Glover, and a hard hitting left fielder, Alexander Hamilton.

Peter Winske

Even at the oldest ballpark in the U.S., a modern day problem exists. As soon as the last out is recorded in an inning, loud, blaring music erupts from the speakers. It is almost impossible for us bleacher fans to discuss the last half inning without shouting at the person sitting next to us.

During the middle innings, a discussion arose on what should be done with Fenway Park. It must have been a mirror of what occurs throughout Boston because there was no clear agreement. One participant has been coming to Fenway since 1945 and now when he pays $60 per ticket, he wants something more than tradition. Others who come in once every X games want Fenway to remain as it is. I confess that although I grew up attending Wrigley Field, I feel that there is a time when enough is enough. Pittsburgh has proven that a fan-friendly park can be built that combines the best of the old and the new.

THE FENWAY EXPERIENCE

Jim Sandoval

I was born and raised in the shadow of the Big "A," Anaheim stadium, home of the Angels. Attending ballgames at both the Big "A" and Dodger Stadium (Chavez Ravine) was not entirely the experience that baseball is meant to be. Notorious for late-arriving and early-leaving fans, in both ballparks baseball talk was at a minimum. At Angels' games frequently fans of the opponents outnumbered those of the hometown club. As an adult I have had the privilege of attending games at 31 major league ballyards and about a dozen minor league ballparks. None compares with the Fenway experience.

The adventure began with a short stroll from the hotel to the "T" station. Dropping my token in the slot I followed the signs to the train. Fenway Park was about three stops away. I thought we would never get there. On the train I saw many Red Sox hats and jerseys. Around me the conversations were about tonight's game. "Who is pitching?" "Oh no, not Maddux" "You think we can beat him?" This was about three hours before game time and people were already focused.

A surging mass of people detrained alongside me at the Kenmore Square station, one of the Fenway Park stops. At that point I was surprised anyone remained on the train. We climbed the stairs and began to follow the signs to the ballyard. As I walked excitedly down Brookline Avenue, I saw the Citgo sign famous from the view over the Green Monster in left field at Fenway. Yankee haters selling T-shirts were everywhere.

Many in the crowd began to enter local establishments for food, drink and conversation. I spotted a "Chicago Bar and Grill" which gave me a chuckle here in the heart of Boston. As I crossed over the Massachusetts Turnpike I saw it: the back of the Monster, Fenway's landmark. Large Coke bottle advertisements above the wall drew one's attention to it. As I moved closer to Landsdowne Street I saw a sign saying, "The Outfield welcomes Red Sox fans." I guess Yankee fans have to eat elsewhere.

I turned left onto Landsdowne Street, behind the left field wall. I had decided to walk around the ballpark and soak in the experience. In my experiences in California, parking lots surrounded the field. Here it was a neighborhood. I could smell meat cooking somewhere nearby. I looked right and saw the brickwork of the back of the ballpark. To my left I saw a sign measuring the distance from home plate. 514 feet if you hit a ball over the wall and onto the top of the building across the street.

I strolled down the street, cruising through a souvenir store behind left-center field. It was now about 4:50 and the talk around me was still about baseball. I saw many families preparing for the game. What appeared to be fathers and sons, even three generations of a family strolled by me. I saw kids with gloves, male and female, ready to get that foul ball when they got inside. As I continued down the street behind center field, I noticed some local watering holes with crowds gathering.

Continuing on around the outside of the park I moved to what should be the right-center field area. I saw a parking lot! Alas, it had a sign establishing it as a lot for those with press permits only. We freelance writers have to walk. This was Ipswich Street and at 189 there was an inside parking lot with the name Red Sox Garage and 600 Club. Continuing toward home plate I saw multiple TV trucks and vans setting up for their broadcasts just outside the Media entrance. I was tempted to enter one of the vans and apply for a position but was able to restrain myself before the local constables would have needed to. As I neared the corner I noticed parts of this street were blocked off to traffic, with some cars behind the barrier. The smells began to grow at this point.

When I reached the corner, turning right I entered Yawkey Way. This is what the Fenway experience is all about. People were hanging out all over the street. Vendors were everywhere, selling food, t-shirts, col-

lectibles, anything a die-hard Sox fan might need for the game. The first vendor I saw up close was an African-American gentleman selling Italian sausages in a city known for its Irish population. 1510 "The Zone" radio station was broadcasting live from the window of a souvenir store across Yawkey Way from Gate D of the park.

Looking up I spotted the modern addition of the 600 Club. The rest of the front of the park looked like all the pictures. The trees near the Fenway Park sign. A monument dedicated to Mr. Yawkey on the wall. It was "from those who knew him best. His Red Sox employees." How many Major League baseball owners today would inspire such a sentiment? A 90th anniversary flag flying proudly. I heard, in a strange accent to my California-raised ears, "peanuts, programs."

Hearing a loud noise and realizing it was my stomach growling I decided it was time to partake of some local cuisine. I looked around and saw many of the ballpark staples. Then something you can rarely find in a ballpark caught my eye. Being near the Atlantic Ocean my pre-game meal of fish and chips was quite appropriate I thought. As I waited for the food I watched the crowd outside the ballpark. The crowd on Yawkey Way was growing at about the pace of the Republic of China's population. I finished eating just in time to join a line to enter the ballpark. A few minutes later the gates opened and the excited crowd poured into the cathedral that is Fenway.

I turned left to check out the location of my seats down the left field line. I was here with a large group from the Society for American Baseball Research (SABR). Some of us were in the grandstand and others in the right field bleachers. I chatted with a couple of fellow SABR members and then excused myself to wander the ballpark. Down near the field people were lined up to try to snag a Braves foul ball during batting practice. I wandered down to touch the wall in left and say hello. I looked closely at the hand-operated scoreboard. I knew one of our SABR members would have the privilege of going inside for part of the game. I looked back at the press box, knowing SABR members would be there as well.

I wandered around the ballpark, end to end. I found something I had never noticed before. Down the right field line there was a seating arrangement that is rather unusual. Along the back wall there is what looks like a long bench like you would see in a high school or Little League dugout. It had numbers painted on it for seating assignments. It must be a tough place from which to watch a game as it is behind the walkway. I would imagine there is constant foot traffic there throughout the game.

Everywhere I looked there were Red Sox hats and jerseys. Martinez and Garciaparra seem to be the most predominant. There was a buzz in the park as more of the crowd filed in. As I began to make my way back around to my seat, I saw a grounds crew worker place a ladder against the left wall and climb up to retrieve baseballs from the screen above the wall. When I approached the home plate area I was struck by a sight that brought a smile to my face: in this sanctuary called Fenway Park I saw a nun getting ready to enjoy the game. I decided it was time to do the same.

BAR HOPPING

Denis Repp

The first sounds you hear as you emerge from the Kenmore T station come from the small group of men gathered at the top of the steps. Softly spoken, yet with a bit of urgency, they speak their two lines, over and over: "Who needs tickets? Who's selling tickets?"

Most people can answer both questions with a "not me," and they walk a few steps down Commonwealth Avenue to the corner of Brookline Avenue. The intersection is crowded with people and cars. A few stragglers stay behind to negotiate with the scalpers or to make a final visit to an ATM, and a few cars are directed into a small parking lot by orange-flagged attendants, but most of the crowd crosses the bridge above the Mass Pike to join the throng surrounding Fenway Park.

17:45

There is a line to enter the bar on the corner of Landsdowne Street, the Cask & Flagon. The crowd parts briefly to allow an elderly couple to leave the bar. Dressed for a night at the park, the wife is in a dress, and the husband is in a blue blazer. After gently making their way down the steps, he gets behind his walker, and the two of them begin the slow walk across the street toward the center field bleachers.

A well-built young man walks his bike past the bar's door, to the railing along the building. He's not going to the game; like several others before him, he hoists his bike up onto the railing, locks it there, and walks into Gold's Gym for a workout.

Across the street, a dozen fans gather on the sidewalk outside WEEI's Landsdowne studio to watch the Big Show, one of two pre-game shows being broadcast from the neighborhood. A caller chides one of the hosts, calling him "a stupid little idiot;" the host protests, saying that he stands well over six feet tall.

A little farther down Landsdowne, the Sausage Guy's grill is fired up, filling the area with the aroma of hot meat.

17:55

In front of the Landsdowne Souvenir Store, three young women from Starbucks offer samples of their frozen coffee to passersby. With the temperature approaching ninety degrees, plenty take advantage before crossing the street to Gate C, the entrance to Fenway's centerfield bleachers.

Just beyond the Starbucks van sit Axis and the Embassy Club, quiet and dark.

Things will pick up there a little later in the evening.

18:05

It's already plenty loud at Atlas Dance; there's a line to get in, customers have spilled out through the open windows and doors to enjoy sidewalk seating, the beer is flowing, and the music is playing. Across the street from Fenway's clubhouses, Atlas has opened long before gametime, and will be a busy place long after the final out. Next door, the bar on the corner of Landsdowne and Ipswich is open, but there are not many people enjoying the dueling pianos inside.

On Ipswich, across the street from Fenway High School, cars drive into the garage behind Fenway's right-center seats. This parking is all pre-sold; drivers trying to get in by flashing a twenty at the attendants are turned away. The only people allowed in have their official Red Sox parking passes. The passes just get them into the garage, however; they still need their game tickets to get into the ballpark.

18:25

At a hot dog stand on Van Ness Street behind the first-base stands, business is brisk. One guy works the grill, and hands out the dogs and sausages; his partner takes the $4 for each sandwich. There's a condiment table on the sidewalk, and as they work on their food, two fans discuss the shortcomings of the 1938 Pirates.

(Bostonians don't have a monopoly on disappointment.)

Where it passes behind Fenway's third-base stands, Jersey Street was long ago renamed Yawkey Way, and it's a busy place tonight. It's closed to vehicles on game nights, and it's clogged with vendors and pedestrians. There are no seats, so people lean against walls, sit on the curb, or just walk around while eating their sausages and fried dough. In tonight's heat, cold beverages are selling well, too. One fan leans against a wall across the street and doesn't mind much when he is accidentally showered by the condensate pouring off an air-conditioning unit.

Across from Gate D, a giant Red Sox cap adorns the façade of the largest of the three souvenir stores facing Fenway. There's another small radio studio facing the sidewalk here, and a few sidewalk critics listen in. In the store, a boy tries on a new Sox cap, creasing the bill to make it fit just right: his dad blanches, saying "At least wait until I pay for it before you ruin it."

18:35

A man, his right arm in a sling, passes by, dragging his friend along with him: "I want a sausage and I can't put the mustard on by myself." A minute or two later, the two reappear. The injured man has a half-eaten sausage in his left hand and traces of mustard around his smiling mouth.

The cards 'n' collectibles store next door has a steady stream of window shoppers coming and going.

Just beyond yet another souvenir store, at the corner of Yawkey and Brookline, a fan on the street breaks into a recitation of the Pledge of Allegiance, with heavy emphasis on the "under God"; he gets raucous cheers and a hug from a friend when he finishes.

18:50

A man driving a minivan full of kids pulls up in front of the Boston Beer Works and stops all traffic on Brookline for a moment; he has spotted his wife waiting for him on sidewalk. His kids pile out, he hands the game tickets to mom, and drives off to find a place to park the van. A moment later, another car stops, this time just to allow its driver to chat with a friend she's seen on the sidewalk. The honking horns behind her quickly remind her that this is sort of rude, and she drives off.

18:58

Those fans still arriving on Brookline—and there are plenty of them—quicken their strides when they hear the strains of the National Anthem coming from within the park. People in the bars down the last of their beers, and they begin to cross the street, too.

19:05

A fan heads into the Boston Beer Works; there's no line, but he feels like a fish swimming upstream as the crowd inside him pushes its way past him as they head out to the game. He finds a stool, and is happy to see that on one side of him, there are 17 beers on tap for him to choose from, and that on the other, all eight televisions within sight are tuned to the ballgame.

No choices there.

Red Sox caps are clearly the headwear of choice in this neighborhood, and many fans wear Red Sox jerseys featuring the numbers of their favorite players, past and present. Pedro, Manny, Yaz, Ted—they're all represented. Even fictional players are remembered; a fan walks into the bar wearing a Sox jersey #16 on the back, honoring Sox closer-turned-bartender, Sam Malone.

19:20

Kevin and Bobby sit down

for a quick one before going into game. They have a banner mentioning NESN, and they're hoping to catch a cameraman's eye tonight. They're wearing t-shirts— gifts from Kevin's wife—featuring pictures of Kevin's new twin girls, Abby and Gaby. The front of the shirts show the girls smiling beneath the words "Red Sox Rule"; on the back, there's another picture, this one featuring a rear view of the diaper-less pair of girls, and an uncomplimentary reference to Yankees. Bobby advises that most of the people in the bars are "jackasses, but some of them are all right." Properly fortified, Kevin and Bobby cross the street in time for the third inning.

19:41

Third inning starts.

Roy Gedat

Several lasting memories of the game... "Chipster" Jones looking lost playing in left. He blew one ball off the Green Monster and looked weak on a number of other plays. Watching Tim Wakefield warm up—could anyone throw any slower and seem more nonchalant?

Fenway Park is such a pit. Horrible sight lines, uncomfortable seats and the largest collection of drunks this side of a detox center. Even some of the SABR faithful who were charmed at the age of the place had to agree that big changes/improvements are needed. Save Fenway Park? How about giving fans some value for the highest price ticket in Baseball.

19:50

Brookline Ave. is still a busy place, with people still arriving for game, on foot and in cars.

The ballgame is not the only sporting event taking place in Fenway Park tonight. One flight of stairs below street level, under the left-field stands at the corner of Landsdowne and Brookline, fifteen or twenty people are bowling a few lines of candlepins. The TVs are tuned to the ballgame going on upstairs, but most of the bowlers are concentrating on rolling their cantaloupe-sized balls down the centers of the lanes. As noted Red Sox fan Stephen King is interviewed from his seat during an inning break, a dozen exchange students come to the lanes for their first bowling experience. It's not clear that they are aware of the spectacle taking place above them. A

French teenager rolls a strike, her first, and her pleasure is at least equal to any she might have had at the ballgame.

20:20

Everyone has seen the small mobs of fans that gather on Waveland Avenue in Chicago, waiting to pounce on any home run ball that leaves Wrigley Field. There's none of that in Boston. The combination of the narrow street and the high screen atop the Green Monster make the prospect of a ball landing on Landsdowne very unlikely. As the game progresses, the only person anywhere near the Monster is a man who sits on the sidewalk, his back to the wall, his donation cup to his side, his bongos between his knees. He beats out a steady rhythm as three teenage girls stroll by after leaving the game.

They're together, but totally ignoring each other as two of them are involved in separate conversations on their cell phones, while the third wonders aloud, "Well, should I get mine out, too?"

20:33

The Landsdowne souvenir store is now empty, except for the three workers there. The pre-game rush is long over, and now they wait for the fans to return after the game. They know that their sales will not depend too much on whether the Sox win or lose. They also know that, win or lose, the most popular shirt they sell will be the one with "5 Garciaparra" on the back.

20:40

With the game past its midpoint, there is now a much smaller crowd at Atlas Dance. A few booths in the front room are occupied by people enjoying a leisurely meal, and only three people sit at the bar. Emily and Amber, the two bartenders, pour some drinks, and whirl around behind the bar occasionally to entertain themselves. There are two large-screen TVs side-by-side behind the bar. Like every other TV in the area, they're both tuned to the same game.

21:05

Emily combines a great look with a smart mouth. While she's dancing around during a slow moment, she notices a that customer is dividing his attention between what she's doing behind the bar and what Shea Hillenbrand is doing on the screen.

She calls him on it: "Do you like looking at me or something?" The customer, busted, gives the only answer he can: "Who doesn't?"

The game is into the seventh inning now. Amber says that she likes it over here a little better during the game. It's a little quieter, and slower, so she can chat with her customers a bit. She knows that after the game, Atlas will become a much busier and a much louder place. Except for the occasional lout you see in any bar, most of the people who come will be nice, and fun. As at the Souvenir Store, the behavior of the crowd won't depend too much on whether the Sox win or lose. She does note that it will be a different sort of crowd if the Yankees are in town. On those nights, Yankee fans will likely outnumber Sox rooters, and there will be a lot of loud, good-natured jabbering between the two camps.

Two women in bartender outfits sit down for a beer. They work at Axis, the dance club two doors down. Axis will open at 10:00, and they know that they will be in for a long hot night over there. They finish their drinks, and leave to get their own bars ready for the rush.

Mike and Gary, having left their pal Adam in the bleachers across the street, sit at the bar to enjoy the rest of the game. Between the desire for a cold beer, and the sweat that was fogging Mike's glasses, they have decided to watch the rest of the game from barstools. The Sox second baseman appears on the screen, and Gary calls out "By land, by sea, By-erga!"

21:30

Make no mistake; people in the bar are enjoying their drinks and their conversations, but everyone keeps half an eye on the TV, as the Sox are threatening to rally. The Sox have scored, and are threatening to do more when Manny Ramirez sends a fly toward the Green Monster. The barflies cheer, and then groan when the fly ball falls just short. Amber says that on some nights the music in the bar isn't so loud; if this had been one of those nights, she would have been able to hear the crowd across the street groan when Ramirez flew out.

21:35

Shortly before the game ends, SABR's John Zajc appears on the screen, in an in-seat interview.

The game does end, and Amber is right; the bar is once again packed, and there's no indication that the patrons are saddened by the Sox loss. Adam has made his way through the line and appears at the bar just as Mike has to leave. He's got to get to South Station in time to catch the late train to his suburban home. Adam and Gary will carry on; this is just the one of several stops he and Gary are making tonight.

22:55

The game is long over, but the Landsdowne nightlife is going strong. There is now a long line to get into the piano bar, and the sidewalk seats outside Atlas are filled again. Cars and limousines slowly make their way down the street to the now-busy dance clubs. The Souvenir Store is closed, but the Sausage Guy still has a hot grill and several customers. The exchange students have left the bowling lanes under Fenway Park, which have been transformed into "Mystic Bowling," complete with flashing lights and smoke machines. The light show is easily visible from the street, and it draws bowlers in like moths to a flame.

23:10

Kenmore station is still crowded with people coming and going. A woman steps off a train and asks who won the game. Like most everyone else in town, she's disappointed at the answer. She can only be doubly disappointed that she wasn't here to see the whole spectacle, but no matter; it will all repeat itself tomorrow night.

Randall Chandler

It was my first interleague game, Atlanta Braves versus Boston Red Sox. Being a St. Louis Cardinal and a National League fan, I was naturally for the home team Red Sox as any National League loss would eventually help my team if they won their own game that particular night. Seeing the game in what is now baseball's oldest park made my mind wander backward to 1954, to my first game in what was then one of baseball's oldest parks, Busch Stadium, the former Sportsman's Park.

As to the game itself, there were some great fielding plays like Chipper Jones catching Ramirez' fly on the track. Of course watching Chipper strike out twice and eventually go 0-for-5, it looked like the game was going the way I wanted it to go. We were not treated to any home runs or triples, but a double check of the box score shows we saw a number of good things that happen in baseball: double plays, errors, men left on base, and stolen bases. Not the greatest pitching duel one would expect from two first place clubs with two good pitchers going, but every once in a while the bats do come alive, and someone eventually prevails. The Braves did overcome their high number of LOBs and their bullpen rose to the occasion to notch another victory toward their pennant quest.

A good game in a great old ballpark that was completely sold out.

FENWAY FAITHFUL

Allen Tait

Baseball in the new millennium. In many ballparks, the best seats are corporate, and knowledgeable fans are difficult to find. In these same ballparks, management focuses on attracting the oxymoronic concept of the "casual fan." Non-baseball entertainment is emphasized to encourage this "fan" to stay at the game. To assist, these "fans" the scoreboard tells them when to cheer.

Tonight, the above irritants are a non-issue. I am at Fenway Park in the bleachers. Tonight, I am going to enjoy focusing on the ebb and flow of the game as detailed by crowd reaction. In theory, the game could turn on any given pitch. However, the fans can't get in a frenzy before all 240-plus pitches in a game. The fans need to pick their spots based on anticipation of the situation. With the knowledgeable Fenway faithful, I can enjoy the game with the crowd.

Tonight's game had eight peaks, starting in the first inning. Two on, one out with Manny Ramirez in the cleanup slot at bat. Oh, how quickly the crowd was deflated when Carlos Baerga was picked off second.

The next excitement spike occurred in the third. Nomar Garciaparra up with two out and the tying run on third. Nomar responds quickly, once he sets himself in the batters box, and ties the game up on the first pitch he sees in the at bat. The excitement is short lived, as Manny is unsuccessful in keeping the rally alive.

Concern permeates the crowd in the fifth. Bases loaded, one out, one run in and the heart of the Atlanta order (Gary Sheffield and Chipper Jones) coming up. Tim Wakefield is warming up but the relief is in the crowd as John Burkett works out of the jam without giving up any more runs.

Hope rekindles in the bottom of sixth and a beach ball is punched about the stands as Kevin Gryboski, in

relief of Greg Maddux, issues back to back walks with two out. However, Shea Hillenbrand can't get the ball through the infield and the inning is over.

The crowd is in their feet in bottom seven. The score is tied, the bases are loaded and Darren Holmes is brought in to face Manny. Alas, the ball is given a ride, but it is caught in front of the Green Monster for out number three.

The top of the eighth brings the roller coaster effect. Deuces are wild with a 2-2 score, two on, two out and Rich Garces ready to battle Rafael Furcal. The crowd is on their feet cheering for the strikeout, then is down as a walk is issued loading the bases. The crowd is up again and cheering as Matt Franco is retired.

In the top of the ninth, the crowd is quiet as Tim Wakefield is hit, though not really hard, and gives up two runs.

Bottom of the ninth, rally time and the crowd is ready. But alas, John Smoltz has a 1-2-3 ninth and the Fenway faithful leave knowing tomorrow will be another day.

Claudia Perry, president of SABR in June 2002, threw out the game's ceremonial first pitch, as did former Boston Braves ballplayer Sibby Sisti. Here is Claudia's recollection.

I could blame the erratic nature of my first pitch on the weight of history, since standing in front of the mound at Fenway was a place I would have never expected to be given the Red Sox history with people who looked like me. Pumpsie Green and Tommy Harper look like me, which might offer an explanation to those who are familiar with Red Sox history. Pumpsie gave the Red Sox the opportunity to be the last team in the majors to integrate, and Harper sued the club for discrimination.

Also, my only previous trip to Fenway was not exactly awash in hospitality with a few drunks in the bleachers tossing out racist theories about the Oakland A's, the opponent that summer some 25 years ago. I sat among them afraid to move lest my presence provoke them to more overt hostility.

So, with that complicated history behind me, I stood in front of the mound with Sibby Sisti. The former Boston Brave was there that night since the Atlanta Braves, on their second city since leaving Beantown, were playing the Red Sox.

The people in the stands were friendly, and it seemed a different place than one that had burrowed deeply into my memory.

With all that, I still had a ball to throw. So I threw it and spent the rest of the weekend trying to offer an appropriate explanation for a pitch that sent Lou Merloni sprawling. Frankly, Bob Uecker said it best in the movie "Major League." It was just a bit outside, and that's the line I'm sticking to.

TALKING HEADS

Scott C. Turner

Ted Turner's WTBS, "The Superstation," broadcasts most Braves' regular-season games. If the Friday, June 28 tilt between Atlanta and the Boston Red Sox is indicative of the norm, TBS' interest lies just there—on the game itself. If pre-game or post-game breakdowns are what you seek, find a source other than the cable giant. However, their coverage of this Friday evening's game proved to be more than adequate.

Hoping to find insight into how WTBS would approach this Friday game, I logged on during the pre-game hours to TBSSuperstation.com. "The Choptalk Weekly Review" on this site placed its emphasis on the intradivision Mets/Braves series from earlier this week rather than this interleague set.

Upon seeing the "Scorecard" icon, I took a chance that this might be their cryptic doorway to knowledge about the upcoming game. Instead I found that I could print off a blank scorecard "to know how your favorite Brave is playing." Fine, but I already have a supply of scorecards.

I did find that rookie reliever Tim Spooneybarger is writing about his experiences in the Braves' clubhouse in his "Diary of a Rookie." With a fastball compared to Mariano Rivera's and a "down to earth" personality like Mark Fidrych's, Spooneybarger found himself on Sunday, June 23 writing from AAA Richmond.

He was sent down after being plagued by early control problems on May 10, but his emphasis on "putting up the numbers" paid off. I found on ESPN.com that he was recalled the previous Wednesday after going 1-0 with eleven saves and a 0.90 ERA in International League action. He took the place of the injured Albie Lopez.

This practice of posting a player's diary on the web

is not exclusive to Atlanta. Other teams are doing it, but I've yet to find a rival for either Ring Lardner or Jim Bouton amongst them.

Having abandoned the WTBS website and its general, weekly coverage, I further found on ESPN.com that today's pitching matchup would be one of former teammates Greg Maddux and John Burkett. Burkett, attempting a jab at Bud Selig, has declared a personal boycott of All-Star Game festivities this year at Miller Park in Milwaukee.

Indeed ominous signs continue to swirl over MLB's latest pissing contest between millionaire players and billionaire owners. During the second inning of the broadcast, Skip Caray and Joe Simpson made reference to the labor problems. Simpson asserted that Jim Thome of the Indians will not waive his no-trade clause as a "five and ten man," preferring to negotiate with his current team at year's end. A seemingly dejected Caray noted, "It may not matter for a while."

These announcers did attempt to trace Burkett's recent cold spell (0-3, 4.58 in his last three starts) to the frosted blonde hair he currently sports in a show of support for his son's colorfully hirsute science project.

The TBS pre-game coverage could best be described as brief. At 6:58 EDT Erin Andrews, who also provided an occasional EA Sports MLB update during the game, announced that interleague action would resume at the top of the hour. After a final snippet of "Friends," Caray and Simpson opened the short game introduction by informing viewers that the Braves' 12-3 interleague record had bolstered their jump to the top of the NL East in June. This day's drama would revolve around the returns of Maddux to the hill and Boston's Manny Ramirez to the lineup in a struggle of division leaders. TBS's high-tech lead-in featured cartoon figures of Brave "superheroes" Maddux, Sheffield, Chipper Jones, and Furcal.

In the top of the first, as Burkett set down Atlanta in order, Simpson extolled Boston and its fans, especially the university crowd from the numerous institutions in the area and those New Englanders who drive down from ME, VT, and NH for weekend series such as this

one. Pete Van Wieren would later note when the camera landed on author Stephen King in his Red Sox cap that baseball in New England is more like religion than sport.

Skip noted that traffic was "a little rough" and that it was a late-arriving crowd which would eventually swell to its usual Fenway size—a sellout. Indeed, a stadium that reportedly holds 32,933, held 33,137 on this Friday. Caray went on to extrapolate that interleague play's 16% greater attendance figures over those of intraleague games meant that the fans like it and it should stay. Sounding ill, he also berated MLB for its $2500 fine which was assessed to the Braves because Sheffield's elbow pad exceeded regulation size during this week's series with the Mets.

The announcers concurred that RF is tougher to play in Fenway than the famous LF. As evidence they cited that RF is the sun field during day games and that the circular layout in right often results in unusual caroms for fielders. They arrived at this subject after noting that Chipper Jones had spent quite a bit of time playing balls off of "The Wall" during BP.

A physical challenge not related to his ailing left calf was presented to Maddux almost immediately. Number two batter Carlos Baerga lined a pitch off of Maddux's right leg. The leg ballooned under his sock. He continued the inning, even picking Baerga off at second base, and gamely hurled five innings of three-hit baseball. The TBS cameras caught trainer Jeff Porter's attempts to stem the tide of swelling with ice and wraps.

In fact I found the camera crew to be most impressive throughout the game at focusing on reactions by players and those in either dugout. Neither team appeared pleased with the work of home plate umpire Tim Timmons, but Bobby Cox and Leo Mazzone's agitations played out vividly for the camera. As usual, the Braves' coaches expected a strike zone as wide as the James River for their studious Cy Young winner, and their favorite expletive aimed at Timmons was "Horse****!"

Hometown hero Nomar Garciaparra also exhibited a fascination with equine excrement in the sixth after being charged with an error on a low throw which was dropped by Brian Daubach. Even the most inexperienced lip reader could have picked out Nomar's invective as he pointed to the press box, apparently at the official scorekeeper, and spewed. Acknowledging the shortstop's displeasure, Simpson and Van Wieren, who came over from the radio side in the bottom of the fifth, added properly that Daubach's failure to stretch also came into play.

A wet ball could have also contributed. Several players struggled to grip balls wetted by the soggy turf, and Red Sox centerfielder Johnny Damon plowed a large divot up in the fifth as he charged hard attempting to prevent the Braves' second tally. The announcers noted that Thursday's deluge flooded both dugouts and flowed even into the clubhouse tunnels. Fenway Park, opened in 1912 on the day that the Titanic sank, lacks a modern drainage system.

From the perspective of someone who doesn't have cable or the "Dish" and therefore doesn't see many Braves' telecasts, I found the broadcast to be professional and refreshing. Simpson held things together with timely discussions of statistics (pointing out that 2b Keith Lockhart with one out in the bottom of the fifth had had a hand in ten of the thirteen outs recorded by the Braves, for example) or personal insights (in eleven years as an Atlanta announcer, he's never heard Bobby Cox criticize his players in the papers, for example). Joe also gave a wide berth to the curmudgeonly Caray.

Skip, while overstating his displeasure with the commissioner's office and Boston's official scorer, proved entertaining with quips like "Baerga was out from here to Peoria!" "Baerga turns right after striking out." "Ramirez' pants are so long that they cover his shoelaces." "The official scorer has been horrible for fifty years in Boston." Utilizing an Anglicized, John Wayne-like Spanish he also alerted true speakers of that language to the wonders of the SAP button.

Van Wieren remained smooth as silk and reminiscent of the local weatherman. For my money, his greatest contribution today was his discussion of Sunday baseball in Boston. Noting that there were no Sunday games until 1929, he also mentioned that, even after that law went by the boards, the Bosox had to borrow Braves Field for Sunday games because their proximity to a church forbade playing at Fenway. The Junior Circuit club was not averse to the extra cash garnered in the larger park on those Sundays either, he intoned.

The broadcast also had features similar to those found around the major leagues. I mentioned that the EA Sports update broke in occasionally with reports from other contests. Further, a ticker ran every ten to fifteen minutes at the bottom of the screen, "AOL in the Booth" provided fans the opportunity to have an e-mail question answered on the air, and, at times when a split-screen would be helpful, the "Supershot" was employed.

Trivia also had its place. "The AFLAC Trivia Question" let viewers know that the five pitchers to make 25 or more starts in each year of the '90s were Burkett, Maddux, Tom Glavine, Andy Benes, and Chuck Finley. Simpson chipped in with his own barroom stumper by asking for the only two players to have at least one homer for 24 consecutive years. The two are Ty Cobb and Rickey Henderson.

After John Smoltz extinguished Boston 1-2-3 in the bottom of the ninth, TBS presented one last EA Sports update, someone reiterated that Saturday would be a rare radio-only broadcast, Joe mentioned his love for that "traditional" matchup between Arizona and Cleveland, and Skip finished up by noting that Atlanta's lead over Montreal was 6 and 1/2 games. No player reactions or post-game interviews; just "'Murder at 1600' with Wesley Snipes and Dennis Miller is next on the Superstation."

A MINNESOTAN IN FENWAY PARK

Howard Luloff

Since Met Stadium shut down after the 1981 season, many Minnesota baseball fans like me have been deprived of seeing the game in its natural habitat. The best way to escape the inadequacies of the Metrodome is to do one of two things: see a minor league game or go to another major league ballpark such as Kauffman Stadium, Bank One Ballpark or the oldest surviving stadium in the majors, Fenway Park in Boston.

It was a Friday night in June when I joined about 750 people who attended the national convention of the Society for American Baseball Research at baseball's holiest shrine, Fenway Park. Fenway Park is everything the Metrodome is not. It is compact, has real grass and a close view of the field. There's also the Green Monster, the hand-operated scoreboard in left field, and the illuminated Citgo sign past the left field wall. A haven of history and a haven of heartbreak. Hitters like Hooper, Speaker, Ruth, Williams and Yaz. Pitchers such as Leonard, Shore, Lonborg, Clemens and Pedro. Even Red Sox players with big last names like Monboquette and Win Remmerswaal have called Fenway home. But on this summer night in June, more history could be in the making.

THE GAME

More history took place that night at Fenway when two teams with long, established roots in Boston took the field in interleague play, the Atlanta (nee Boston) Braves and the Red Sox. Before the game, I took my microcassette recorder outside Fenway and asked several fans to give their memories of the Boston Braves. I had a goal of ten but ended up with five. It wasn't easy since most of the fans who remember the Braves' stay in Boston are senior citizens. Here are memories from the

Braves fans I asked:

Gregory Cosmos of Framingham, MA remembered the game where Brooklyn Dodger outfielder Carl Furillo threw from The Jury Box (Braves Field's right field bleachers in fair territory) to retire Sibby Sisti at home plate.

John Girard of Berkley, MA saw Warren Spahn's first game at Braves Field. He described the game as "kind of boring, 'cause all he did was strike everybody out."

Frank Wisdom of Halifax MA saw Jim Tobin pitch a no-hitter. He couldn't recall the year it happened, so I consulted The 2002 Sports Encyclopedia of Baseball and found out that Tobin's feat was accomplished on April 27, 1944 when he shut out the Brooklyn Dodgers, 2-0.

Robert Carr's greatest memory was a pitcher's duel between Spahn and the Reds' Ewell Blackwell. "Ewell Blackwell had the most unusual delivery that any of us have ever seen to that time," stated the Henniker, NH resident. "It was underhand and he lasted maybe three or four years but he was some good."

The last fan I interviewed, Jack Shields of Beverly, MA lamented the Braves leaving Boston after the 1952 season. "We were all heartbroken 'cause they left us for Milwaukee."

Now to the game. My vantage point was in the 40th row of the right-centerfield bleachers. With all of Fenway's differences from the Metrodome, there is only one similarity, the sightline was far away from the batter's box, making it difficult to follow the trajectory of a ground ball in the infield. Also, the seats were cramped. To borrow a quote from a commercial for a defunct airline, I didn't get "three feet for my two legs."

The public address announcer, Ed Brickley, talks to you. He doesn't scream like the long-time Twins PA voice Bob Casey. He wasn't a homer when he read the Red Sox lineup. Fenway Park is one of the few ballparks that plays organ music. Most of them, including the Metrodome play rock and roll. Fenway does play some rock and roll between innings. The scoreboard doesn't play commercials between innings. The National Anthem was sung by SABR member Joseph Mancuso, a singer-songwriter from Ann Arbor, MI and the first ball was thrown by the first female, African-American president in the society's history, Claudia Perry. She's been in the spotlight the last few months with an appearance on the game show Jeopardy!

On the diamond, two veteran pitchers take the mound. The Braves use Greg Maddux and the Red Sox start John Burkett. Maddux left in the sixth due to a sore left groin. He was hit in the foot in the bottom of the first on a lne drive by Carlos Baerga. Both starters struggled at times, getting out of major jams. The Braves used five relief pitchers, including John Smoltz who picked up his 26th save. His career has gone through a renaissance after missing a year due to injury. He has become the first pitcher since Dennis Eckersley to win 20 games in one season and save more than 20 in another. Also, Smoltz is on pace to break the franchise record of 39 saves, set by Mark Wohlers in 1996.

The Red Sox used three relievers, including a former Twin, Rich Garces. The losing pitcher was one of the few knuckleball pitchers in the majors, Tim Wakefield. Knuckleball pitchers have become rare in the majors because there are few pitching coaches who can teach that specific pitch.

Another former Twin was also involved in the game. He played third base in the late 70s and was one of the few players to have his own fan club at the Met. That night, he served as the Red Sox third base coach. His name: Mike Cubbage.

The game had more twists and turns than a ride on the rollercoaster at your local amusement park. There were missed opportunities and a large number of men left on base with the Braves outnumbering the Red Sox 14-8. The Red Sox offense couldn't solve Atlanta's dominant pitching.

The Braves showed why they have been one of baseball's dominant teams throughout the '90s. One reason besides outstanding pitching has been a potent lineup. Their lineup is full of power hitters including Chipper and Andruw Jones. The additions of Gary Sheffield and Vinny Castilla have also helped the Atlanta attack.

One aspect of the game that should not be overlooked is defense. The Braves second baseman Keith

Lockhart had an outstanding game. He was their ninth batter but on this warm, Friday night he played like a Gold Glove winner going 11 for 11 in fielding chances without an error. In one stretch, he had five straight assists.

BASEBALL'S BEST FANS

The one thing that really touched me at Fenway was the fans. Red Sox baseball has a major cult following throughout New England as well as other parts of the United States where people moved out of the region and remain fans. Red Sox fans are from all age groups, starting from the youngsters who follow the current crop of players to those in their 70s, 80s and possibly 90s who remember Bobby Doerr, Ted Williams and the last time the Red Sox won the pennant, 1918.

They know when to cheer and know when to boo. The scoreboard is not an electronic cheerleader that exhorts them to be loud like it does at the Metrodome. A large percentage are dressd in Red Sox clothing, ranging from the familiar red and white home uniform wthout a name on the back to a dark blue jersey with names like Ramirez, Garciaparra and Martinez.

But Red Sox fans, like Twins fans, can be fickle. Case in point, September 16, 1965. On that day, Dave Morehead pitched a no-hitter. Fenway looked like a Cape Cod village after Labor Day weekend with only 1,247 in attendance. On April 27, 2002, Derek Lowe threw the franchise's first no-hitter in 37 years as 32,837 packed the park. The team's recent success was evident when I got out of the Kenmore subway station en route to the game. There were several fans pleading "Tickets, tickets" thanks to another Red Sox sellout. According to Scott Greenberger's article in the July 1, 2002 *Boston Globe*, Fenway has drawn over two million fans 15 of the last 16 years. An incredible feat, despite the small seating capacity and the highest ticket prices in baseball.

POSTGAME WRAPUP

For someone who has spent the majority of his adult life watching baseball in the Metrodome's antiseptic atmosphere, Fenway Park was a welcome relief. It was nice to watch baseball played on real grass before a packed house instead of a quarter to half full stadium. The Braves showed why they have baseball's best record with outstandng pitching and timely hitting. Even the backup catcher, Henry Blanco, who entered the game with a sub-.200 batting average, solidified the victory with a ninth inning double. The Red Sox had a tough night with only five hits. The fans in the bleachers had no souvenirs to take home because there were no home runs.

As Fenway begins its tenth decade as one of baseball's historic stadiums, time could be running out. Greenberger's article stated that the park could be replaced or renovated. For many fans like me, going to the original Fenway Park is one of baseball's great experiences.

Fred Peltz

Being from Southern California, I was drawn into the Fenway experience by the contrast: the street vendors and program hawkers, parking fees. I told my wife that I'll never complain about paying $8 to park at Edison Field again. (She doesn't believe me.)

I enjoyed the intimacy of Fenway, the nonexistence of Disney/Fox electronic cheer leading and the sincere, loyal support of the fans. They were in the street waiting to get in, and didn't leave in the 7th inning.

INTERNET RADIO

Zack Triscuit

Rich Klein's Notes

I have not done a sheet like this since I did a paper on a 1977 Yankee/Red Sox game. Every fan should do this once in his life.

Carlos Baerga—truly bad game—pickoff in 1st. Bad toss to lead to a run and broke a back.

Fri night w. Zoc. I usually play an AOL Friday night trivia game run by Tom Zocco. I got to walk with him to the game but I liked my seat much better than his and did not sit with him as planned.

In the 6th, the guy sitting next to me introduced himself and we fell into a nice chat about baseball. Larry Meyers is his name.

I work in the card memorabilia field and there is nothing at the game I needed to catalog.

Glad to see the real El Guapo pitch.

No beer vendors.

Rotisserie thoughts: good—Awfulman stealing 2nd. Wakefield giving up 2 in 9th.

Slight blockage by a pole. But nothing too bad.

Many girls come in 2 or more sans dates.

Mike Remlinger—when we used to travel home from our job, one of my compatriots once met Remlinger's fiancee on a plane (she was a stewardess). He did not make it to majors fast enough—she dumped him. He is now married to someone else.

Although I feel I have completed my Red Sox tour of duty, I still see myself as an amateur soldier on the Fenway green. I have been enlightened through the tales of *The Curse of the Bambino* and *The Boston Red Sox Reader*. Entrenched in my mind are visions of Fisk and Buckner along with other images of preemptive joy and utter ignominy. Boston University, my chosen four year institution, I found to be a Pesky's Pole away from Fenway, home of these aforementioned ghosts. This life changing decision at the same time seems so essential and ultimately influential to my philosophical maturity. For a proponent of Jefferson, Adams' staunchly Puritan homestead can only help to mold a reasoned worldview out of an optimistic, good-natured clay. And with the Olde Towne atmosphere comes its tragic ball team and its both erudite and embittered fans. While today's baseball vistas hurl continual stimuli at the casual fan, Fenway Park remains a hardball fortress that does not beckon the baseball weak at heart.

Fenway's red brick exterior lends not even a glimpse of the emerald diamond to an outsider. Although I can vouch for this elusive view from my inaugural walk around Fenway, I remain incomplete as a baseball fan until I have passed through the park's antiquated gates.

Nevertheless, I find myself in the midst of an oxymoronic situation on a clear summer night. Through 21st century technology I seek to connect to an early 20th century relic, built to house the 19th century crank. However, the friendly but straightforward voices of Red Sox radio broadcasters Joe Castiglione and Jerry Trupiano help to bring together a collaboration of both worlds.

A newcomer fan such as myself, with very little Sox baseball experience, invokes his SABR mind in undertaking the history of the Beantown club. The crimson hose's match-up with the Braves ball club of Atlanta reminds one of the early days of Boston dominance of the game. From the late 19th century up until Frazee's tragic sale of Ruth in 1920, Boston was America's baseball mecca. The Boston Beaneaters, as the National League descendant of the great Cincinnati Red Stockings were known, won the pennant three straight times from 1891 to 1893 and added two more in 1897 and '98. After winning the first 20th century World Series, the Boston Red Sox would go on to collect titles three more times in the next fifteen years. The "Miracle Braves" would even give Beantown an amazing comeback by leaving the National League cellar in July of 1914 and eventually sweeping the powerful Philadelphia Athletics. The Olde Towne was even on the brink of having its own "Subway Series" when the Sox fell in a one American League playoff to the eventual World Series champion Cleveland Indians. However, Boston had seen its last opportunity at a cross-town match up in the Fall Classic. The Braves headed west to Milwaukee in 1953.

Nevertheless, this series can rekindle the glory days for the few octogenarians who still frequent Fenway Park.

I find myself listening to this game on WEEI, 850 AM over the Internet on MLB Radio. For a mere fifteen dollars a season, up from the original cost of nothing, a hardball fanatic can listen to every game of the season in English, Spanish, and for you handful of Expos fans, even in French. One minor drawback about MLB Radio is that it is a quarter of a minute in the past. Yes, every crack of the bat you hear has reverberated over the ionosphere for 15 seconds before it leaves your desktop's speakers. However, oh how the moment of utter failure could have been pushed back for the lifetime Sox fan on MLB Radio. Pesky could have had a brief interlude before his hesitance in 1946 was ingrained in the minds of New England listeners. Yaz's final pop up in the 1978 American League East playoff could have been suspended in air with just a moment of solace for Boston's embittered backers. While that sums up the minor glitches, the major ones can give any baseball follower gray hair. Often times I find myself entranced in a pivotal late inning moment of a major league contest only to be whisked away from the action by the fickle ebb and flow of cyberspace. I defy anyone to try to listen to 60 minutes of continuous MLB Radio. Today's communications technology will not allow a smooth connection between the worlds of baseball and the Internet.

Nevertheless, the stern but enthusiastic voices in the booth calm and inspire any fan to weather this technological storm in the name of the national pastime. Through their insightful commentary and embodiment of the New England spirit, Joe and Jerry remind one that in this high tech age they simply broadcast baseball on the radio.

After a Papa Gino's pizza ad and a superfluous update of the Boston disabled list, common sense to any Red Sox fan, John Burkett delivers the first pitch.

Home plate umpire Tim Timmons barks out strike one on Rafael Furcal.

Burkett proceeds to retire the side in order with Furcal popping up to Hillenbrand, and Franco and Sheffield going down on strikes. With more of a symbol of the apocalypse than a Red Sox offensive opportunity taken advantage of, Greg Maddux's first pitch evades the strike zone. However, Maddux regains his command enough to get Johnny Damon to ground out, 4-3. After two straight singles from Baerga and Garciaparra, Carlos does his best Luis Aparicio impression stumbling back to second as Maddux picks him off for the second out. Jerry commenting on Maddux's inability to hold runners immediately preceded this.

Following Ramirez 5-4 fielder's choice to end the inning, the Society for American Baseball Research gets a warm welcome from the booth. Both Jerry and Joe discuss the joy of being part of SABR's media panel for this year's convention. I am sure if the Red Sox could have commented they would have warmly welcomed 700 people who can historically document that the franchise is truly cursed.

After a Pepsi and a bathroom break I am ready for the second inning. Burkett remains sharp, delivering strike one to Chipper. In John's second straight 1-2-3 inning, the booth has just enough time to discuss Andruw Jones' position as the best defensive centerfielder in the game. The bottom of the second sees the second unsuccessful Red Sox offensive spurt with Shea Hillenbrand's one out, Wall Ball double being squandered by the bats of Varitek and Nixon. Jerry and Joe, aware as the rest of New England is of their owner's ability to hit triple figures in millions of dollars devoted to the team payroll, discuss Maddux and Glavine's status as free agents after this season. Perhaps the twelve-time Gold Glove winner Maddux may find himself going for 300 wins in Fenway's friendly confines. Of course Red Sox fans can always hope.

After starting his first two innings off with strikes, John Burkett proceeds to walk leadoff man Darren Bragg on four straight pitches. Stepping to the plate in the eighth spot, light-hitting Henry Blanco, serving as Maddux's personal catcher, proved the fact that good strategy can always beat solid pitching. Blanco fisted a hit-and-run ball past a maneuvering Baerga to put men on the corners for Keith Lockhart. With the next batted ball, Burkett cleared the bases with a 4-6-3 double play putting two outs and the game's first run on the board. Bringing the top of the order back up for the Braves, Furcal hustled down the line to make a groundball to Baerga a little too close for comfort at first base.

In the bottom of the third, Maddux started things off by walking the nine spot, Boston fan favorite Jose "Awful"man. While Jerry "smells a hit and run," Offerman showed the speed he can utilize once every five times he comes to the plate to take second base. Damon followed with a groundball to the right side of the infield moving Offerman to the hot corner. With two outs, Nomar and the

Red Sox capitalized on what the official scorer would rule innings later as an error on Castilla, bringing Offerman in to tie the game. After Nomar stole second base, Manny Ramirez, deliverer of men on base, rolls a weak ground ball to Lockhart to end the Boston side of the third.

To lead off the fourth, Julio Franco connected with a Burkett offering and ripped a single. After Sheffield's fly out and Chipper's check swing strikeout, Joe discusses the possibility of Jim Thome coming to Boston with that chance being very slim. And if disturbing news comes in large packages, the booth follows the Thome discussion with an update on the Yanks five run third inning putting them ahead, 6-1. And of course the scribe of horror, Stephen King is attendance. Nevertheless, a Castilla flyout to center puts any further Braves offensive terror on hold.

After a swig of water and one of mom's fudgie no-bakes, I am back in time to hear the fielding clinic put on by Keith Lockhart as Maddux retires the side on three straight groundballs to the right side. After a dearth of offense from the middle of the Atlanta order, Darren Bragg's reemergence at home plate leads to an infield single with Baerga's dugout toss issuing the Atlanta right fielder a free pass to second base. As Blanco steps to the plate, the official scorer has the aforementioned revelation in changing Nomar's RBI single to an error. Back to the present, Keith Lockhart shows he has prowess with the bat driving in Bragg from second base.

Jerry's mentioning of Ellis Burks' possible trade to Beantown elicits a "huh" from my brother Caleb, who hopes

Lawr Michaels

Going to SABR, seeing friends like Bill Gilbert, Mat Olkin and Tony Blengino, and attending a game anywhere with them is always a dreamy pleasure.

At Fenway the dream became exponential. It was a great and entertaining game, with a lot of runners and chances. And walks and squib hits around and by offensive juggernaut Darren Bragg was, well, crazy and wonderful.

No dot racing. No gimmicks, though one wave.

The stands were full at the start and most everyone stayed till the end. Oh yeah, and to put the icing on the cake, my wife—and best friend—attended with me.

his ears aren't bringing him more news of the Indians dismantling. While my father, his father, and his father's father have borne the shameful years of the Cleveland franchise, my adolescent sibling has been primarily reared through the Tribe's glory years. Getting the fifth inning under way, a Furcal bunt single and Franco's second hit in as many innings loads the bases and brings Tony Cloninger out to the mound to talk things over with Burkett. With the heart of the order before him, Burkett retired Chipper and Sheffield on two flyouts into the glove of Manny Ramirez.

Looking to stay in line as for the win, Maddux continues to patronize Keith Lockhart as he records his sixth straight assist on a grounder from Nixon.

Indulging in this defensive showcase, Joe recognizes "Greg has his 4-3 pitch working." Jose Offerman proceeded to join the 33,137 in attendance and watch Maddux master the strike zone, gazing at strike three. Following suit, Johnny Damon rung up on strikes as Maddux's fourth strikeout victim.

Jump-starting the offense in the sixth, Andruw Jones rips a single. Castilla would continue the Braves' hard-hitting attack only to be denied a hit by a spectacular catch from Trot Nixon. As Darren Bragg steps to the plate, the booth runs an ad for Fenway Park tours. Being that I have both the New England obsession with the 90-year-old relic and a very anal retentance as far as baseball knowledge, tour guide might be a great job to pave my way in the world of sports while I attend BU. During my pondering of this, Bragg provided the second Atlanta hit of the inning. With men on first and second there is action in the Boston bullpen with righty Rich Garces and lefty Chris Haney getting loose. More good news follows Blanco's flyout to right. Timo Perez's long ball has pulled the Mets within one of the Yanks at 6-5.

Nevertheless, Keith Lockhart continues to terrorize Boston pitching as he induces Nomar to throw offline to first. However, Burkett is able to preserve the one run deficit with Furcal grounding out with the bases loaded.

While I must say I had yet to test the fortitude of MLB Radio all summer, I found the computer had a complete lack of sync with the tempo of a ball game. Unknown to my Compaq was the essential fact that in baseball there is not a sixth inning but a seventh inning stretch. However, this technological ignorance would only keep me from hearing the first two batters retired on ground balls by Atlanta reliever Kevin Gryboski. Thus MLB Radio can often cut the red tape of the Boston melodrama and take the tortured Red Sox fan closer to the night's climax. Of course technology would be back in order for another brinkmanship inning of Red Sox baseball as Shea Hillenbrand's fielder's choice leaves two Sox runners stranded.

Burkett headed out to the mound for the seventh inning. Providing another masterful inning, Burkett got groundouts from Julio Franco and Andruw Jones and a flyout from Chipper, leaving Sheffield in scoring position. While Burkett kept the Sox right on the Braves' heels, and the 25th sellout of the Fenway was announced, the Big Apple brought Joe and Jerry more crushing news. "Yankees now up 8-5 on Posada's home run," Joe disgustedly updates. "Sounds like your dog just got run over," Jerry replies. In reality much of Massachusetts canine population has perished in the minds of her Red Sox fans. Nonetheless, the chalk foul lines, often the red stockings' only defense from their downtrodden, Calvinistic fandom, enfold a match up that is not yet out of reach. Varitek leads off the bottom of the seventh by lacing a single off reliever Chris Hammond. Nevertheless, even in an often-long ball friendly park such as Fenway, the fans demand the merits of small ball from their team. Trot Nixon's inability to move Varitek over and his eventual strikeout brought boos and jeers from the crowd worthy of Jose Offerman, who just happened to follow Nixon and reach on a walk.

While the booth reminds the Red Sox nation that they are assured of their fifth interleague losing season in six years, Damon's popout to third base brings a lifetime .424 hitter against Braves pitching to the plate in Carlos Baerga. And if stats ever meant anything, Baerga proved so with an RBI double off the monster to even the score. With Offermann on third and Baerga at second,

Garciaparra was intentionally passed, sending Hammond to the showers and setting up a bases loaded match-up between Darren Holmes and Ramirez. Jerry's Red Sox pessimism escapes him for a moment as his exaltation at Manny's fly ball is followed by the Fenway sigh of despair and Chipper's easy grab in front of the wall.

Putting a gem into the hands of the Boston pen, Burkett passed the baton to Alan Embree, who followed a ground ball out with two bases on balls to the soft underbelly of the Braves' batting order, drawing a spirited response from the Boston faithful. And when the fans speak, apparently Grady Little listens as he summoned Rich Garces to face the announced batter Wes Helms. Of course the late inning machinery baseball is famous for what ensues, with Matt Franco taking Helms' place. After retiring Franco on a 1-3 ground ball, Garces makes his contribution to the Red Sox walk fund with Furcal taking first to load the bases. Borrowing Maddux's famed "4-3 pitch," Garces and the Red Sox avoid trouble and put the key to opening the dead lock in their hands.

With arguably the best reliever in the Braves pen on the mound in Mike Remlinger, Rickey Henderson stands in for Brian Daubach and draws a walk. However, the lower echelon of the Red Sox lineup were unable to create the offense of the previous inning. Hillenbrand's strikeout was followed by a Jason Varitek 6-3 double play to complete the rally killing

After a rough start to the ninth inning with leadoff batter Gary Sheffield's double, Tim Wakefield appears to have recovered after two fly outs to center. However, Vinny Castilla is determined to stay at the Mendoza line for the night, and he comes through with a single to center bringing in Sheffield. Following a Wakefield walk to Bragg, the offensive barrage would continue from the 7-8-9 men in the Braves' order. Adding salt to the Boston wound, Blanco bloops a run-scoring double in front of a diving Trot Nixon, making it a two run Boston deficit. While they still threatened to create a non-save situation, Wakefield struck out pinch hitter Jesse Garcia to retire the side.

For a team not known for comebacks, facing a Braves team that had found a closer to match the past dominance of Mark Wohlers in John Smoltz, the Red Sox did not appear up to the task of putting two tallies on board with Smoltz' 96-mile-an-hour heat to contend with. Bobby Cox's diamond in the rotational rough let Nixon and Offerman spray the ball to short and second, respectively for ground ball outs before he blew away Johnny Damon to send the remaining Boston faithful out into the nightly sea of "Yankees Suck" merchandisers awaiting them on Brookline Avenue. Mike Remlinger collected the win, staying a perfect 4-0, while Tim Wakefield took the loss, falling to 2-3.

Retiring the Red Sox 1-2-3 in the ninth, John Smoltz acquired his 26th save of the season. Wanting to avoid the rehearsal of the tragic denouement ingrained in the mind from every Boston defeat, I headed across Lansdowne Street and up Brookline Avenue past Citizens' Bank, skipping the postgame wrap up. There in Kenmore Square I gaze at the financial center's fickle reminder—"Reverse the Curse"—as I turn down Commonwealth Avenue and head towards the Warren Towers of Boston University....

In reality I climb the carpeted stairs from the basement of my home to the first floor. It is not September just yet, though another Sox squander brings another sad autumn to mind.

Rich Gibson

Having previously visited Old Comiskey, Wrigley Field, and Tiger Stadium, I was eager and excited to visit the "oldest and smallest" ball park left. With the stories about Fenway being replaced with a new park in the near future, I was very happy to hear that SABR 32 was going to be in Boston. My wife and I knew we would be going to the conference, but visiting Fenway was a big reason to go to Boston. I immediately started reading up about the park and its history. It is hard for me to imagine all of the players who have played there and the special events that have happened over the years. The excitement was building.

After arriving at the convention, we heard that a tour of the city's former and current ball parks was being planned. Having toured several other parks, we decided that we had to take this tour if Fenway was included. These tours usually allow you to see and hear things that are sometimes not known to even long-time season ticket holders. Before the tour started, we gathered and sat in the lower box seats. Immediately, we noticed how tight these $60 seats were and how little leg room there was. The tour was great. The guide told stories, like why there is one red seat in the sea of green outfield seats, and pointed out features like the Morse code hidden in the painted border of the Green Monster scoreboard. One of the tour's highlights for us was when we got to walk out and actually touch the fabled Green Monster. Following the tour, we returned to the hotel so that we could rest up before that night's game.

As we were preparing to walk into the park for the game, we noticed that all of the men were being frisked, but not the women. This is slightly more drastic security than we're used to at Cinergy Field where they just check inside bags and purses. After making it through

security, we found our seats. They were number 1 and 2, so we thought they must be aisle seats. Well, not really. They were on the end, but blocked by railings, so we had to go in through the other end of the row. That was a surprise. I was pleasantly surprised to find the $44 seats were actually wider and more comfortable than the closer, more expensive seats. As we got situated, we noticed that columns blocked second base for me and home plate for my wife. Being in the last row of the lower deck also meant that we couldn't see popups.

Since we saw most of the park during the tour, we decided to stay put and watch the game instead of wandering around. We had to describe the missing action for each other as the game proceeded. It was refreshing to see that Boston has very supportive fans who really get into the game. Near the end of the game, we walked down and went through the gift shop before heading out to catch the train back to the hotel.

After we got back to the hotel, we decided to stop and have a cocktail or two and discuss our impressions of Fenway and the game. The first thing that came up was a greater admiration for the Boston fans and what they go through to see games. They seemed to be very appreciative of their team as well as good baseball. This was true even though they were paying very high prices to sit in very small seats that sometimes didn't even point towards the field, not to mention having to look around columns that blocked their view. We were not able to come up with any particular reason why, but for us, this park just didn't seem to have the same "magical" atmosphere as we felt at Wrigley or Old Comiskey. Even several weeks after being there, I still do not have an answer. Don't get me wrong. I am very happy I was able to see and tour this historic place, but I doubt I will make a return visit. It will make seeing Boston home games on TV a little more special.

AMERICAN ANTHEM

Joseph Mancuso

We live in the reality of our beliefs, the mental image of our world. For certain things, the ideal image that we hold of them is crucial to their preservation and appreciation. Behind the reality, which can both disappoint and elate us, exists that ideal, the very real and living spirit of it. For these things in life, that spirit is at least as important as the strict reality, if not entirely paramount.

I believe that for us, our culture, and our history, baseball is such a thing.

For over a century baseball has surprised and exhilarated and endeared itself to our people. Its spirit—its ideal—is something that has transcended and withstood countless tests of time. Through everything from worldwide wars to sportwide scandal and corruption, the spirit of baseball has persisted. It has dodged the fallout of challenges to its existence and integrity, flowing effortlessly between past and present, from the major leagues to Little League, always finding lasting love somewhere in the hearts of the American people.

I emphasize American people here not to imply that there is any shortage of love for baseball outside of North America, because there is plenty. Rather, I do so to prepare the point that our very nation, and our patriotism, are akin to baseball in that they, too, thrive on their ideal, their living spirit.

I am certain that I do not need to embark on an in-depth historical or political diatribe to demonstrate the trials our nation's spirit has withstood, or to enumerate the long legacy of disparities between its ideal and its reality, which have been regrettably frequent from our founding age right up through present days. However, be they shared by fellow citizens or unique to me, my frustrations with the realities of our nation only lend weight to the fact that my persistent love for it is rooted in its spirit. Like baseball, we love our nation for what it can be, for all of the times when it does move and astound us, and for that for which it stands. Like baseball, the ideal of America persists, despite the upheavals and disappointments, and keeps us endeavoring to help it survive, improve itself and be there for generations to come.

The spirit of baseball and the American spirit—in my mind, the two are forever precious and entwined, not only in their persistent ideality, but in their inextricable historical and cultural connection. "Our Game," as Walt Whitman called it and Ken Burns echoed, was born as we know it on our own soil, and has become a part of our identity as a nation. Our National Pastime is just that, a pastime, an activity for the people at the game, defined as much in the appreciation of it as in the playing. From the mid-Western descendants of the pioneers, to the widespread children of the immigrants of our fathers' and grandfathers' day, to the urban newcomers to our nation today, it is common to us. From the inner cities to the endless farmlands, it knows no bounds. From Jim Thorpe to Ted Williams to Jackie Robinson to Joe DiMaggio to Sammy Sosa, it has become, thankfully, for all of us.

What, then, is more sacred to those who love the spirits of both baseball and our nation, and who feel the innate and deep connection of the two, than the moment at the beginning of a game when we rise to our feet to sing "The Star Spangled Banner"? So moving is this unique instant when, already electrified with anticipation for the game, be it amidst tens of thousands around a sprawling pristine field or on aluminum park bleachers watching a child or sibling stand in a makeshift uniform, we pause in reverence for our country. In this moment we feel our love of our nation and our game swell in concert over the natural exhilaration of hearing and raising our voices in song.

For me, as a baseball fan, this moment is one of the highlights of any game. As a musician, the idea of singing on the field and leading my fellow fans in the anthem, especially at a major league game, had long

been something of which I could only have dreamt. When, through a few twists of fate, that very opportunity came my way, I was thrilled and charged with excitement.

I was also, perhaps quite understandably, filled with what one might call some very "un-Buddhist" idealistic expectation. The Buddhists say, if I dare paraphrase, that suffering comes only from incorrect perception. It is not reality, but instead how we perceive reality, that is the true cause of pain. As a layman, I have yet to expand my understanding to the point where I can exercise this concept in practice.

It all began as a simple and small thing. My father, Peter Mancuso, a SABR member and baseball historian, had plans to attend SABR 32 in Boston in June of 2002. Given the 550+ miles separating us on a daily basis, he thought the event might make a nice weekend trip for the two of us to catch up outside the usual buzz of holidays and major family gatherings, which had been our only chances to see each other of late. The itinerary sounded good: take in a game at the historic Fenway Park on Friday, have an opportunity to find out more about SABR and attend some events, and take some time to myself in Beantown. I accepted the invitation, and we made plans to get to Boston, he from my family's home in eastern Pennsylvania, and me from mine in Ann Arbor, Michigan.

Not long after things were set in motion, Bill Nowlin of SABR's Boston chapter sent an alluring email down the pipeline. As part of SABR's involvement and experience at Friday's game, he had arranged with the Red Sox for the National Anthem at Fenway that night to be led by a SABR 32 attendee. He was making the submission of materials to the Red Sox himself on SABR's behalf, and was requesting audition recordings sent to him by the first of June.

I had been an independent musician and vocalist for about seven years, but I had never performed the anthem at any game before, outside of singing along in the stands. The honor of having my first time be at a Major League Baseball game, and furthermore at Boston's legendary Fenway Park, was nearly unimaginable to me. Despite my feeling that sheer numbers would make for low odds of being selected, this opportunity was too fantastic to pass up. Amidst a hectic week at work, I found an evening to put up a microphone after hours and belt out the best audition tape I could. It was a rough live cut recorded after a long day, and I honestly didn't expect it to fly, but I figured I would at least be able to say that I tried. I sent out the tape, and life's hectic grind took over. I didn't feel the weeks pass, and by the time I was preparing for the trip to Boston, I had assumed that my initial estimate of declination had been correct.

It was sometime in mid-June when I received email from Bill, via my father, to the contrary. He informed us that the Red Sox had liked my recording, and that he needed some information regarding my status with SABR. I had submitted my audition as a SABR 32 attendee, but with it I had also indicated that I was officially attending the conference, my first SABR event, as a guest of my father, and was not yet a member of SABR. This technicality had been Bill's concern, and we soon concluded that formalizing my connection with SABR via membership would be the most fair and appropriate course of action.

Knowing SABR membership would be something I would definitely enjoy in and of itself, this was more than agreeable to me. With the help of Bill and John Zajc at SABR's main office, I immediately put together the materials necessary to do so. Faxes back and forth and more email ensued, throughout all of which I endeavored to tell myself that things were not completely certain just yet, and I should psychologically prepare for the possibility of losing this once-in-a-lifetime opportunity. My nervousness notwithstanding, all was well when the dust finally cleared, and I had received confirmations all around that everything was set. I could finally allow myself to get excited.

In my immediate family, of course, there was euphoric chaos. My mother Camille and my brother Matthew were now determined to make the voyage from home and attend the game, and the necessary travel and lodging arrangements had to be made. Again, when everything at last settled, all was well. The logistics had been worked out, and Bill had even managed to have the Red Sox provide us with four tickets in the correct location in exchange for our original pair in the SABR block. My gratitude over all of this had increased tenfold, but with it, unbeknownst to me, so had the emotional stakes.

As the last of this was falling into place, I emailed Bill with my thanks and a few final questions. I had performed at a variety of venues in my years as a performer, but never before at a place anything like a baseball field. Knowing Bill had arranged this many times before, I asked him what he knew about the technical aspects of the performance, such as pacing of the tempo, microphones and monitors, and other details of the sound system. In his reply he explained that he would happily pass my questions on to the Red Sox if need be, but he also mentioned a small particularity that caught me off guard.

"Maybe you didn't understand, though, about the singing of the Anthem," Bill kindly explained. "What will be played over the sound system is the tape which you sent in. You will actually sing live into a microphone, but that's only a backup in case the tape breaks."

As my eyes moved over the words, I physically felt my heart sink.

I could not believe it. Moreover, I started to wonder what it meant. Were all the anthems at all of the games in the majors done this way? Had it been done this way at every game I had ever seen throughout my life—Yankee Stadium—Veterans Stadium—Tiger Stadium? What about when Billy Joel sang at the opening game of the 2000 Subway Series, while my housemate, bassist and fellow Native New Yorker Markus Nee sat beside me in front of the TV as we zealously cheered him on? The idea was heartbreaking.

It did not take long for my cynical side to take hold. In the darker light of simple realism, the reasons seemed obvious. They had to eliminate variables. There were TV stations counting on set amounts of valuable commercial time. There was the expectation of the general populace, raised on spoon-fed, squeaky clean, overproduced entertainment since the dawn of the mass media. There needed to be the retention of control. Suddenly I wondered how I could have been so naive.

But I knew why I had been naive. I had been naive because this was baseball. This was different, I had thought. This was something sacred enough to transcend the laws of day to day practicality. In today's day and age, in the aftermath of one of the most devastating tragedies in our country's history, this was singing the National Anthem at a baseball game. In what time within recent decades was the idealism and integrity of our Nation and its Pastime and its Anthem needed more than now? Surely there was none, I had thought.

The philosophy is clear. I am a citizen, attending the same baseball game as my fellows, walking into the park alongside them wearing similar workaday clothing, and watching from the same grandstand, eating the same hot dogs. I rise to my feet with them when the ball is hit deep and the outfielder runs to the wall. I despairingly sigh with them as the last pitch of the inning sails over the plate and into the catcher's mitt. So then, let me stand before them as I am, and let them hear me as I am, as I perform not for them, but with them, in this nigh-unto-Holy ritual. Let me be sincere with them, singing as one of them, and if my voice slightly falters, or if I slur a word to take a breath, let them hear it. This is not an enactment, and I am not an entertainer here. I am simply an American like themselves, chosen for one brief moment to lead before sitting down beside them a moment later. Perhaps I am asked to carry out this task because I am musically-suited to it, but let that aspect remain in appropriate discretion here. Let this music dissolve away the line between performer and audience, rather than become part of the endless sea of pop culture designed to emphasize it.

This is not a contrived presentation of prefabricated illusion. This is baseball.

It seemed, however, that this philosophy sadly did not reign, at least not in the world of the Major Leagues. The people making the choices here had to think about the people bringing in the money, the "demographic majority," who I could only then suppose weren't exactly

Peter J. Mancuso, Jr.

SABR 32 was my second pilgrimage to Fenway. The firs, was two years ago when youngest son Matthew, was on his way to a three-week summer camp at Wellesley. My wife Camille and my mother Mary made it a foursome. For me and Matt, it was awesome. For the ladies, it was a night out, part of a larger mini-vacation. I knew then, however, that the old park was indeed a special place. My own thoughts, then, drifted back to my boyhood solitary journey from my native Staten Island, across the harbor to the home of my beloved Dodgers, Ebbets Field. Oh, how I try to conjure up every fleeting image of that summer day in 1956. Oh, how I wish I could go back to Flatbush and revisit that great place, hear the sounds, smell the air and taste again that orange drink in the waxed cardboard container. Fenway has become the symbol of what should have never happened in Brooklyn. Fenway, made it all the more justifiable, important, necessary to get to Boston, to get to SABR 32.

"Dear, would you like to go to Boston with me for the annual SABR convention?" Her smirk said, "no."

"How about you and Matt tour the town while I'm at the meetings and we can take in Fenway again?" The roll of her eyes said, "definitely not."

"Maybe I'll ask Joe, he can fly in from Detroit, it will be a great father-son get away." She said, "that sounds great." And Joe said, "that sounds great, count me in." For the two of us, it would be our first SABR convention and for Joe his first visit to Fenway.

Then came the invitation to audition to sing the National Anthem at Friday night's game. Joe is a singer and songwriter and was already looking for-

ward to the Music & Poetry segment at the conference. When he received notice of his acceptance to perform the Anthem, there was no holding his mother back. Suddenly, the uncomfortable seats, the noisy crowd, the six-hour drive and the associated expenses vanished into thin air. Her son, her first born, her parent's grandchild, was going to sing the National Anthem, at Fenway, no less! The Red Sox even made it a foursome again, with tickets for her and Matt, Joe and me. What a night. She got in her 35mm for the stills and her camcorder for the video. She was loaded for bear! It all happened, right before her very eyes and ears. She had tears coming down her cheeks and was saying something about how unbelievable it all was.

I stared out at the 90th anniversary logo centered on the Green Monster in left field. 1912 to 2002, ninety years of baseball. In times of peace and war, hardship and prosperity, triumph and frustration, people have come here, I thought. This special place that is now forever buried within the crevices of so many memories that its very name arouses the collective consciences of perhaps millions, still stands for millions more to experience; how wonderful, I thought. As I looked down at Joe, performing the National Anthem, as I looked at his brother clicking away with the 35mm, and over at his mother with the video, I thought about the future. I thought about the future families of our line and about the legend of when great grandpa Joe or great-great grandpa Joe, or great uncle Joe sang the National Anthem at Fenway. Then I prayed that those yet to be born would still be able to visit this electric place called Fenway, and that they would be able to wonder what it must have been like for their ancestors on that Friday night in June, the 28th of 2002 to be exact, when Joseph David Mancuso sang the National Anthem at Fenway.

reverent baseball fans steeped in history and tradition and untainted spirit. This was, after all, reality, the real world, and the real America. This was the America weaned on MTV and Hollywood, expecting very much to be dazzled, but not necessarily moved. This was the America who spectates, not participates, except as directed, be it explicitly, or via the implicit suggestion of a perpetuity of marketing. This was the America that pays for what they're told to want, and unforgivingly rejects all else. This America was the audience as they saw it, and in the eyes of the Big Show, the rules of Show Biz must apply.

For an idealist and musician, this philosophical difference between reality and a simulation bordered on the sacrilegious. The act of "faking" a live performance is suicidal taboo in the world of self-respecting musical artists. While thankfully not the absolute heresy of "lip-syncing" to another person's voice (as per the "Milli Vanilli" performers of years past), this plan nonetheless went against much of my nature as an independent singer/songwriter, especially one who had cut his teeth in the honest and open-hearted world of folk music. Even with all of the aforementioned emotional preparations, I had not prepared for this.

So began the pseudo-radical ventings to housemates and friends, the heated phone conversations with family members, and the soul-searching. Much to the surprise and disbelief of many, I seriously considered passing on the opportunity entirely. Despite all the investments made on the part of my family, despite the inevitable embarrassment of having to decline at such a late hour, I strongly felt that I might not want to support what I felt was a dishonest representation of something sanctified. Still crushed from having been given the realistic truth, the loss of my idealistic preconception was all that I could see.

To make matters worse, the audition tape I had submitted was something I was not fully satisfied with. I had submitted it with the belief that it was just an audition, and that it would not be presented publicly at all. If the Anthem absolutely needed to be performed their way, then I wanted to at least follow suit with a recording worthy of a pre-produced presentation. Being denied both live integrity and studio quality was surely the worst of both worlds. Additionally, I had, mostly for fun, added a reverberation effect to the audition audio to loosely simulate ballpark acoustics. I was concerned that, in combination with the real thing upon playback, this effect might make it sound unnaturally awkward.

As the thoughts and conversations snowballed onward, it became apparent that what I really needed to do was gather more information. After all, I really had no understanding of exactly why the Anthem was performed in this manner, only my guesses. Perhaps, I thought, this was merely the default arrangement, but other options existed. Maybe the league, for some reason, actually thought I would prefer to do it this way. I decided that I needed to go to the source, ask some questions, and not make any final decisions until I knew the specifics.

Bill Nowlin had given me the name of his contact at the Bosox, and my father, anxious to have the matter settled, helped me acquire their number. (He rattled it off so readily during the phone conversation that I started to wonder if he had the whole MLB roster in his personal address book, a scenario I could almost believe.) I made the call, and, getting a recording indicating that the rep would be out of the office for a few days, I left a message. At the same time, I took a look at the Red Sox website and managed to guess at an email address. I sent an email, thinking that perhaps it might make for faster communication. I honestly didn't know what kind of response to expect from a busy major league executive, and anticipated every kind of reply ranging from nominally helpful information right on down to "It's our way or the highway, kid." Dad had clearly reminded me that while this was a landmark event for us, this was just one of this season's eighty-some-odd home games to the people running the park. I recognized this, and knew that all I could do was try and hope for the best.

To my surprise, the best was even better than I had guessed. A reply came promptly from the contact Bill had provided, Red Sox Promotions and Special Events Representative Rick Subrizio—and he couldn't have

been more accommodating.

Rick opened his email explanation with a comforting fact: "Your concerns about doing the anthem pre-recorded have been echoed by other performers in the past." Rick seemed to understand my feelings all too well, and went on to list about half a dozen reasons for the policy of using pre-recorded material.

The first reason Rick enumerated was acoustics, and this was one explanation I was able to technically understand. Because of the size of the ballpark and the natural propagation time of sound, a word uttered into the microphone at one instant and emitted from the loudspeakers the next doesn't make it to the ears of the performer until as much as a half second (or sometimes even much more) later. This delay creates a distracting effect, making it very challenging for even trained performers to maintain smooth rhythm and consistent tempo. For musical shows, especially for concerts in large arenas and stadiums, complex monitoring systems on stage solve this problem by allowing the performers to hear themselves in real time. Fenway doesn't have such a system, and I could imagine that the complication of providing one would, for most people, be difficult to justify for only ninety seconds of performance.

Timing with television breaks was also one of the reasons Rick mentioned. Especially with the long acoustic delay, it's apparently very easy for a performer to slow the Anthem tempo down significantly while singing live. In addition to appearing slow to the listeners (who can only hear the performers voice post-delay via the sound system), the piece will often get extended in duration making for difficult transitions during broadcast of the game. A pre-recorded anthem guarantees that the timing of the game's start is predictable, facilitating the necessary television programming. While my personal views of our television culture and the commercials associated with it didn't lend much compassion to this particular reason, I could at least understand its importance to the team from a business standpoint.

Rick also listed a few reasons related to insuring the Anthem's quality and respectability. Despite its role in everyday life, the Anthem is commonly known among vocalists as a somewhat difficult song to perform, especially a cappella, mostly because of its extensive pitch range and tricky accidentals and tonicizations. The performance is also potentially affected by a human factor; for most singers, Fenway's attendance represents the largest audience for which they've ever performed. The Anthem's presentation ends up being subject to a variety of challenges, which is uncomfortable to a venue trying to preserve the song's importance.

In addition, ensuring a reasonably traditional rendition of the Anthem was of great concern. "We are a pretty traditional ballpark and team," explained Rick, "and the prerecording makes certain that the anthem is presented in a reverent way. We're not averse to people taking it out a bit, but especially in light of recent patriotism, we prefer that the versions done here remain more traditional, and the recording is a way to make sure that we know what we will get once the performer goes out to sing."

Rick also mentioned what he described only as "The Roseanne Barr situation."

This group of reasons, while somewhat contrary to my musical ideals, were at least in line with my philosophies about the Anthem itself. I did still feel it was unfortunate that the performer's skill, professionalism and respect for their task could not be trusted, but I could understand the desire to minimize any risk. In the end, it was about respect for the Anthem, and what it means to the fans. It was a different approach than the one I would take, but the end goal was the same.

It was in this thought that I found the peace and clarity I sought. Thankfully for all of us, it was clear that Rick Subrizio was a genuine baseball fan.

On top of all of this, Rick was also perfectly amiable to me providing a better recording, and even offered me the resources of Fenway's in-house studio, should I be unable to line things up in time back home.

With my view on things refreshed by Rick's attentive and friendly assistance, I felt informed and emotionally positive enough about things to acquiesce to the necessities of the situation. I confirmed with my family, much

to their relief, that I would in fact be performing the Anthem at Fenway. I was able to schedule a recording session with my employer, Robert Martens, at our company's primary studio, Solid Sound. The session went well, and with minimal effort we had a clean, reverb-free recording of the Anthem which fell within the ninety-second duration limit prescribed by the Bosox. By then the weekend was upon us, and it was time to make the journey.

On Thursday afternoon, the 27th of June, CDs, luggage and SABR literature well-packed, I was dropped off by my girlfriend Kim Walbridge at Detroit Metro Airport about 3:30 PM. I eagerly strode in only to find my flight to Boston cancelled.

Puzzled, I transitioned rapidly from excited to slightly panicked. I looked at the departure list curiously; every flight into Boston, New York, Newark, Philadelphia, Pittsburg, Baltimore, Washington, White Plains... all cancelled. After joining the innumerable ranks of lost passengers in the roughly three-hour line to see one of the two agents dispatched to assist us, I was informed that a major storm system had taken out the early evening's flights into the entire region, and that I had been booked on a replacement the following morning. Unsuccessful in contacting anyone at home to pick me up, I decided to hold off on the livery option and kill some time by watching the surrealistically quiet eastern airfield, and then by making some long-shot phone calls.

Almost as if it had all been serendipity, I got lucky. The agent at the ticket counter had been unable to locate any available flights into the region, but the agent I finally reached via phone found a direct flight into Providence, Rhode Island, an alternate destination I had not considered. A quick call to Hertz verified the affordability of a one-way rental car between the two locations, and I at last hung up the phone with about a half-hour to make my new flight. Off I was.

My next challenge was encountered at security. Having managed to avoid flying since September 11, I had packed my one carry-on bag in the usual manner, filling the main compartment with clothing and such, and ignoring the outer compartments, which I always left packed with a collection of small items I use during travel. I had forgotten, however, that within that collection was a four-finger lockblade pocket knife, of perfectly legal length, with which I had always traveled since my Scouting days. After being staunchly informed that I had, albeit unwittingly, committed an arrestable offense, I convinced security that it had been an oversight, and they reluctantly decided not to confiscate my heirloom and allowed me to check it with my bag. Now, carrying only what I had in my pockets, I ran full-tilt and non-stop to my distant gate, suddenly reminded of my currently poor cardiovascular condition.

My in-flight entertainment was comprised mostly of resignedly reading the only magazine available, within which I fortunately stumbled upon an interesting piece about an old collectible baseball card game unearthed by the author in his attic. After briefly chatting with a friendly woodturner from England (who had been snoring for most of the trip), I silently celebrated as we touched down in Providence. I retrieved my bag and acquired my rental car and directions, and hit the road for Boston. The drive went smoothly except for a midnight traffic jam on the downtown freeway, during which I wondered what else would go wrong. At long last I arrived at the Park Plaza Hotel, greeted my father, and finally, at about 1 AM, lay down to sleep with a feeling of exhausted success.

The next day, while Dad attended a series of conference events, I had one last task to complete: I needed to deliver my updated CD to Fenway so that it could be reviewed and prepared for gametime. After a leisurely morning of recuperation and playing phone tag with Rick Subrizio, I set out on foot to make the delivery.

The day was intensely sunny and humid, and I tried to take in the sights and sounds of Boston's Back Bay while still keeping up the pace. I walked along Newbury Street, watching pedestrians bustle in and out of the brownstone-style shops and restaurants. I emerged onto Massachusetts Avenue, and followed the directions I'd gotten from a friendly UPS driver onto Ipswich Street toward the Park. As I sampled the strange blend of

quaint, urban and ex-industrial neighborhoods along my route, I thought on Boston. It had been quite awhile, maybe nearly fifteen years, since I had been there, and memories were dim. Such a rich city, I thought, somehow more restful than the powerfully charged streets of my birthplace, New York; rigid and municipal like Washington, but concealing a twist, a defiant ancient hum of revolutionary spirit; dense and walkable, unlike

Anne Campbell

An afternoon at Fenway is the perfect summer activity. When Lib Dooley was alive, I spent many a pleasant game in the seat next to her. I have fond recollections of Lib—she sat right by the on-deck circle where the batboy kneels, and she had a small tray laid out on top of the wall on which she placed candy and "healthy" snack offerings. These she always opened carefully with the scissors she brought; they were also offered to those seated nearby her. She was a schoolteacher but always wore elegant attire to every game, including a fur coat when the weather was chilly. I remember the huge jar of jelly beans she regularly sent to Mo Vaughn's father—the wonderful stories about her enduring friendship with Ted Williams—the birthday cake she always sent to the batboys. She was a truly wonderful character—always positive and supportive of team and never nasty—except when fans in the area got obnoxious near the end of a game when she might quietly signal an usher to remove them. They never knew what happened. She was appalled when my daughter-in-law brought her six-month-old baby to a game one night. She thought it was way too dangerous for a baby to sit in the seat right behind the on deck circle. That same grandson is now an avid Sox fan.

the cities of the mid-West and beyond, and well-aged with history.

I turned a corner, and history stared me right in the face. There, in the middle of it all, stood the almost mythical Fenway Park, a weathered brick fortress casting its spires of lightwork and netting into the afternoon sky. It wasn't some huge contrived artificial thing, buffered by parking lots and sterile surroundings. It was rough and real, rooted deep in the past, but alive, like an old and massive tree trunk still sprouting fresh leaves sunward, simultaneously epic and thriving. It spoke for the city, as part of it, almost pulling the surroundings into it with its character, wholly connected.

I approached it and blindly walked its perimeter, feeling like a wandering knight coming upon a sleeping keep well before its time of open invitation, seeking the one gate that would grant me passage.

I entered already worn, sweating from the heat. The representative at the door greeted me with an assuring smile, and directed me upstairs. The Red Sox offices were slick and modern, deceptively nestled in the Yawkey and Brookline corner of the edifice. Rick, as he had warned, was not around, and so I left my materials with the receptionist as he had instructed. In between the nearly two dozen phone calls she fielded in the few minutes I was there, I asked for a pen and paper. I left the CD, along with a thankful note to Rick, complete with the location of the backup copy I had had my housemate Dave Morris place on the Internet the night before—just in case.

Grabbing a cold drink at a local grocery mart, I made the journey back, taking the more cosmopolitan route, direct down Boylston, past the city sights. I nodded to the enviable students at Berklee; popped in with an impromptu greeting to the folks at WBCN radio (as I just happened to be wearing a T-shirt from WCBN, Ann Arbor's university station); made note of the convention center, public library, amphibious vehicle tour booths and homey-looking diner advertising authentic Italian food; people-watched my way through the Trinity Church park; and headed back along the street to the hotel.

After regrouping and making the various preparations, including changing into my virgin SABR 32 T-shirt, the time came. Upon my recounting the deceptively long walk I'd had, my family decided a taxi ride would be preferable. The driver dropped us on Brookline Avenue, and we followed the stream of people into the heart of the pre-game festivities on Yawkey Way. The sports shops were open, the sausages were hot, and Bosox fans buzzed about the gates excitedly. In the middle of the street, a loose crowd gathered to watch the live pre-game WEEI radio broadcast through a window that overlooked the scene. My father and brother purchased some dinner from the vendor outside our gate, and I donned my brand new Red Sox cap, a gift from Dad, and the first fitted baseball cap I'd ever owned. At the time and place of rendezvous Rick had specified, we passed into the high brick walls and waited.

Rick Subrizio was even nicer in person than he had already been via email and phone. He was a tall, lean, youthful gentleman in a sharp black suit, but with an air of relaxed informality that was welcome, given my increasingly jittery nerves. He guided us into the Park, and we emerged into the grandstand behind home plate from a short stairwell. Rick pointed up into the crowd, indicating the location of our new tickets, and my parents and brother headed up to the seats. With the ease of someone who had done this countless times before, he then led me down the aisle to a gate in the fence just to the right of the cage. He opened it, and gestured, and I stepped out onto the field at Fenway Park.

I purposefully raised my eyes slowly, trying to take in every blade of grass between the plate and the Green Monster. I looked out over the outfield at the bright sky and the scoreboard and the crowd. With a smile I gazed at the huge American Flag raised triumphantly over the bleachers. I breathed the air consciously, trying to soak in every shred of energy the place and time had to offer. I knew the next few minutes would fly by.

I moved along the wall to the center of the cage, right behind the plate, as directed. Rick and I chatted a bit as we waited, and I took my microcassette recorder from my pocket and tested it for the third time. He was a Boston native, and a Bosox fan all of his life. I offered my assumption that he therefore must really love his job, and he confirmed it with a smile. Handling the Anthem and color guard at the games was actually only a small portion of his responsibilities, he had said, and the hours required were long, but the tasks were enjoyable, and it was a great place to work.

Amen to that, I thought, and as the lineup started to come out over the loudspeakers, I looked out again over the Park. Ruth played here, I nearly mumbled aloud to myself, even before he built the mighty House back home. Nearly a century of baseball, and some of its greatest moments, had happened here. There had been agony, too, I recalled, even in my own lifetime, and I darkly cast my mind back to the first time I became a Bosox fan, back in Junior High School, when the Mets stole the 1986 World Series. I was certainly both a Yankee fan and a Sox fan that week; so much for the infamous rivalry.

Rick mentioned a few last items, and my mind returned to the task at hand. I had asked earlier about not having the microphone on the field at all, my last-ditch attempt for the elimination of deception, and he reminded me that it was needed as a backup, so I had to use it. He also gave a few pointers, like starting with my head down so as to hide any misalignment between me and the very start of the recording. He indicated when to walk out, and, with my tape recorder already running, I took the field. I stood at the microphone facing the grandstand, the Flag now incorrectly behind me, and sighed, reminding myself that this was the Big Show, after all.

I listened as they announced the Anthem and introduced me over the loudspeakers, and, with my hat over my heart and my head down, I took a breath and waited for the first note.

When it came, I started singing along as powerfully as I could. I felt at least my microcassette should hear more of me than of the recording that was blasted out across the Park. I wanted the people in the front rows to hear me, or maybe even the players in the dugouts. Someone, dammit, is going to hear this thing live, I

thought, at least insofar as I can muster. I sang my heart out, trying to stay in the present, but there was, admittedly, still some anger in my voice. I had even premeditated the idea of blowing their cover, maybe stepping away from the microphone for the last line, exposing the truth to the fans over "the home of the Brave." As the words rolled by, however, I found myself needing to focus on staying in sync with the recording. It was very unnatural and somewhat difficult at points, and I tried to shake off the feeling that everyone could tell what was really going on.

As the ninety seconds drew to a close, the crowd started to roar. By the time the last two lines were upon me, there was no more room for regretful feelings. I raised my head up as the *ritardando* began, and my eyes found the Flag, waving regally "o'er the land of the free" from a pole high atop the press boxes and windows above the grandstand. As my last breath gave way to the din of thirty-three thousand people, I couldn't help but be elated. Whether they were cheering for a live performance, a recorded one, the game, or for our Country, didn't matter anymore. I had done what I had come to do as best as I could do it, and with a sincerely grateful wave to the crowd and nod to Rick, I put on my Bosox cap and walked back to the gate. The only thought on my mind was pure, simple and entirely unspoiled: play ball!

Making my way up the stairs to my seat was like crossfading between two worlds. Just inside the gate, Rick congratulated me, and fans rose to shake my hand and offer kind words, and I started to wonder if maybe it did truly appear live to them. As I ascended, the handshakes turned to waves and the waves to nods, and by the time I neared my family's row, Rick had vanished, I was just another gamegoer amidst my fellows shuffling into our seats. With a feeling of relief I made for my spot, still feeling unsure about how it must have looked.

The folks directly around my parents, of course, had already doubtless been notified that it was me who had performed. They were graciously congratulatory as well, and quick conversations rose up here and there as I settled in, the last of which was with the gentleman to my right, whose name I may never have gotten.

"So how does that work?" I think he finally asked, "Is it pre-recorded?"

"Yeah," I nodded with a surrendering smirk, "that's how they have to do it."

He nodded back, explaining he'd figured it had to be, given the magnitude of the whole thing.

Ah, sweet catharsis. An opportunity for honesty, and an understanding soul upon which it was well-received. We both didn't want it to be that way, but that was how it was, the reality of the thing.

Then, as an afterthought, he added something akin to, "Well, what do you expect after that whole Roseanne Barr thing?"

I laughed out loud. What do we expect, indeed?

I spent the rest of the game reveling in the Park and the atmosphere, letting my mind unravel. I marveled at the sheer number of people there, an impressive turnout, especially relative to the largely empty CoMerica Park I had recently visited back home. I cheered hard for the Bosox, and felt the stabbing disappointment when, after such a low scoring game, Atlanta took a hard lead so close to the end. I watched the grandstand fans loyally pass hot dogs and large bills up and down the long rows as the concessions staff made their rounds. Good, I smiled to myself, here is proof that there is still plenty of honor left in the game.

After the 2-4 loss, we leisurely took the walk back to the hotel, retracing my return trip down Boylston, this time by night. During the walk, a handful of strangers afoot in the city stopped to ask us about the outcome of the game. One white-haired gentlemen groaned when he heard our report, and thanked us, moving along and shaking his head. My father couldn't help but smile, remarking that one could easily tell that this was "a great town for baseball."

Behind us, Fenway Park agreed, now eclipsed by the synthetic horizon, slowly returning to its palatial sleep and its nonagenarian dreams.

Late that night I sat at the desk in our hotel room and took a few moments to notate my thoughts. Recalling the relieving feeling of having shared my secret with my neighbor at the Park, I pondered upon my plan to make the issue central to my contribution to The Fenway Project. Perhaps many SABR members already knew the facts of the situation, or at least assumed something similar, but it needed to be brought to indisputable light. Bill Nowlin's bold initiative to capture so many personal accounts of a single game seemed a relevant venue, and the readers thereof an important community with whom to share my concerns. Certainly there would be others who felt as I did, and just maybe, over the years to come, things could change. In the idealist's reality, hope springs eternal.

As I wrote, I thought, too, on Boston. "It's a town I always liked," I wrote, "but never really had more than a cursory opportunity to connect with... until now, perhaps. I'm sure that while I still feel very much a visitor here, my experience tonight will bring me closer to a real link... and when I was on my feet in the bottom of the ninth hoping we'd gain back the game as the batters cracked the ball and ran for first, for at least one moment... I felt like I'd been born here."

The remainder of the weekend was spent enjoying time with my family, and exploring the community at the conference. Every event I attended or person with whom I shared ideas made me more pleased with my new official status as a SABR member. It was very truthfully an honor to have represented the organization at Fenway, a special initiation for which I will always be grateful. Several people thanked me for my work over the following days, and with each I felt my sentiments reinforced. As someone who had at first felt a bit out of place, I was thankful to be welcomed so warmly by so many brilliant and talented people, all brought together by a shared love of our American game. It is to this fellowship that I offer this contribution, hoping that my amateurish verbosity will be tolerated, if not outright embraced, by a colleagueship enamored with the importance of documentation, both public and personal.

"What are we, after all, but time incarnate, experience concentrated for a moment, a tiny and temporary fragment of Everything sliced off to peer at itself from a direction never seen before and carry its study home?"

My journal captured my reflections over ginger ale and pretzels on Northwest flight 393 to Detroit Metro. "We are that, or nothing at all."

And what are the time-stained bricks of the towering walls of Fenway Park, and its aching seats worn and reworn by five generations of the seventh inning stretch, and the deep earth beneath its baselines consecrated by summer upon summer of pounding hits and steals and slides, and its cold steel housing and concrete foundations still invisibly rattling with the residual power and sound of hundreds of thousands of unrepeatable rushes of emotion, and the lifetime of voices that have called out over its green enclosure with hearts covered and eyes raised to the stars and stripes?

What are all of these things but dust called together for a cosmic instant and given life with the divine breath of human memory?

In strict reality they may be nothing. But in the reality in which we each truly live, in the world of our perception, they are a gift from those who have come before us, a link to an ideal that we must not forget.

Long live the Spirit of Baseball.

Rick Subrizio and Joseph Mancuso

Bob Buege

The Red Sox hosted the Atlanta Braves, but I came to see Fenway Park for the first time. Winning and losing mean very little to me. That's what happens when you have a hometown team like the Milwaukee Brewers. I liked watching Greg Maddux and Nomar Garciaparra, but Fenway was the star.

Before my visit, Fenway lived only on the TV screen and in the mellifluous words of John Updike. Media images of the Green Monster and the right field fence that falls away from Pesky's Pole are simply inadequate. The intimacy and the immediacy of the ballpark, the seats, the neighborhood, and the strangely-configured playing field recall a distant past.

I enjoyed communing with the spirits of Smoky Joe and Teddy Ballgame. I sat in the first row in the bleacher area, above the Red Sox bullpen, enjoying the game through a wire fence, from a narrow seat, with a constant parade of vendors hawking their wares and obstructing my view. Someone once sat where I sat and watched Speaker run down a fly ball. It was wonderful.

I searched my video memory and the seats for the spot where Williams' final home run landed. The whole experience was wonderful. Fenway is a jewel.

IN THE BRAVES CLUBHOUSE

Stew Thornley

After picking up my credential about two-and-a-half hours before the game, I made my way to the field. The Red Sox were taking batting practice with few Braves around yet, but some of the coaching staff, including dugout coach Pat Corrales and pitching coach Leo Mazzone, were in the dugout as was manager Bobby Cox, smoking a cigar. I was working on a children's book on Chipper Jones and had had the chance to talk to Jones on the field for a few minutes when the Braves were in Minnesota for a series two-and-a-half weeks before. This time I decided to talk to Cox—who had been general manager when the Braves drafted Jones with the first overall pick in 1990—about their decision to take him. Rather than ask Cox about why they took Jones over pitcher Todd Van Poppel, who was the next player selected, I inquired as how much interest they had had in Tim Costo, a shortstop from the University of Iowa. Cox wasn't effusive but did say he remembered Costo well and that one of their scouts, Joe Caputo, had wanted them to draft Costo. Jones, like Costo, was a shortstop at the time and played that position in the minors. However, the Braves planned on playing Jones in left field in 1994, only to have Jones injure his knee in spring training and miss the entire season. In 1995, Jones ended up playing third base. Cox said the plans on where to play Jones were entirely a result of their defensive needs at the time and not a result of his poor performance at shortstop in the minors. Cox pointed out that many players make a lot of errors in the minors and that Jones's experience had not soured the Braves on using him at shortstop.

Since I was also planning a book on Game Sevens in the World Series, I asked Cox if he had any special memories about Game Seven of the 1991 World Series, a classic in which Cox's Braves lost to the Minnesota Twins in

10 innings. Perhaps it was because he didn't want to think about that loss, even nearly 11 years later, or because he was tired of talking to me and wanted me to get lost that he just growled, "I can't even fucking remember Game Sevens." I wrote the quote in my notebook, thanked him for his time, and got up and left.

I headed up the dingy ramp from the dugout to the clubhouse. It had rained heavily the night before, and the runway still contained puddles of water. At the end of the runway was a door that went right into the Atlanta clubhouse. Greg Maddux was sitting by his locker. However, I knew he didn't like to talk prior to a pitching performance, so I instead approached Kerry Ligtenberg, who was sitting at a table and working on a crossword puzzle. I had done public-address announcing for the Minneapolis Loons when Ligtenberg pitched for the team. Feeling a bit of a connection with Ligtenberg, I talked with him a bit about the Loons. Chipper Jones and a few others were also at this table, playing cribbage. Most of the players were lounging on a couch around a big-screen television. Next to it was a rack loaded with DVDs and video tapes. Music is banned in some clubhouses because of the conflicts it creates over what type of music to play. I wondered if the fights over which movie to watch ever broke out among the players.

I wanted to talk with John Smoltz, who had been the starting pitcher for the Braves in Game Seven in 1991, but he was engrossed in conversation with someone by his locker. I looked around for bullpen coach Bobby Dews, a longtime member of the Braves' staff in the majors and minors. Two years before, I had had a nice conversation with Dews in the National League clubhouse before the All-Star Game in Atlanta. Dews had managed Jim Bouton in Savannah in 1978, the year that Bouton was attempting a comeback and we had talked about that in Atlanta. Bouton became the subject of a *Sports Illustrated* article which also focused attention on Dews, who felt that the article was the impetus for the Braves calling him up to the majors as a coach the following year. Dews worked in various capacities, including as director of player development, for the Braves

over the years and was happy to be back, in uniform, as a coach. Dews again had good things to say about Bouton. Dews also told me that he had written a book of his own, *Twelve Voices*, a collection of short stories that will be published next year by Longstreet Press.

I went on to the field for a while, then back to the Braves locker room. By this time, Smoltz was in the trainer's room-off limits to the press-working with some weights. Earlier, I had seen Greg Maddux in there, getting his left calf wrapped. Maddux had missed his previous start because of a strained calf muscle.

Along with Bill Nowlin, I went upstairs, ate in the dining room, and settled into the press box. In around 1990, the old press box had been converted into luxury seating and a new press box built on top of it. From the top row of the press box, we had to lean over to see home plate. This was probably the worst vantage point I had ever had in a press box. I considered moving outside and finding a place to sit, but although the view wasn't the best, I enjoyed the company and decided to stick around. Sitting on my left was Bill Francis, a researcher from the Hall of Fame. Bill and I had sat next to each other in the auxiliary press box at Yankee Stadium during the World Series the previous October and November. In the third inning, we were joined by Eric Enders, a former researcher at the Hall of Fame. Eric and I, as well as Bill Nowlin, had been on the same baseball tour to Cuba in February 2001. Eric was a scoreboard aficionado, as is Bill. In Cuba, the two had been able to operate the scoreboard in Pinar del Rio. For the Fenway Project, Eric had the assignment of spending a couple innings in the scoreboard inside the Green Monster.

In the game, Maddux came out after five innings. He had allowed one run, unearned, and had a 2-1 lead. It was figured that his bad calf was the reason for his early departure although in the first inning he had also taken a hard shot off his right shin. The Braves relievers allowed a run in the seventh, wiping out Maddux's chance for a win. Having the bullpen blow a win was something Maddux had probably gotten used to, but this year's crop of Atlanta relief pitchers was better than many they had had in the 1990s.

The score stayed tied into the ninth when Gary Sheffield of the Braves led off with a double on a drive that bounced off the top ledge of the scoreboard in left. Chipper and Andruw Jones both flied to Johnny Damon in center, but then Vinny Castilla hit a soft fly to center that dropped in for a hit as Sheffield came home with the go-ahead run. After Darren Bragg walked, Henry Blanco blooped a double to right to score Castilla and make the score 4-2. John Smoltz worked the last of the ninth, retiring the Red Sox in order.

The game over, I joined the herd of reporters rushing to get downstairs to the Atlanta locker room. We went down on an elevator that also stopped at other levels to let fans on and finally got down to the bottom level. Reporters ran out of the elevator, dodging fans as they weaved through the concourse to get to the door to the locker room. Inside I looked around but didn't see Maddux at his locker. (One of the reporters asked me if I'd recognize Maddux and to point him out if I saw him.)

As is often the case, players and managers have little of substance to say after the game. I often think reporters would be better off staying at their computers and write a description of what actually happened in the game rather than bolt for the locker room to get mostly meaningless quotes.

The only real issue was why Maddux had come out after only 74 pitches. In his office, Cox confirmed that it was concern over Maddux's calf that caused the early departure. Back in the main part of the locker room, Maddux emerged and the press posse rushed toward him. I led off with a comment/question about him allowing only one fly ball. Maddux responded nicely but not to the question I had asked. He said would have liked to pitch longer but "looking down the road, looking at the big picture, I wasn't right." He praised the bullpen, even though it had lost the lead. Asked if he had asked to come out of the game or if it was the manager's decision, Maddux shrugged and said, "I don't know." (He didn't know if he asked to come out?) He added that he didn't complain about coming out and

pointed out that Cox runs the show.

Maddux commented about his mound opponent that night, John Burkett, who had pitched for Atlanta the year before: "I've only seen Burky pitch good—never saw him pitch bad. We miss Burkett in the clubhouse. He ran the pools."

We all jotted down Maddux's comments as if they were really earthshaking stuff, and many of his quotes ended up in some of the game stories in the Boston newspapers the next day. Here's a few I spotted in Rich Thompson's story in the next day's *Boston Herald*: "As far as my calf goes, this was my best game since the last two, so it's going in the right direction. It's not hard to pitch. I don't have any problems pitching. It's playing baseball.... I like to pitch well, obviously, but we are kind of looking down the road and looking at the big picture a little bit. I thought our bullpen was outstanding, like they have been all year, and they were good again tonight.... This is a good one, it's a cool place to pitch. It would have been nice to have stayed out there facing Burky. He's a good dude, and it would have been nice to battle him some more. We've only seen Burky pitch good, we've never seen him pitch bad, and we expected a tough game because we saw it every day last year. He knows how to pitch."

On my way out of the locker room, I queried Atlanta general manager John Schuerholz on the deal the Montreal Expos had made to get Bartolo Colon. Schuerholz seemed unconcerned about the Braves' main competition in the National League East strengthening its rotation.

I went back up to the press box to get the official box score and check it against the tallies on my scoresheet. A few thoughts about keeping score. This is something I've been doing for nearly 40 years. Like others, I've refined my system over time. In addition to keeping score of games I attended when I was young, I enjoyed going through *The Sporting News Official Baseball Guide* that my dad got each year. These contained complete play-by-play of the All-Star Game and World Series. I'd use these accounts to practice my scorekeeping, entering the games and individual plays into my scorebook.

About 10 years ago, I designed my own scoresheet, something Eric Enders has also done (Eric has even bound his into scorebooks and now sells them). To me, a completed scoresheet is a work of art. It's not the person entering the hieroglyphics who is the artist; rather it is the players on the field, creating the events that are then recorded. At the end of the game, the scorer has a unique piece of art, as individual as a snowflake or a fingerprint, no two games ever being the same.

The Campbell Family

Anne Campbell—grandmother:

Although I'm an enthusiastic Red Sox fan and we lost to the Braves, I can't think of a more pleasant summer evening than sitting in the bleachers and soaking up the pleasures of attending with an old high school friend and my son and grandson (who was watching his first major league game). The weather was perfect. The sausage and beer a ritual; the grass was green; the sky was blue and we just relaxed and enjoyed. Trot Nixon made a great catch right in front of us. This is life as it should be!

Jim Campbell, age 10:

My first impression was that it was very green. My second impression was that it was very huge. It was kind of dirty around your feet. The Coke bottles and Hood milk cartons were weird because I expected to see that on an electronic screen. All the players were really good and I was psyched. It was my first major league baseball game. The pitchers threw the ball so fast you couldn't even see them. It was amazingly fun and I definitely want to go again.

James Campbell, age 38:

I hadn't been to a baseball game for several years, and was attending with my mother, an old friend of hers, and my son, who was seeing a ballgame for the first time. I've never seen a pro game anywhere but Fenway—Fenway Park IS baseball as far as I'm concerned. The sound of the pre-game announcements on the PA and the crowd, coming through the entrances as you enter the park and make your way to your seat, along with the sights and smells of the concession area. evoke a flood of childhood memories.... I was glad there was a fan "tussle" in the bleachers—it wouldn't have been a real ballgame without one!

IT'S NEVER ABOUT THE GAME

Irv Goldfarb

Name's Goldfarb. Saw my first live baseball game back in '62 at Yankee Stadium and screamed Roger Maris' name for so long that he was finally forced to turn around and acknowledge my presence. I was too scared to speak for the rest of the day.

First saw the Mets in June of '63 at the Polo Grounds, where, naturally, they never played polo. The Duke had tied it up with a two-run homer, then the Mets and Cubs battled all day, until one Tim Harkness hit a grand slam in the bottom of the 14th with two out, and the Mets won 8-6. I've been a Met fan ever since. (Fill in sarcastic remark of your choice here...) I've run into lots of folks over the years who claim to have been there that day, but I don't believe most of them. I just know I was there.

First game at Shea was Memorial Day, 1964. If you know your baseball, you'll remember it as being the longest doubleheader in baseball history. The Mets and Giants lasted through 27 innings of game two, until Mays' team won it in the bottom of the 27th inning. My childhood was fraught with extra innings, but I did learn one thing early: It isn't always about The Game. Sometimes it's about everything else...

JUNE 28, 2002: My birthday. And Boston is my first SABR convention. How thoughtful of them to schedule a game for me to see that very night! I lived in Connecticut for 19 years and had been to Fenway Park many times. I saw Gary Carter homer twice there in Game 4 of the '86 World Series, when the Mets came crawling back from the dead to prolong the Red Sox century of agony. Sometimes it's just about luck.

I call a friend of mine in Connecticut and invite him to spend my birthday with me at the game. He's a Sox fan, so he readily agrees. Tonight, the Bosox are facing the Atlanta Braves, a team that, in turn, has tortured the Mets for almost a decade. I have already seen them twice this week in New York and both times they've pulled out annoyingly agonizing victories. I know even before we leave the hotel that they're probably going to do so again tonight. But it's my birthday and I'm going to sit in the bleachers of the second oldest park in baseball, with hundreds of fellow SABR members, and drink beer and watch the sun set behind the Monster. So who cares who wins? Sometimes it's only about the atmosphere.

6:00 PM: My friend Phil arrives at the Park Plaza Hotel, just as I am choosing my outerwear for the evening. For me, choosing the appropriate shirt, jacket, or jersey is half the fun. I've brought along a T-shirt depicting the screaming Milwaukee Braves' Indian head from the '50's, that everyone at the convention has commented on; however, I refuse to wear anything that might construe me as a Braves fan—I'll save that shirt for my trip to Miller Park later in the summer. Instead, I lovingly choose my authentic, cost-way-more-than-it-should-at-the-Clubhouse Shop Mets road jersey, with "Koosman 36" stitched on the back. Jerry was my favorite and I am always stubbornly proud about being a Met fan.

6:30 PM: Phil and I take a taxi to Fenway to avoid the prospects of "parking lot hell." Along with the charm of a ballpark that opened in 1912, comes the knowledge that the parking situation around Landsdowne Street has not been upgraded since 1912. If you can find a spot within walking distance at all it'll cost you at least twenty bucks, and that usually puts you in a fast-food joint's lot, boxed in by four other vehicles. We decide to cab it.

6:40 PM: We're not out of the taxi five minutes when a tall, pony-tailed, rock-'n-roll type dude, who looks as if he knows absolutely nothing at all about baseball stops me and says, "Cool—'Koosman!' Is that a real jersey?"

"Oh, yes," I answer proudly, slowly rotating like Nikki Taylor on the runway, as I allow him a complete look at the back of the shirt.

"Where d'ya get it?" he asks, studying it carefully.

"Mets Clubhouse Shop," I answer, and in case he doesn't understand the full force of the comment, I add: "In New York."

Suddenly, Mr. Pony Tail snorts and points. "Yeah, but it's got this black drop shadow here, so it's not *really* real, is it?"

I am suddenly appalled; my eyes narrow and I snort back: "Sure it is!" I resist the urge to show him my Master Card bill as incontrovertible proof.

"Naww," he replies, daring now to touch the shirt while outlining the lettering on the Mets logo. "See, it's got the black outline under here, and the Met jersey didn't *have* any black in it back then, so yeah, it might be real, but it's not really authentic!" With one last snort he spins away and disappears into the pre-game crowd. I want to stop him and laugh at his irrelevance, demand to know how he learned so much about the evolution of the New York Mets' uniform, and let him know that he can't tell me *anything* about baseball tonight, because tonight I am among the largest and most well-informed group of baseball researchers in America! But I don't do anything, because he's right, of course. The original Met jersey *didn't* have any black drop shadow around the lettering, and being among the largest and most well-informed group of baseball researchers in America, I surely should have realized this before I even took my Master Card out of my damn wallet! I am terribly embarrassed and want to rip off the jersey and throw it in the nearest trash can. Instead, I simply sigh and continue on toward the bleacher entrance. Wish I had worn my Milwaukee Braves shirt with the screaming Indian head instead.

7:00 PM: Phil and I purchase our first beers of the evening and we actually get carded! I have more gray hair than the girl at the beer stand has cutesy dimples, but she wants to see my ID anyway, so I shrug and show it to her. "It's my birthday," I add sarcastically. "Do I get a free beer?" Smiling at me, she quickly pours two and hands them over. I figure her phone number is out then, huh?

Finally locating our seats high up in the bleachers,

Phil and I settle in to watch the last of the groundskeepers as they spruce up the field in preparation of the contest. It seems that everyone in our section is wearing their SABR name tags except for me and Phil. Phil has a reasonable excuse: he's not a SABR member. I, on the other hand, have always had something against name tags. Maybe it's just me, but wearing a 'convention name tag' is kind of akin to walking through midtown Manhattan with a camera around your neck. It fairly screams "Tourist!" Convention name tags only make me feel like Oliver Hardy in "Sons of the Desert," so if I affix them to my clothes at all, it's usually at the belt buckle, where they invariably fall off sometime during the convention and people, if they care, have to ask me who I am.

7:05 PM: I am studying the names on the SABR tags around us, when suddenly I notice that we are sitting next to the estimable Mr. Norman Macht. I have never met Mr. Macht, but his is a name I see every morning in the e-mail folder in my computer at work, the one marked "Baseball Stuff." He has answers to questions that SABR members need to know quickly, and he helps Deadball and 19th-Century members with obscure facts, and he comes up with ideas for committees, and he has his work published in *The Baseball Research Journal* and *The National Pastime*. I am suddenly a little nervous, aware that he is sitting next to me at a baseball game. Immediately, Norman leans over and says, half in jest: "Now, I'm at the age where I might be getting up and down a lot, so you guys will have to be patient if I have to leave my seat a few times...."

I smile. "For you, Norman, anything!"

"Well," he remarks to his companion (could this be Lois?), "we may have to test them on this!"

7:06 PM: Norman tests us on this. Leaning over to me, he says, quite seriously, "Can you ask that gentleman right there if he'll please sit down?" I am not sure to whom he is referring. "Right there," Norman points. "That guy writing the lineups in his scorecard. Can you ask him to please sit down? He's in my way." I feel stupid—I'm still confused. In the way of what? I look out at the field, and see only the last of the groundskeepers lugging their water hoses down the foul line.

"*That guy?*," I ask quizzically, pointing to a fan standing up a few rows ahead of us.

"Yes, please," replies Norman. "He's in my way. I'm trying to watch Greg Maddux warm up, and he's blocking my view of the bullpen..." I suddenly feel very important! I immediately compare this situation to perhaps The Babe returning for just a day to catch a game at Fenway Park, and he's just asked me to please pass his hot dog! I peek around the offending fan and indeed see Maddux winding up and delivering his warm-up pitches to the bullpen catcher. Determined to keep my word, I nod, and head down the bleacher stairs. I get to the guy with the scorecard. Unfortunately, he is not a SABR member.

I lean over and say, as intimately as I can manage: "Excuse me. You see that older gentleman up there?" The guy looks over my shoulder. "Well, he wonders if you could possibly sit down to fill in your scorecard. He really wants to see Maddux warm up and you're kinda blocking his view." I look at him sheepishly and shrug. The guy looks a little annoyed, but merely shrugs back. He sits down. "Thanks!" I whisper, and proudly return to my bleacher seat, mission accomplished.

"Thank you," says Norman nodding. "I like to watch the great pitchers when I can."

"Well, you picked a good one!" is all I can think of to say, as if in affirmation of Norman's opinions on baseball talent. But we've bonded now, both of us aware that it's not always about the game.

My friend Phil has no idea what just happened.

7:10 PM: As President of SABR, Claudia Perry takes the

mound to throw out the first pitch. Our society's presence at the game is announced and our section goes wild! Claudia winds and deals... it is not pretty. "She throws like a *girl!*" someone remarks ashamedly in a loud voice. Another member turns around to me and innocently asks, "Can I resign from SABR?" We are a cruel bunch.

7:12 PM: The game finally begins and, unfortunately, I admit that I'm ready for a second beer. Damn that Von der Ahe and his crazy ideas!

7:55 PM: It's the top of the third and the game is scoreless. Henry Blanco walks for Atlanta, moving ex-Red Sox (and ex-Met) Darren Bragg to second base. *Baseball Prospectus* has just listed Henry Blanco, by the way, as one of the five least productive catchers in baseball, and it makes me wonder why so many major league pitchers always seem to struggle with the Henry Blancos of the world. Then I remember that Blanco is the same guy who beat the Mets with a huge home run earlier this season and now I giggle vengefully to myself. (This, by the way, is one of the reasons I pay no attention to publications such as *Baseball Prospectus*. They concentrate on numbers and only numbers, but they never seem to pay attention to the reality. Yes, if the games were "played on paper," these guys really would be geniuses! But they need to figure out the fact that it's not always about the numbers, either.)

Keith Lockhart (another Met-killer) hits into a double play, but Bragg scores. 1-0 Braves.

8:05 PM: Bottom of the inning—Nomar hits a dribbler to third, but Vinny Castilla can't make the play and Jose Offerman scores to tie the game at one. I'm excited, as the Mets creep inexorably closer to cutting a half-game off the NL East lead.

8:18 PM: There are two kids sitting on the other side of us; the one next to me hasn't stopped talking since they sat down. (I use the term 'kids', by the way, to denote anyone who looks to be under 35. I have earned this right, especially on my birthday.) But they're talking about baseball, and they are SABR members, so I begin to eavesdrop. The trivia question appears on the message board. Now, like most of us, I always think I'm good at these, but the kid next to me comes up with the answer before I even have a chance to finish reading the damn question! (Please don't ask me what the question was—I can't remember. I only know I wouldn't have gotten it right.) I continue to listen in, but by the next inning they've switched their conversation to a detailed study of the Clarence Thomas case. No, really, I'm not making this stuff up! I am absolutely fascinated, as I realize that these guys were probably around *twelve* when the Clarence Thomas case was in the news, yet here they sit, in the far reaches of Fenway Park, discussing the pros and cons of the "Coke Can Defense" and the merits of American jurisprudence. Me, I can't even remember what the hell Anita Hill wanted from us in the first place! Punks! When I was these guys' age, all I talked about was women, the Mets, and Bruce Springsteen... Umm—okay, so I maybe I still—er—never mind...

I suddenly get depressed and head downstairs for two more beers for me and Phil. I remind the girl at the beer stand that it's still my birthday. She smiles at me again, and charges me twelve more dollars.

8:26 PM: Keith Lockhart singles and Bragg scores again. 2-1, Braves. What do these guys do, *practice* or something? I seriously hate this team.

8:40 PM: The score is still 2-1, and everyone seems to have gone into that 6th inning funk. You know the one I mean—when you just kind of look around the stadium and try to pick out things to think about, if you're not already thinking about something else. I look around the bleachers, and listen to the fans as they intermittently scream different chants and phrases, trying to 'rattle' the visiting Braves. I shake my head pitifully.

You know, I try not to be overly provincial and, trust me, *no one* on this great green earth of ours despises the New York Yankees more than I do! But I still manage to sit in the bleachers at Yankee Stadium every now and then. (I was actually out there the night that Psycho Clemens hit Mike Piazza in the head, and when I heard the crack of the helmet, I swore it was a foul ball! I had never thought a human head could make that particular noise...) But I have to admit, for all of their violent, disgusting, animalistic traits, the fans in the bleachers at Yankee Stadium are some of the most disturbingly *creative* people this side of Joseph Mengele! And the most amazing part is, the Yankee Stadium bleachers (out of necessity, of course) are non-alcholic sections! Their call-and-response greetings to each of the Yankee starters at the beginning of every game is nothing short of goose-bump inducing. (I absolutely *love* it when Derek Jeter turns and dutifully waves his glove in greeting just before the next pitch.) And they let no one, I mean *no one* who resembles a celebrity, walk up the stairs without starting a chant. Short guys with glasses get "Wooo-dy Alll-ennn!" every time. Same for fat guys, people with Met hats (yeah, me, too) and large-breasted women (you may allow your basest instincts to run wild on this one).

Now what they've done to "YMCA" would curl your nose hairs! You see, at Yankee Stadium, when the groundskeepers come out to drag the infield, the PA system blares the classic Village People ditty, and the groundsmen dutifully stop at each chorus and do the "spell-out-YMCA-with your-body" thing. The crowd all sings and gyrates along, and I always thought it all pretty silly, until the day I heard it from out in the Yankee Stadium bleachers! The fans out there have kind of—um—altered the lyrics some, and they've sort of changed the meaning of this particular tune. (I can't go into specifics right here you understand, but let's just say these "revised" lyrics question the sexual lifestyle choices of the listener, and we'll leave it at that.) Anyway, I'm a pretty tough bird to shock in my old age, but when I first watched nine-and ten-year-old boys and girls happily singing along with these "new-and-improved" lyrics, I didn't know whether to cover my ears in shame, or run from the stadium screaming! (Unfortunately, instinct usually tends to prevail in these cases, and I just laughed out loud for a very long time.)

Now here I sit, gazing around Fenway's bleachers, and I shake my head once again. Poor, poor, pitiful Red Sox fans—"Hey, Maddux, you stink!" and "Larrr-yyy!" chanted sarcastically in Chipper Jones' direction, are surely poor substitutes for some of the things I've heard in my many visits to the Bronx Zoo.

8:54 PM: The fans at Fenway actually go and make things worse! In this, the Year of our Lord, 2002, the 21st century, mind you, the fans in Boston actually start doing *The Wave!* Oh God, when will it die! *When?* Okay, so they still do it at Shea every now and then, too. But I can proudly say right here and now that in the twenty-odd years since this blight was first forced upon us by some sacrilegious hicks in the state of Washington (or wher- ever it started; believe it or not, fans on the West coast actually argue about whose hellspawn this originally was.), I have never, ever stood up during a wave. Never! And, I am even prouder to state, right here and now, that almost nobody from SABR stood up on this night, either! *Damn* proud!

9:06 PM: Almost as if on cue, though the Red Sox are facing the Atlanta Braves, and there is not a pinstriped uniform in sight, the entire Fenway bleacher section starts a chant of "Yank-ees Suck!" I take back everything I said and join in merrily.

9:10 PM: It's between innings, and The Whiz Kids next to me are out of intellectual discussion fod- der. Obviously bored with every- thing they deem interesting, they reluctantly turn their attention to me.

"You from New York?" the more loquacious of the two asks.

"Uh-huh," I reply intelligently.

"That explains the jersey then,"

he smiles. I look down at "New York" emblazoned across my chest and smile back.

"Good thinking."

"So," he continues, as the next inning has not yet begun, "what committees are you involved with?"

Okay, fair question. I ponder seriously for a moment before answering: "Deadball—19th Century—Negro Leagues. The Negro League Committee was actually the first one I joined."

"Oh," he remarks thoughtfully, and pauses. "So I guess you must like things that sort of—aren't around anymore...."

"Yes—yes, I never thought of it that way." I nod and begin to think about it this way for the first time. "Yes, I guess I do." The kid turns back to his friend, while I am caught up in a miasma of introspection, wondering what it was about my childhood, exactly, that has caused this particular flaw in my makeup. I begin another search for the beer guy. Suddenly I start to wonder if maybe there's a Zoloft guy around. I try not to sniffle. Once in a while I wish it really was just about the game.

9:29 PM: Maddux is long gone; Chris Hammond is now pitching for Atlanta. I remember a time when including the words "Chris Hammond" and "coming out of the bullpen" in the same sentence was a harbinger of only laughter and good things on the horizon for the oppos- ing team. But alas, like every other retread that that cursed Leo Mazzone gets his mitts on, he's turned this one around, too, and Hammond is having another one of those simply 'efficient' seasons for the Atlanta Braves.

On this night, however, the Sox give him trouble: With two out in the seventh, Carlos Baerga (is the whole freakin'

Skip McAfee

I attended the game, sitting in the bleachers with the larger SABR contingent with a high school classmate (we graduated 47 years ago!), Anne Campbell, from Waban, Massachusetts. She brought her son (James) and her grandson (Jimmy), age 10, attending his very first big league game. From our vantage point in the straight- away right field bleachers, up high nearly beneath the scoreboard and, at my advanced age, I couldn't pick up the base- ball after it was hit, owing to the distance from the plate and the sea of white shirts along the 3rd base line.

baseball *world* populated with ex-Mets, or what?) doubles in a run to tie the game at two, and after intentionally walking "No-mah." Darren Holmes (another Mazzone reclamation project), comes in to face Manny Ramirez. It's the situation we've all dreamed of as kids—bases loaded, two out, late innings, tie game. More importantly, it's one of those situations that Dave Campbell always talks about.

I actually know Dave Campbell from my days at ESPN. A light-hitting infielder for Detroit and San Diego in his previous life, Dave's now a baseball analyst, and I know that he likes to sit in bars after games and drink and talk about baseball. One night I mentioned to him that I had been to the Hall of Fame, and had seen the scorecard from Seaver's 19-strikeout game against the Padres in 1970. One thing I had noticed, was that Campbell was one of the two Pods who actually had a hit. (If you really need to know who the other one was, ask the two kids who sat next to me—personally, I can't remember.) Anyway. Campbell was really proud of this achievement.

"Do you remember the hit?" I ask him.

"Sure!" he begins proudly. "See, early in the game, I hit a rope, I mean a *rope*, about this high off the ground..." He holds his hand about an inch off the bar. "I mean this thing was a laser!"

"So that was the hit against Seaver, huh?" I say, obviously impressed.

"Hell, no!" Campbell shouts, grabbing his beer. "Sonuvabitch Cleon caught that one right off the grass! Sonuvabitch! But next time up, I bounce a 23-hopper down the third-base line and I beat it out for a hit!" He cackles. "I was always pretty fast!" I nod and signal the bartender for two more.

Now here we are at Fenway, 2002, and I recall something *intelligent* that Dave Campbell often says: "In every baseball game there are always a few situations that can turn the game around. Not many—maybe three or four. And the team that takes advantage of these situations, usually wins." Not really heavy stuff, but smart and simple. So, here we are: bases loaded for the Sox, tie game, two out, seventh inning. Manny Ramirez versus Darren

Holmes—a situation for the home team to take advantage of if ever there was one. Count goes to 1-2... and of course, Holmes strikes him out, proving two things: why Dave Campbell is a very highly regarded baseball analyst—and that sometimes John Hart actually did know what he was doing.

9:44 PM: With the game tied, also comes the devastating news that no more beer will be served, so I begin to mentally settle in for a long night. Gazing around the park, I focus on the Green Monster that has proudly ruled left field for most of a century. It's glorious—it's intimidating—but I gotta say it right here: the scoreboard part of it really does stink! No, come on, unbiased baseball fans! The out-of-town scores on this thing is incredibly slow! And incomplete. And hard to see. (Well, at least from the bleachers.) Thank God they finally complimented it with an electronic out-of-town scoreboard over the bleacher area, because that one in the left field wall is virtually useless! It's got the Mets trailing the Yankees by five runs, when I know (via my handy-dandy Walkman, of course) that they've cut it to three! C'mon!

Studying the structure across the field from me, I recall the Harry Coyle story I read somewhere, *Sports Illustrated*, I think. Coyle, of course, was the maverick NBC director, who, if you believe all the other stories you read, basically pioneered everything good about baseball telecasts for thirty years. (As opposed to Fox, which has basically ruined everything good about baseball telecasts for the past five yea... oops—sorry—I digress.) Anyway, this story claimed that the whole televised image of Carlton Fisk waving/praying/wishing that home run ball fair, to win Game Six of the '75 Series, was actually caught on tape by mistake!

Supposedly, the camera that Coyle had parked inside the Green Monster was only put there for down-the-line shots and was basically supposed to remain stationary. But just around the time that Fisk was digging in, waiting for that fateful delivery, the cameraman sitting in the already old, decrepit Monster saw a mouse—or maybe it was a rat—creeping along the wall directly in front of him! Reacting as most of us would, this poor cameraman jumped about a foot in the air, and in so doing, hit the camera, spinning it out of position and pointing it up the first base line, juuuuust enough to catch Carlton as he danced his way toward the bag, waving and genuflecting as he went. And without that rodent, the cameraman would have simply had his camera trained directly on the plate, and would have basically missed the whole Carlton Fisk Show! I swear I read this! As ol' Casey might say, "You could look it up!" (Of course, Casey never claimed he was ever telling the truth, he only said "you could look it up." He never said what you'd find.) Okay, so how a-bout that? [Editor's note: the Fisk-mouse-camera story has been largely discredited.]

9:56 PM: Much like death and taxes, the inevitable comes to Fenway Park. Tim Wakefield, whom the Red Sox seem to have never been able to decide is a starter or a reliever, enters the game in the ninth inning and immediately surrenders two hits and a walk. The Braves then take a lead that I know they'll never relinquish. To put a cap on the evening, Henry Blanco smacks *Baseball Prospectus* upside the head once again, driving in another run, to make it 4-2. The Fenway crowd begins to dissipate and by 10:15 the game becomes another page in baseball history, to be examined, studied, and written about by SABR members for time immemorial. Atlanta has defeated the Red Sox and the Mets, losers tonight to the hated Yankees, have lost another game in the NL East standings. Me—I need to find more beer. I'm on vacation, and spending the weekend with hundreds of enthusiastic baseball nuts AND my good friend Phil, who I'm sure is ready to join me in a night of total irresponsibility and full-blown decadence, as I celebrate my birthday in the party town of Boston!

10:16 PM: Phil announces he's tired and has a headache, and he has to get home to walk the dog... He'll join me for a drink back at the hotel, but then he simply has to get on the road, but "thanks, I had a real good time" Sigh... I might as well be married again.

11:25 PM: I accompany Phil to the parking lot, where he gets in his Jeep and heads for the highway. It's a warm night, and I've got money in my pocket, but I'm pretty tipsy and I don't know this town well enough to know where the hell I'm going. I decide to have a Jack Daniels and Coke in every bar I can find within walking distance of the SABR hotel.

June 29th, 1:45 AM: Painfully tired, but comfortably numb, I head back to the Park Plaza, where, to my delight, I run into a throng of SABR-ites enjoying the last of their drinks at the hotel bar. I clamber up onto a platform used for serving brunch and sit studying the room carefully through my sleepy haze. The Deadball Committee is playing fantasy baseball in the lobby. I think Dode Paskert just got a hit off Smoky Joe. A few seats away, I can see 19th-century committee members plotting out tomorrow's meeting. Right in front me at the bar, a semi-attractive blonde smiles at me and looks away. Interesting, but I think I'm a little too lit to make any attempt at intelligent, yet vapid conversation this evening.

Instead, I take my glass and wind my way out on to the street, where, earlier in the day, I had somehow found a parking spot right in front of the hotel for the whole weekend. Climbing up on the hood of my Sebring, I lean back, drink in hand, and watch the stars rotate in the murky Boston sky. I am feeling pensive and alone, and I'm wondering if this really is the right way to spend my birthday at all...

Then I suddenly remember I have to be up early! There's an 8 AM presentation on Lefty Grove's history versus the Yankees, and one immediately after that about the WWII USO tours that I just have to see! And the Deadball committee meeting is tomorrow, and the 19th-century one, and how the heck am I going to catch game two of the Met-Yankee series on TV if it starts at 1:00, and I'm supposed to be at the luncheon, listening to Pesky and Dom DiMaggio talk about Ted Williams?

I hop off my car, empty the last of my Jack Daniels into the street and head back to my room. I have a lot to do and a big day ahead of me, and now that I think of it, I truly don't know of anywhere I'd rather be on my birthday, than exactly where I am! Sometimes, thankfully, it really is about The Game, after all.

LONG TIME PASSING

Paul Parker

From the standpoint of longevity, The Fenway Project intrigued me when I heard about it. Much of what SABR and baseball are about concern sheer time, history and longevity, and of course Fenway is major league baseball's oldest field.

As an employee of the Colorado Rockies since their inception in 1993, I've had the opportunity to work with a great many people, first in the box office for two years, then the season ticket department for two and a half years and now as manager of one of the Rockies' retail stores and as team archivist for the past four and a half years. Over the course of that time, many have expressed their pride, often self-righteously, in having been season-ticket holders since the "beginning"—way back in 1993! *Really?*

In 1995 I paid my first visit to Fenway Park, and made an effort to mingle with the locals and solicit their thoughts and feelings. Of the Boston fans I chatted with, some in their sixties and seventies, a significant number held season tickets where they did because their fathers and even grandfathers had had those same seats since the 1930s and 1940s. So for the Fenway Project I decided to spend some time seeking out the longest-holding or oldest season ticket holder.

I first had a conversation with an usher down the left-field line who, suspecting I was a newspaper reporter, would only identify himself as Dave. When asked about the longest season ticket-holder, Dave said Lib Dooley had been, but she passed away in the off-season.* Dave said Lib had been a "good friend" of Ted Williams.

Since Lib was gone, Dave was quite sure the new longevity leaders at Fenway were Anne and Jerry Quinn, and that they could be located out in Row 1 of Section 41 of the right-centerfield bleachers. Dave wasn't sure if it was 1959 or 1960 when the Quinns started their run, but he was sure it was Jerry Quinn's 81st birthday that day.

At the end of the game I found the Quinns, right where Dave had said. In speaking with Anne, like Dave the usher said, she couldn't pinpoint 1959 or 1960 as the start of their continuous run of season tickets, but she emphasized that it was definitely Jerry's 81st birthday.

Dave had also suggested that I speak with a man named Ed Goode—apparently the longest serving usher at Fenway—who knew *everything*. After tracking down Ed, I found him to be similarly reluctant to give out too much information, being suspicious of what I was doing, like Dave had been.

After explaining what SABR and The Fenway Project were, Ed began to open up a little but only gradually. As I lured him out of his shell, he told me he'd been working at Fenway Park for 22 years, and had always been a Red Sox follower. I asked Ed how long he'd been coming to Fenway, and his reply was since the late 1930s. But Ed's father had been a diehard Boston Braves fan, so most of the time they went to Braves Field. Ed's dad never got over the Braves' departure from Boston, and never switched his allegiance to the Red Sox. But Ed loved the Sox from early on, and it stayed that way for him.

Editor's note: Dave was mistaken. Lib Dooley passed away on June 19, 2000. That evening, the Red Sox suffered their worst defeat ever at the hands of the New York Yankees, 22–1.

BEFORE, DURING, & AFTER

Bill Nowlin

Before the Red Sox could host Atlanta on the evening of June 28, a great amount of preparation was required.

The park was cleaned after the game against Cleveland on Wednesday evening, June 26. Rodger Auguste and Michael Hardy oversee Fenway's post-game cleaning, and they were present with their staff until around dawn on the 27th. They had an extra day, as it turned out, because the game on the 27th was postponed due to rain, and there was a lot of water in the runways between the clubhouse and the dugout. This presented additional challenges for the grounds crew, headed by David Mellor in his first year as Director of Grounds and for the venerable Joe Mooney, Superintendent of Park and Maintenance. As Michael had once told me some hours after a game, "A lot of pressure goes along with doing the job. The average player's making over a million dollars a year. They couldn't do that if the place never got cleaned. Everybody would be upset, from the front office all the way down. It has to get cleaned."

Cleaned it was, and the daytime cleaning crew takes over from the night crew around 7 AM. Throughout the day, deliveries arrive at Fenway's one entrance. The park was built in 1912, before loading docks became standard. At Fenway, most deliveries are unloaded on the sidewalk and brought in by hand-truck. Paid attendance on the evening of June 28 was a fairly typical 33,137— it was the 25th sellout of the year at Fenway (out of 35 home games) bringing total attendance to 1,149,362 on the year. Through the delivery entrance, concession-aire Aramark had to receive enough hot dogs, soft drinks, other foodstuffs and souvenirs to supply a large temporary town (population 34,000).

Other full-time and day-of-game employees arrive at

different points during the day, in preparation for the evening competition. Red Sox President/CEO Larry Lucchino had one task away from the park that day. He attended a Community Fellowship Luncheon at the Hilton Boston Logan Airport—reception at 11:30, lunch at noon. Proceeds benefited the Red Sox Foundation, which then made donations to the Crossroads Family Shelter and to the Red Sox' RBI program (Reviving Baseball in the Inner City), as well as the Boston Area Church Little League.

The television crew for the New England Sports Network (NESN) and the Braves' television superstation WTBS begin checking their equipment many hours before the game. Newspaper reporters begin to filter in three to four hours before the game, trolling the clubhouses for quotes and watching both teams take batting practice. Security people, ushers and Boston Police Department officers on paid detail begin to assemble, more or less around the time that stand workers for Aramark arrive—the gates open 90 minutes before the scheduled 7:05 start and the park must be staffed to welcome the throngs.

Outside Fenway, the street vendors selling sausages and soft drinks and souvenirs have all positioned themselves as well, settling in for the late afternoon and evening. Many will still be there after the game, working the "out crowd." It may be counter-intuitive, but Jim Parry has been selling sunglasses outside Fenway for over 15 years and he's still there in the dark after 10 PM selling sunglasses to folks leaving Fenway.

The tempo picks up as more and more as game time approaches. The seats begin to fill, and the starting lineups are announced by 2002's public address announcer Ed Brickley—himself a member of SABR. The ballpark rituals are carefully scripted. At approximately 6:57, Ed intones, "Ladies and gentlemen, please rise for our National Anthem. Performing "The Star Spangled Banner" this evening is a singer-songwriter, and a member of SABR, the Society for American Baseball Research, Mr. Joseph Mancuso from Ann Arbor, Michigan." The Anthem completed, Ed continues the pre-game ceremonies, "Ladies and gentlemen, boys and girls, please

direct your attention to the pitching mound for tonight's ceremonial first pitch. This evening the Boston Red Sox are proud to welcome over 750 members of the Society for American Baseball Research. And now to throw out this evening's ceremonial first pitch, please welcome SABR President Claudia Perry along with former Boston Braves infielder Sibby Sisti."

Sibby's throw was more accurate than Claudia's; after all, he was a former ballplayer. Ed then continued the introductions, "Ladies and gentlemen, boys and girls, we now ask you to direct your attention to the field microphone behind home plate as 9 year old Justin Ames from Methuen, Massachusetts now says the words we are all waiting to hear." Justin then shouted "Play Ball!" into the microphone, as his photograph was taken by one of Fenway's photographers, so the Sox could send his family a memory of the occasion.

The umpires took the field. The crew for the evening saw Tim Timmons working balls and strikes behind the plate. Paul Emmel was at first base, Gary Darling at second and Rob Drake at third. The managers exchanged lineup cards, and—it being the first game of the series between the two clubs at Fenway that year—went over the ground rules with the umpires.

The sound system featured, as it always does at Fenway, John Fogerty's "Centerfield." Alternating with the pre-recorded music was Fenway organist Ray Totaro, who's been alternating as house organist since 1994 with Richard Giglio.

Temperature at game time was 76 degrees, winds from the E-SE at eight miles per hour. First pitch was only slightly delayed, coming at 7:06. Rafael Furcal took John Burkett's first offering for a called strike. The game was underway.

Later, as the game progressed, Ed Brickley had other announcements to make, and the electronic message board had other messages to convey.

Birthdays were celebrated for: Heather Doiron, Steven Marcoux, Brian Cristello, Riley Young Morse, Gary Rodrigues, Jennifer Lee Sabounjian, Amy Walsh, A. J. Trustey, Fran Torrisi, Jason Bouffard, Jim Carney, Brittany Fournier, Lesley Cunningham, Herbert Miller,

Brad Kenney, Nicole Schmalenberger and Ruth Lawrence. The scoreboard also read, "Congratulations and Good Luck, Mark and Susan" and "Congratulations Matt Tavares on getting married." Presumably his bride was congratulated as well. "Congrats Tim and Jen from your family at Bader Architecture" read a final congratulatory note.

Other than SABR, with its 750 seats, the following organizations were in attendance, and recognized: City Year Boston (230 seats), William Damon's group (100), Katherine Brown's group (100), Mass/Rosene Anatomy & Neurobiology Lab (80), Universal Reality (50), Town of Hartland, Vermont (48), and groups of Richard Edgerly, Mary Hegarty, Paul Place, James Rodrigues and the Morley family.

Suites for the night included Pfizer, Staples, Hewlett-Packard, Frito-Lay, Ameriquest Mortgage Co., McCormick & Epstein and Bingham Dana.

At the end of the third inning, the Poland Spring logo was displayed on the message board. "A proud sponsor of the Boston Red Sox" offered a Lucky Winner contest where a patron could find a free Poland Spring coupon inside specially marked copies of the official game program. Many other features kept the message board lively. Some SABR members were pleased to note that the Red Sox were the first team in major league baseball to offer stats such as on-base percentage and OPS (on-base percentage plus slugging), statistical measures that were first really promoted within SABR.

Nearer the end of the game, Ed infomed all Riverside MBTA passengers that there was a problem with the tracks at Fenway station and that there would be MBTA representatives outside Fenway Park and at the T stations to direct public transportation passengers to express buses, or how to proceed via the Kenmore station stop via the C line through Cleveland Circle.

In 2002, the team had opened its street-level "Diamond at Fenway" function room to fans from the seventh inning on, and for up to two hours after the game. Food was available, but it was more like a sports bar than anything else. It was the first time a member of the general public could order a glass of Cabernet Sauvignon at Fenway, other than in the VIP "600 Club" upstairs or in one of the suites. This evening, Budweiser was staging a promotion in the room, giving out T-shirts and coozies. There was a Bud Light table hockey table set up near a back wall painted with the image of the Green Monster. It was the opportunity for players to "Win A Budweiser T-Shirt." What was it like to play hockey at Fenway Park? "Intense!" said Colin Stack of Concord, Mass. "Ecstatic!" was the one-word reaction of winner Christina Bercury of Falmouth.

For those heading back into downtown, the subway was working fine. The Braves' Tom Glavine and Boston's Lou Merloni both stopped to sign autographs for a few fans, who waited hopefully outside the gate as players left the park an hour or so after the game. The main field lights were turned off and the night cleaning crew was already in action with their Poulan Pro 442 model blowers driving the accumulated trash down from the upper grandstand in left field.

The press box was for the most part silent, with the front row beat writers on deadline keying in their stories after gathering the final post-game remarks from players, coaches and managers. A couple of hours earlier, during the eighth inning, as portly Red Sox reliver Rich Garces fielded a come-backer, dropped it and then made a hurried throw to first instead of starting an inning-ending double-play, a writer snapped off a quip: "He wouldn't have dropped it if it was a hamburger!" Now it was a whispered, "See you!" as a writer departed. Larry Stephenson was the Pinkerton guard that night; he would be staying through the night, in charge of Fenway Park until daybreak on June 29.

I hopped on the T and ran into two Atlanta fans (from New Jersey!), pleased with their first visit to Fenway (and their team's victory as well.) The trip to Boston was a wedding present for the young groom from his new bride. While Boston fans looked back on this night and saw the start of the slide that took the Sox out of the playoffs, this young couple presumably held better memories. Their Braves made it to the playoffs for the 11th year in a row.

FENWAY PARK EXPERIENCE

Jeff Campbell

It was a beautiful night for a ball game. It was hot, but not oppressive. I enjoy a stroll from my hotel to Fenway Park with several SABRite friends. We talked of baseball, of course, but also of life and current events. Along the way we happened to walk alongside a father and son who were also taking in the game. As it turns out it was the boy's first game. What a first game! Greg Maddux and the Atlanta Braves versus the Boston Red Sox at Fenway Park! As we walked along we began to see a glimpse of Fenway Park. I pointed this out to the young boy as Fenway became more clear. His jaw dropped. He didn't say anything, but his eyes said "wow!" and he noticeably became more excited as he anticipated his first baseball game.

We mingled with the throngs of fans outside Fenway before the game. Thousands of people: men, women, girls, and boys of various races, shapes, and sizes all readying themselves for a baseball experience. A group of men discussed the pennant races as they polished off their dinner: hot dogs and beers; a patient father explains to his son why he doesn't need another $10 baseball card of Nomar Garciaparra; a group of college kids, already beer-buzzed, lets everyone know what they think of the Yankees; a mother wipes mustard off her daughter's face; an indecisive young man mulls over the plethora of baseball cap choices as the front counter attendant gives him an impatient stare. These are just a few of the human interactions I experience before the game.

We make our way to the line forming outside our gate entrance to the bleacher seats. Security has tightened since 9/11 and everyone is scrutinized. We slowly make our way to the head of the line. As I approach security he notices my backpack, which I keep all my essentials for a baseball game: a scorebook with two #2 pencils and a small sharpener, binoculars, a bag of peanuts (cheaper on the outside!), and a couple of baseballs (never know when there's an opportunity for an autograph). Also, for this game I added a notebook and pen so I could take notes on the ballpark music experience. The security looks at me sternly and shakes his head.

"Sorry, no back packs."

"What am I supposed to do?" I reply.

"There's a place next to Gold's Gym that will hold it for you. It's ten bucks, though."

"Uh, thanks, I guess." I mumble.

I make my way to the bag/backpack holding area and leave my backpack along with at least two score of other assorted bags and backpacks. They give me a number receipt to redeem my property after the game. I have to pare down my ballpark essentials. I take with me the binoculars, scorebook and one of the pencils and sharpener (don't want to be stuck with a broken pencil lead) and head back to the gate entrance. The security lines and the detour to the bag holding area cost me about 20 minutes and now it's only a few moments from first pitch. I was unable to hear any of the pregame music. I'm slightly agitated at this point, but it dissipates as I see the green of the field.

One of the first things I noticed after I'm seated is that I can't hear the PA system very well. The music was very faint. It's probably a combination of my hearing loss from listening to music loudly for many years and the quality of the PA speakers. At this point I kind of lost interest in the music experience of the ball park. There were too many other distractions, like the game for instance. I did manage to notice that a Beatles song was played (maybe it was "Help!" when the Braves made a pitching change), as well as the baseball classic "Centerfield." During the seventh inning stretch my fellow SABRites and I joined the crowd for the traditional singing of "Take Me Out to The Ball Game." One thing I've noticed, attending games with SABR members, is they tend to sing "Take Me Out to the Ball Game" louder than most fans.

Michael Freiman

In the bottom of the inning, Rickey Henderson drew a pinch walk, extending his major league record for walks in a career. Thus the fans at the game were treated to the first 2,159th career walk by any player in history. Alas, Henderson never made it as far as second base (being erased on a double play grounder by Jason Varitek) so fans hoping to see the first 2,273rd run or the first 1,401st stolen base by a major league player went home disappointed.

VIEW FROM THE OWNER'S BOX

Daniel Levine

Before the game, the Owner's Box is full of kids—what looked to be 10 to 15 year olds, mingling, jousting for position, and yelling for players and coaches to come over and sign their ticket stub, or ball, or cap. At some point, the box itself is cleared, but not the seats immediately adjacent. So, the metal bar that separates the two becomes a crowded boundary. A group of three or four tow-headed boys had claimed that space, and their demands moved from very polite cries of "Mr. Little, Mr. Little," to frustrated "Mr. Henderson! Over Here!" to, finally, dropping the honorific altogether: "Manny! Mannnnny!"

The requests continued up to gametime—despite our efforts to convince the kids that, at this point, the players were getting ready to go to work, and the likelihood of them breaking that ritual to come over was, in fact, even less than the likelihood of my having regular access to such seats.

Initially, I was at a bit of a loss as to what I would/could contribute to the Fenway Project. However, I was fortunate enough to receive a ticket in the Owner's Box through an auction held at the Annual Business Meeting. So, the answer became a bit easier, as the vantage point (literally closer to both the mound and home plate than Grady Little) is one that I, at least, had never held at a Major League game.

After the top of the first, a theme for the night emerged. At the change of inning, Manny Ramirez had to only run from his position in left field to the dugout. The Red Sox batboy, in contrast, had to refresh the home plate umpire's supply of baseballs and gather various and sundry equipment for the on deck circle, resulting, usually, in a series of 3-4 trips between the dugout and home plate.

In spite of this, Manny hit the top step of the dugout a mere step before the batboy had finished his chores. Hence, a race was born. In all, Ramirez must have been fully rested before the game: the first was the only inning where he arrived sooner than the batboy.

Each time Nomar came to bat, as he moved from the on deck circle to the plate, a cheer would go up. From our seats, it sounded like a deep roar, starting beneath and behind us, then rolling through the entire park. It was remarkable: the affection for Garciaparra by the Fenway faithful is obvious.

There is growing interest and buzz about the idea of "self-organizing communities," groups that manage to come together and create complex structures without the presence of top-down guidance. The canonical example is that of an ant hill. For someone who, as a norm, attends games at Enron-cum-Minute Maid park, where electronic guidance of crowd behavior is constant, Fenway was fascinating. Chants would develop, grow, gain momentum, and fade (Let's Go Red Sox! Boom-Boom-Boom-Ba-Boom!), on their own, in different parts of the crowd.

And I'm not one to badmouth new parks: I really don't mind the silly car races, the get up and do the twist segments, the free pizza for the loudest section, etc. But being at a game where the baseball intelligence was such that the game itself was enough to dictate the behavior of the crowd was awfully impressive. It lends credence to the myth of New Englanders having baseball knowledge bred in the bone.

We had a hard time spotting the other SABR members in the park. Luckily, in the middle innings, some enterprising souls in right field started the wave. As it moved around the stadium, the SABR sections were easy to spot: the wave would be in full force down the right field line, past us just inside first base, around home plate, and then, just beyond third base, a depression would appear—a visible trough. Again, just beyond the Red Sox bullpen, another noticeable patch of stillness in the motion. Yep, SABR seats in both cases. Curmudgeons and spoil sports!

Tim Wakefield took the mound for the Sox in the 9th. We had all agreed that it would be fantastic to see a knuckleballer from this angle, and that, given the previous day's rainout, Wakefield was likely to see some action. Wow. We had, of course, a horrendous angle to see left/right movement, but just about a perfect one for up/down and changes in speed.

Wakefield's knuckleball looks, from the side, as if it skids on the way to the plate, much like a car when it hits a patch of wet road: my guess is that our eyes anticipate that the deceleration of the ball on its path to home plate will remain constant. So, when the knuckler slows down suddenly, it leaves an impression of a pitch sliding liquidly towards the catcher.

Red Sox principal owner John Henry watched the last two and a half innings from the seat directly in front of me. When the Braves scored in the top of the 9th, as Sheffield rounded third giving Atlanta an 3-2 lead, and as the crowd expressed its displeasure, he leaned forward, putting his head in his hands. "Aha!" I thought, "An owner showing disappointment in his team's fortunes." As he leaned back, his fingers still by his head, it was "Aha, an owner... cleaning his ears?" No: he was putting in ear plugs. The final two innings passed for him with the clear plastic plugs firmly in place, removed only when he got up to walk onto the field and through the Red Sox dugout after the game.

Jean Hastings Ardell

Packed together on the rush-hour subway, we followed the crowd up, up into the street, past scalpers, fans, commuters, to Yawkey Way, with its storefront pizzas, hot dogs, and souvenirs—in danger now of being squeezed out from their businesses. Turnstiles are proposed, so the Bosox owners can reap more food and drink income. Fenway's crammed onto the site, this urban ballpark, so unlike Eddie Field's expansive parking lot and sight lines at home. We file through narrow brick corridors to the blue, red-trimmed slatted seats, so narrow your arms and legs touch your neighbor's, sweaty, companionable. The famous Green Monster, the jagged lines of the outfield—an anomaly of the field's symmetry today, but surely reasonable in 1912. The wall is not painted the expensive British racing green of Jaguars and neo-nostalgic ballparks, but a softer tone, the hue seen on hospital scrubs. Fenway is a sellout this cool evening.

WEST COAST VIEWER

R. Plapinger

Bottom of the 1st: 4:21 PM Pacific time. I awaken from my nap to hear Braves TV announcer Skip Caray saying "That is not good" (when he says this, he sounds like the apocalypse is imminent) and the camera showing a shot of Greg Maddux in the dugout, his ankle taped and swollen to what looks like 2-3 times its size. I wonder, can you tell this if you're at the stadium, or is this a "tv only" insight?

Maddux takes the mound anyway. Nomar rips a ground ball past Vinny Castilla at 3b. It was a hard hit ball, but appeared to me to be fieldable—Castilla doesn't make the play and what could have been a dp (Baerga was on first) leaves the Sox with two runners on.

Baerga rectifies the situation by getting picked off.

Manny Ramirez is up and the Braves announcers comment on his uniform, Caray noting that his "pants are under his shoes" (they are long and almost baggy) while his partner Joe Simpson, playing to the home folks (the Braves announcers are good at this) notes that Manny probably "bought last year's shoes at Bennie's in Atlanta." Maddux gets out of the inning.

Following top of the 2nd: 4:33 PM. As the inning closes, Caray notes "these have been the two easiest innings of the year for Burkett."

In the bottom of the inning the Sox have a runner on second with two out and #9 hitter Trot Nixon due up. Caray actually starts discussing the possibility of an intentional walk until he realizes he's broadcasting an interleague game in an American League park and duh—the pitcher doesn't bat. Simpson tries to bail out his cohort by noting that a slumping Jose Offerman follows Nixon and "it may be worth it to get him." The Braves do not follow their announcers' dubious strategy and somehow Maddux retires Nixon.

Top 3rd. Following his "two easiest innings of the year" Burkett can't throw a strike. At the same time Caray notes this, a microphone picks up one of the "idiosyncratic" Boston fans (that's what Simpson called them when giving the perfunctory "how great it is to be in Fenway" speech later on) yelling "Throw a strike, Burkett," a nice confluence of announcer and fan.

Caray and Simpson note that the Braves are 34 and 12 when they score first, 18 and 5 in June (if they win tonight they'll set a team record for victories in the month)—I think to myself, "no wonder we're eight games back" (I'm a Mets fan) and figure there's hope, because they certainly can't keep this up.

Bottom 3rd: As the camera pans the stands at the beginning of the inning, I'm reminded of my friend David Nevard's (editor and publisher of the great "fanzine" *A Red Sox Journal*) comment that Fenway on Friday night is the world's biggest singles bar. As I scan the faces looking for SABRites that I recognize, I wonder about the mingling of intense baseball reseaches with David's "singles" and how that could lead to some interesting interactions. Unfortunately the Braves cameramen seem far more concerned with the game than the action of the fans, so I found no evidence of SABR or partying singles, not to mention intermingling SABR singles... all night long.

The Red Sox score a run when third baseman Castilla bounces a throw a few feet in front of Franco at first. The ball gets by Franco and it's scored a hit for Garciaparra—a decision with which Caray and Simpson emphatically disagree. They're speculating as to whether the error will be charged to Castilla or Franco (they seem to vote for Franco) when the scoring is announced. As the inning ends Simpson says disdainfully "It's a hit cause they're in Boston."

Game tied 1-1: 5:04 PM.

Throughout the fourth inning, Caray and Simpson seem almost distracted by the game, preferring to spend their time criticizing the official scorer and his ruling the "error" a hit. In fact, Caray leaves the booth saying "I'm going to find that guy," presumably to confront him and find out what he was thinking. He returns apparently without having located the scorer—or at least he's not telling us what happened.

As the top of the fifth opens, Garciaparra's hit is taken away and an error charged to Castilla. This hardly mollifies Caray and Simpson—they continue to complain saying it was really Franco's error, not Castilla. When the Red Sox mascot ("The Green Monster" c'mon) appears on the field, Caray speculates that he's taking a break from his scoring duties.

Meanwhile, Boston kicks, drops and throws the ball away allowing the Braves to score the go-ahead run. But, with the bases loaded Burkett gets Sheffield on a harmless pop up to left (though Manny does try to throw the ball into the dugout) and then does the same to Jones, and wriggles out of the inning.

Bottom 5th: 5:36 PM. Maddux is cruising. As the inning closes, the broadcasters note that second baseman Keith Lockhart has eight assists so far, approaching a record, Maddux has allowed no fly ball outs, has struck out four and retired seven in a row.

Top 6th. With one out, the camera shows Maddux leaving the Braves dugout. Simpson comments that his ankle "has finally caught up with him."

The Red Sox display more fine defense as Garciaparra's throw short-hops Daubach for an error. The camera catches Nomar seeming to stare or point at the official scorer's box as if he's complaining that the error was charged to him when it should have been Daubach's. The misplay helps the Braves load the bases but Burkett escapes yet again. As he's running off the field Garciaparra again seems to be looking up at the official scorer.

Wait a minute! This is Nomar Garciaparra—the ultimate "team guy." Surely he wouldn't care if he had one or two more errors than he deserved—it's the team, not stats, that count—isn't it ? Can't figure out if perhaps

Nomar isn't the guy portrayed in the media, or if he's just having a bad and frustrating day, or if the announcers are misinterpreting a totally benign gesture by Nomar due to their antipathy to the official scorer. Again, I wonder if any of this is apparent to the fans in the stands watching the game.

Bottom 6th: Kevin Gryboski pitching for the Braves. As his stats flash on the screen, the Braves' bullpen's ridiculous 2.37 ERA comes up—a figure inflated by a horrible six or eight-run John Smoltz inning early in the year. They can't really be this good. Can they? This bullpen success can't last. Can it?

Top 7th. Burkett wriggles out of yet another jam. The Braves have now left 9 men on base so far. Of course, they still lead 2-1. It's 6:13 PM.

In the bottom of the seventh another Braves reclamation project, Chris Hammond, is in to pitch. He gives up a single to Daubach—the Red Sox' first hit since the 2nd inning. "Gamer" Nixon, strikes out, fanning on a high hard ball after twice fouling off bunts. The fans boo, but Joe Simpson's favorite player, Jose Offerman, walks and scores on Baerga's double, tying the game. The Braves then walk Garciaparra intentionally to pitch to Ramirez (proof positive that Manny isn't himself). Manny almost trashes the strategy, sending a long fly ball to left off reliever Darren Holmes (Darren Holmes? Chris Hammond? It's like watching the 1995 Rockies or something—what happens to mediocre pitchers when they get to Atlanta?—it's sure not the water) which Chipper catches easily.
Score tied 2-2: 6:31 PM.

Top 8th: Newly acquired Alan Embree pitching for the Sox. He immediately shows why he's both tantalized and frustrated all of his earlier teams by easily retiring Castilla on a ground ball, then proceeding to walk the next two hitters. Rich Garces replaces Embree. He induces Matt Franco—batting for Wes Helms who batted for Lockhart, to hit a double play grounder right back to the box, except Garces drops the ball, gets only one out and then walks Furcal, loading the bases. And then retires Julio Franco. The Braves have left the bases loaded for the third time in four innings.

Bottom 8th: 6:51 PM. The Red Sox go down quickly. Caray and Simpson barely have time to tell any Rickey Henderson stories (he pinch hit and walked), before Remlinger retires the side.

Top 9th.   And here we go....
I said it earlier, I'll say it again: I'm a proud Mets fan. Among other things, that means I've spent the last few years being continually frustrated by the Braves' success against the Amazin' Ones. Said frustration made all the worse by the way the Braves end up winning: Kenny Rogers walks Andruw Jones with the bases loaded—on four pitches!; the "unhittable" (against the rest of the world at least) Armando Benitez gacks up a ninth inning lead as the Mets are attempting an unbelievable run at a miracle... and there are doubtless others which I've forced to the back of my mind so as not to have to relive them over and over and over. It's as if, my sister and I have often speculated, Cox and Scheurholtz and Turner—the whole gang of them—Smoltz, Maddux and Terry Pendleton too!—have made some sort of deal with the devil—that allows them to pull yet another Braves victory out of the grasping hands of the futile Mets.
Apparently, it's not just the Mets. Gary Sheffield blasts a double off the wall versus Tim Wakefield. But the knuckleballer then gets the Braves next two best hitters, Andruw and Chipper Jones to hit easy fly balls. Two outs... No problem. For the Braves... Just as Simpson is saying "no one's hit the ball hard..." Castilla dinks a single to center scoring Sheffield with the go-ahead run. Darren Bragg (Darren Bragg? c'mon...) walks and Henry Blanco—batting .198 or something like that, then pops up to right—only the ball eludes the plodding second and first basemen and the hustling, diving Trot Nixon and falls—Bobby Cox couldn't have run out there and placed the ball in a better place—for a single. Another

run scores. Stupid, cheating Braves do it again. 4-2 Atlanta.

Bottom 9th: Smoltz pitching for Atlanta, a virtual lock and Simpson and Caray really get going now....

While giving the scores of the night's other games, one of them notes that the Yankees have slaughtered the Mets, 11-5. Simpson says that they (the Mets) spent "all that money" in the off-season and it's gotten them nowhere and now he's "hearing" (his far flung sources...) that they "might dismantle" the team. Caray recalling an incident earlier in the week when Mets GM Steve Phillips objected to the size of Gary Sheffield's elbow pad... (Hey! It was too big!), twice!, says the Mets shouldn't be worrying about things like elbow pads and the Braves.

Simpson, pointing out that tonight's defeat leaves the Mets barely above last place Philadelphia, chirps that "they should be worrying about the Phillies... I was always told you can't worry about first place until you're in second place."

Oh yeah, Smoltz retires Nixon, Offerman and Damon in a blink. Caray and Simpson seem disappointed that the game is over and they can't trash the Mets any more.

7:58 PM. Final score:
Stupid Cheating Braves! 4, Red Sox 2.

Mike Spatz

Fenway Park. The home of the Boston Red Sox since 1912. Fenway, created the same week the Titanic sunk was the place I spent my night on Friday, June 28, 2002. I had heard about this park from classmates and other SABR members, and I had seen it on TV before. But never had I been in this historic structure. When I was seated and ready to watch the game, I observed my surroundings, and they were nothing like I had heard. Living only about forty minutes from Baltimore my whole life, Oriole Park at Camden Yards would be what you could call a "base-line" for my grading. That is a high bar, and I wondered if Fenway could live up to it. It wouldn't from what I heard. Baseball fans I know told me Fenway was a dump. Remembering this thought I took a look around. Okay, there were a few popcorn boxes on the floor, and there were some pieces of trash near the stairs, but nothing strange. All parks are going to have trash on the cement floors once in a while. Camden wasn't that much better in the "dirty category." Then, I remembered someone telling me that it would be very dark in the lair of the Green Monster. As I looked around, the lighting was fine. Maybe I had to wait till the late innings of the game, so I did. But still, the field looked fine, light-wise. Then, I tried remembering that last negative attribute someone told me about Fenway Park. Oh yes, the seating is tight. I looked down, and moved my legs around. Never hit the chair in front of me. But I am only 13, so I have no say in this. So in a sentence, I believe Fenway is the Jamestown of baseball.

Now, the actual ball game. Atlanta Braves v. Boston Red Sox. A typical game. No home runs, but some could have gone over the left field wall was it not for the Green Monster, but it has been that way for 90 years, so, nothing new. Nothing on the field that I knew of affected both team's playing. The crowd was loud during bases loaded situations, and those two times the Red Sox scored, but that's just the way Boston fans are, I guess. So in a nutshell, the ball game was good, the fans were loud, and Fenway Park must stay. For a few more seasons, at least.

A MARRIAGE PROPOSAL

Bill Nowlin

On the night of June 28, 2002, during the course of the game, Danny Szecskas proposed marriage to Kristen Hanley.

The proposal was flashed on the electronic message board between innings. The couple were seated on the roof on the right field side, in Box 19, Row D, their party in seats 1 through 4. Szecskas runs the Braintree Athletic Club at the Sheraton Braintree. He met Hanley at another club, the Varsity Club in Quincy—this one being "a local drinking establishment." Hanley is a hairstylist. I asked him to tell me his story a month or so after the game.

Bill Nowlin (BN): How did the whole "proposing at Fenway thing" come about?

Danny Szeckas (DS): We paid to be on the screen. I paid $100 for it to be [up there]. My brother's wife made all the arrangements with the Red Sox on the Internet. She was told they were going to take pictures and mail them to her. My brother and his wife took some pictures. She has a picture of it right on the screen. It was after the 4th inning.

BN: What did the announcement say?

DS: It said, "Kristen Hanley, in roof box... whatever the numbers were, Danny wants to know..." The fans were going crazy. And then it said, "...will you marry him?" And that's when I did my knee thing. It was pretty cool.

BN: Have you known each other long?

DS: We've pretty much been married for five years. We've lived together for that long. We have a child together. Our son's four. Jake. Financially, I wasn't ready to get the ring and stuff. It's time. Now it will be official. We're looking for a year from September, down the Vineyard. Finally. We're getting around to it. The parenting thing's tough enough!

BN: Are you guys big Red Sox fans?

DS: We go to a lot of games. I played baseball for years in Babe Ruth and all that. Yaz was my favorite player. I just thought it would be a little different. She likes it there in the summer; Fenway is gorgeous—it's just a beautiful park. I love it. I'm one... I don't want to change Fenway. I like it the way it is. I like that you can sit almost anywhere and pretty much see. I haven't been to many other parks, but you go to other parks and you can't see. You might as well get a TV set.

BN: Did Kristen expect a proposal in the Park?

DS: She had no clue. Well, she knew it was coming, kind of. For some reason, I think she thought it was going to be at the hotel later. She definitely didn't think it was coming at the game. She was shocked it was at the game. Up on the screen, especially. I was trying to plan how I would do it, in correlation with the screen. I thought they would show us real quick on the screen, but I don't think they did. I guess there was someone taking pictures, but I was so into my engagement that I didn't notice. That's a tough area to get a camera up there. It was a blast, though! We had a nice time.

BN: So, did she accept?

DS: She said yes. That would have been something... but she did. I've heard that happens once in a while, that they say "No." This was a no-brainer, though—we've been together forever. We're so happy.

BN: Now, how about the ballgame that night? My wife and I held a wedding reception at a Fenway function room for the people who couldn't make our wedding in Texas. It was freezing cold and the Red Sox lost 10-0. You couldn't have been too happy to see the Red Sox lose the night you proposed...

DS: That was the boringest game I've been to in ages. Wasn't it awful? I was so nervous, but it was just not good. Just awful. I didn't like the game. But I didn't care. Of course, I want to win, but that wasn't my focus that night.

EXPECTATIONS

Francis Kinlaw

My first visit to Fenway Park in Boston came a half century after I began listening to Red Sox games on the radio and a mere 47 years after my first view of the classic ballpark on television. Growing up in North Carolina, I had developed a familiarity with the unchanging dimensions of the playing field and the height of the outfield walls by listening to Game-of-the-Day broadcasts on the Mutual Radio Network while flipping through a well-worn copy of a Red Sox yearbook that had (for some inexplicable reason) appeared on the shelves of the only newsstand in my small town. Then, a couple of years later, I was able to watch the few national Game-of-the-Week telecasts that magically originated from faraway New England! As Dizzy Dean entertained his audience with jokes and antics, I became fascinated by the idiosyncrasies of the place and by players from Harry Agganis to Norm Zauchin who wore the colorful Bosox uniform in the 1950s.

And now, as I prepared to meet the Green Monster in person, I was naturally curious as to whether my long-held images of the historic site would prove to be accurate. For months I had wondered: How would I feel sitting in the packed bleachers on a warm Friday night in late June when the talented Atlanta Braves came calling?

Before departing from the Tar Heel state for Beantown, I had jotted down a number of preconceptions about Fenway Park, its atmosphere, and its environs.

THE BALLPARK WITHIN THE NEIGHBORHOOD: I had anticipated that the structure would be located in an old part of the city, near many residential properties similar to those that surround Chicago's Wrigley Field. To my surprise, I observed very few residences in the immediate area. With cars zipping along the Massachusetts

Turnpike just beyond the left field wall, the gem in Boston actually seemed a bit reminiscent of Detroit's Tiger Stadium or old Comiskey Park in Chicago—- both of which existed in close proximity to expressways in their final years. But, while those two masterpieces were easily spotted as one approached them on foot or by car, the relatively low height of Fenway and its light towers allow small commercial buildings in the neighborhood to shield the ballpark from view until the fan is within "shouting distance" of it.

NEIGHBORHOOD STREETS: I knew before my train pulled into Boston that the city is filled with narrow streets. I also knew that the game between the Braves and Red Sox would attract a near-capacity crowd. I therefore expected to find small streets packed with people before and after the game. Did I ever!

SENSE OF HISTORY: As I thought they would, historic baseball moments popped into my mind throughout the evening, and the presence of former players—- from the stars of my boyhood like Ted Williams and Jackie Jensen to more ordinary characters like Milt Bolling and Sammy White—-was almost perceptible.

SENSE OF INTIMACY: Fenway Park always appeared on television to be small and compact in comparison to other stadiums. I was looking forward to experiencing its unique environment and to sitting closer to players than I had in any other major league park. I was not disappointed in the least as my seat in the fourth row of the bleachers provided a nice view of centerfielders Johnny Damon of the Red Sox and Andruw Jones of the Braves while putting me nearly in position to shake hands with Boston pitching coach Tony Cloninger or anyone warming up in the Red Sox bullpen.

DOMINANCE OF THE LEFT-FIELD WALL: Who could possibly ignore the Green Monster, looming over the playing field like the landmark it is? I was confident before entering the park that the tall barrier would be in my conscious or subconscious thoughts throughout the

game but—-lo and behold—-it actually slipped from my mind as the game proceeded. Perhaps my perch in centerfield reduced my awareness of the wall as a factor that could affect the action on the field and ultimately the game's outcome, or maybe my frequent conversations with friends distracted me from the Monster's unusual influence upon everything from managerial decisions to the thought processes of individual players. But, for whatever reason, the famous target for hitters did not lurk in my mind constantly.

SIGNAGE: From watching games on television, I had developed an assumption that fewer visual advertisements would be evident in Fenway Park than in most other ballparks. Such signs were present, of course, but I was pleased to observe that their designs were more subtle than those of ads in other parks (with the notable exception of Wrigley Field).

PUBLIC ADDRESS SYSTEM: To my pleasant surprise, my 57-year-old ears were granted a respite from the press-box screaming which has unfortunately become a standard ingredient of modern servings of baseball. The announcer offered information in an understandable and dignified tone, and the absence of blaring music between innings and during pitching changes made my evening as a spectator much more enjoyable. Now, if only the other major and minor league teams would stop assaulting my hearing....

SEATS AND LEGROOM: I thought that my personal space in an old park like Fenway would be limited, and it certainly was. My assigned seat was located far away from an aisle, so it immediately became evident that trips to a crowded restroom or to a busy concession stand would be an ordeal. Let's just say that I got to know the fans sitting in nearby seats well, and I had plenty of time to study the cracks in the decaying concrete beneath my feet.

FANS: Prior to my trip to Boston, I had been informed by many supposedly reliable sources that Red

Sox fans were knowledgeable, cynical, and vocal. The ones around me certainly understood the game, and they did exhibit their full share of cynicism. They did not seem to be any louder than their counterparts in other stadiums, but I was later told that I was among an unusually sedate group of people. Friends seated several rows above me reported that the rowdy behavior for which Fenway's bleachers are unfortunately known was indeed rampant elsewhere in our general vicinity.

In a quiet hotel room on the Saturday morning following the game, I weighed reality against expectations and determined that the two were surprisingly similar. That realization was reassuring because it confirmed that this devoted baseball fan had indeed been fostering reasonable mental concepts of Fenway Park since childhood. But an even greater sense of satisfaction was derived from the first-hand discovery that such a splendid urban setting does exist for the playing and watching of baseball. Thankfully, Fenway Park was not merely a figment of a young boy's imagination that was perpetuated over the years as that young boy grew into manhood.

A NIGHT IN THE SBN BOOTH

Anthony Salazar

The adventure really started en route to Fenway Park on Friday. Boylston Street was packed with activities, as tourists and natives wandered the streets. I had decided to make the one-and-a-half mile trek to the stadium from my hotel, mainly because I thought it would be interesting, and I figured that I would probably get lost taking the T, Boston's subway.

It was a hot and muggy day in Beantown, just the kind of day a guy from Seattle is NOT used to. So, by the time I got to Fenway, which was around 4PM, the rain that had just started was very welcomed. Unfortunately, the water drops from the sky did not last. I obtained my press pass, and made my way to the 5th floor, where I was to hang out in booth belonging to the Spanish Béisbol Network, the Red Sox's Spanish-language broadcasting partner. There, I met the two announcers, Juan Baez and his partner JP Villamon, the engineer, Uri Berenguer, and producer/company president, Bill Kulik.

After spending some time with these guys over a meal at the press commissary, we made our way down to the field, where the Atlanta Braves were preparing for their first visit to Fenway this season. The Braves in their history, of course, were no strangers to Boston. They began their story in Boston, before moving to Milwaukee in the mid-1950s, staying there only a short period before moving again, this time to Atlanta.

Some parts of the park were showing their age (the place was built in 1912), while other parts looked pretty good. The field was immaculate. I had to reach down and pull a few blades of grass, just to see what it was like.

We watched a few of the players take batting practice, before we headed down into the Braves clubhouse. What first struck me about the clubhouse was the fact that the room was awfully small, at least compared to some of the newer ballparks. Some of the Braves were sitting around a TV watching "Black Knight" with Martin Lawrence. They laughed and were having as good time. Among those I spotted on the couches were Vinny Castilla and Andruw Jones. Some of the other guys were in the back playing cards. I think they were playing gin.

We grabbed Rafael Furcal for interview. He was a nice guy. Shorter and thinner than I thought, and very pleasant. And he definitely looked at least 23. There had, of course, been the controversy affecting many of the Latino players and whether their ages were accurate. In Furcal's case, the issue was whether he was 21 or 23. I tended to believe the latter, as most folks do.

From the Braves clubhouse, we headed back up to the field where we spent just a few minutes checking out batting practice once again. Then, we went into the Red Sox clubhouse. As I watched a bunch of kids reach down toward the dugout trying to get a player's autograph, I wondered if they wondered who I was, and thought how lucky I was to be going to see some of their heroes. The Red Sox clubhouse was just a small and dank as their counterpart's. The atmosphere was a definite contrast. The music blared loudly, as the players were spread about in various stages of pre-game activities. I looked around at the lockers and noticed the uniforms hanging neatly from their hooks, awaiting their owners.

I first looked for Nomar Garciaparra, a favorite of mine, mainly because he grew up near where I did in East L.A., and because we have the same birthday, though I have about eight years on him and absolutely no talent for shortstop.

We ran into Carlos Baerga, who was sitting at his locker just about to get suited up. He's one of those guys who has been around for a while, and has had some setbacks, but has managed to make his way back to the bigs. He was very nice to me as I chatted him up about a celebrity softball game he used to sponsor for charity in Puerto Rico. He said he gave that up when he became an owner of a team down there. We next visited Rolando Arrojo, who sat rather calmly at his locker. Though he spoke somewhat softly, he seemed pretty focused. Again, he was another nice guy. I gave the clubhouse one last look for Nomar and for Pedro Martinez, but they must have been somewhere else. Oh well, maybe next time.

Back in the booth, the guys settled in for the main event. The announcers, Dominicans Baez and Villamon, were funny and very animated. From what I was told, the station's footprint, their range, extends from Providence, RI to southern New Hampshire. Their Latino audience is comprised mainly of Dominicans, though Puerto Ricans come in a close second.

I noticed that the announcers had a tendency to get sidetracked, only to hear the producer snap his fingers to get their attention and point to the field, saying, 'call the game, fellas, call the game.' Actually this happened a couple of times. They simply got carried away with a discussion.

It's easy to do when you love baseball.

The styles of the two announcers were somewhat different. One kept and used handwritten notes, while the other used none at all. Both, though, kept score throughout the game and worked in the ads for their sponsors, as any good announcer would do.

Throughout the game, Uri got into the act, as he filled in some youthful insights to his older counterparts. Uri, I would learn later, is the nephew of former major leaguer Juan Berenguer. The senior Berenguer, 15-year veteran, had been a part of the 1987 World Champion Minnesota Twins. Uri's story goes a little deeper, you see.

Some years ago in his native Panama, Uri had been stricken with a form of cancer. His parents then brought the family to Boston, where he sought treatment through the Jimmy Fund at the Dana Farber Cancer Center. As Uri was on the mend, he met and befriended Red Sox radio announcer Joe Castiglione. One thing led to another, and Uri found himself working various jobs for the Red Sox while still attending high school. He eventually landed a part-time position with the Spanish language broadcast team working the engineering board, where he also gets to throw on the mike and help the crew call the game. He's now a student at

Northeastern University and is cancer-free, living a good life and following his passion in the Red Sox booth.

The game was pretty good, though errors cost the Red Sox dearly as the Braves pulled out a win, much to the dismay of the Red Sox faithful, knowing that their beloved team had been knocked from first place.

I've been fortunate to meet some of baseball's other great Spanish-language announcers, such as Jaime Jarrin (Los Angeles Dodgers), Felo Ramirez (Florida Marlins) and Amaury Pi-Gonzalez (San Francisco Giants). I was pleased to make the acquaintances of the Spanish-language broadcast team from the Red Sox. Their commentaries and insights were colorful, educational, and at times funny. I appreciated their enthusiasm for the game, and felt their pain for every Red Sox error committed. I held my breath as I gave the field of Fenway Park one last look. The green grass that contrasted the Green Monster, the seats below the press box that held fans watched games in 1986, in 1975 and in 1967. There were many memories and many treasures held in those seats. I had my own memory and my own treasure to take back with me to Seattle. Watching another Red Sox game on television won't be the same. I can say I've been there, and it was great!

HAIBUN FOR FENWAY

R. Chamberlain

For K.L.

I had written her a partial letter from my hotel room prior to leaving for the baseball game against Atlanta. Manhattan had stolen her away from me for the summer and I made a certain connection with this city that had personal grudges against New York. That is, if one can compare the statuesque curves of a beautiful woman with the pudgy outline of the Sultan of Swat. It was my first time downtown as a group of us walked to Fenway from the Park Plaza. I felt isolated among crowds and cars advancing to the game and thoughts of her transposed against the city scenery.

Green eyes reflecting
On windows, streets—cornerstones;
Fair-skin red hair smiles.

My goal was to write about Fenway and it was a natural transition for me to make such instant personal connections with baseball's classic bluegrass arena. The stadium was my companion that night as I sat pressed shoulder to shoulder in her rickety wooden grandstand arms. Through summer evening humidity my mind drifted in and out of the game as I finished my Fenway Franks and beer. Neck stretching around the post obstructions—a stark reminder of her elegant, if not estranged, stadium sisters in New York and Chicago. The Morse code on the Green Monster whispering, "Yawkey, Yawkey." A long foul ball to right reminding me of Johnny's home run squeaker around Pesky's Pole.

Fenway marks the past.
Leather mitts and wooden bats
Ever locked in time.

The game ended and I walked home under the city lights and the hustle and bustle of late-evening restaurant patio dinners and after game drinks. The results would be filed under some sabermetric statistical log for experts to compare and contrast against the grand scheme of baseball. I saved my ticket stub and took the game back with me to the hotel. I finished my letter and said goodnight to my New York love, Boston and Fenway.

Joe Favano

Have been to over 20 major league parks and third time at Fenway. First time in Fenway bleachers in over 24 years.

Short comments:

Most fans stayed for entire game (other stadiums, many would have left after Braves scored 2 runs in 9th).

7th inning stretch—not as organized as at other stadiums (nobody sang).

Hokey "Play Ball" at beginning (never any place else).

Don't remember street vendor pedestrian mall the last time here. Enjoyed cheaper alternatives to inside food/concession—will miss them when they put in the turnstiles.

Lack of rowdyness in bleachers except the professional "wave" organizers.

ON NOT SEEING THE GAME AT FENWAY PARK

Angela Jane Weisl

Fenway seems more a part of the city than many of the parks I have visited. For all its beauty and feeling of sacredness, Yankee Stadium, my home park, requires a long subway trip; for all its being in the center of the South Bronx, it creates its own separate space, apart from the city that surrounds it. Like Pac Bell Park in San Francisco, its proximity to water makes it seem on the edge of things, looking outward towards Baseball's national and international legacy rather than its own locality. Even less a part of its own city is the Stade Olympique in Montreal, rising as it does out of a strange concrete wasteland like the Mothership, ready to return to a distant planet. Fenway sits on its own block, the streets leading to it as much a part of the regular traffic as the game traffic. Indeed, the street we walked down to get to the Bleacher entrance reminded me of the walk between Victoria Coach Station and Victoria Train Station in London, a similar mix of noise, activity, and grime; old touches of past ideas about public building rubbing shoulders with vendors hawking hot dogs, programs, souvenirs.

In this post-September 11th world, one of the key features of ballparks is now their security. The Bleacher Guard patted down the men in our group, while contenting themselves with checking the women's handbags. Before leaving for SABR, I bought a pocketbook small enough to pass through inspection but large enough to accommodate sunscreen and a book, my new specialty baseball purse. Most suicide bombers are men, and most wear suicide belts. In New York, the guards do not touch anyone, but men have to show what's under their hats. The guard told me to finish my water and throw the bottle away in an ever-growing pile. No bomb that I know of has ever been concealed in a water bottle, least of all one that someone was drinking out of. The whole thing is as much about comfort as it is about real security, but it works. Outside, the world may close in, but inside, the park is still safe, pastoral, a timeless refuge.

I had hoped to examine the various wares for sale at Fenway. In the middle of revisions on a book that deals at length with medieval relics and contemporary memorabilia, I planned to add to my officemate's little-plastic-catcher-keychain collection while satisfying my own interests. I am an eager observer of fan's desires for memorabilia. How did Fenway's collection of souvenirs differ from other parks', from the slick Giant Shop at Pac Bell, to the tiny concession stand at Cooper Stadium, home of the Columbus Clippers, to the Stan's Sports World outside Yankee Stadium? What could I find out about Red Sox fans from observing what they bought? Objects, lately, seem to take on new meanings and references; my neighborhood in Brooklyn was overrun this Summer with Cyclones shirts and caps, just as in past years Subway Series T-shirts seemed to capture a defining New York spirit of good natured—and sometimes not so good natured—conflict. Aware of other kinds of conflict, I surveyed the caps my friends and I had chosen to wear—my husband sported a Morisi's Pasta Hat, while I chose my academic affiliation over my fan affiliation, wearing a cap proclaiming "Chaucer." John and Ryan, braver souls, wore their Mets caps and shouted "Go Sox" in their best and loudest fake-Boston accents. I bought a program and gave my husband the scorecard.

Climbing to the forty-ninth row of the bleachers and finding my center seat, I had little hope of getting out for my memorabilia survey. I also soon discovered that for all the stories of the intimate bandbox feel of Fenway, the forty-ninth row of the bleachers precluded any feeling of closeness to the action. The Diamondvision dissolved into a fly-eye of pixels, the famed Green Monster seemed small, and the old scoreboard was barely visible, tucked into an angle below us. The SABR member singing the National Anthem seemed impossibly far away, and I could barely see Claudia Perry throwing out the first pitch, although I cheered wildly, loving the unifying qualities of baseball that brought us all together that night.

One feature of my whole SABR experience was recognizing how many different ways there are to see baseball; listening to statistics papers beyond my comprehension, I found little in common with my own mytho-historical, narrative-driven sense of the game. Watching fellow SABRites around me scoring the game via countless different systems, I envied their ability to turn what they saw into representations that would preserve it in their memories. Even more so, I envied those who could translate what they were seeing from what felt to me impossibly far away; used to the third-base side of Yankee Stadium's Upper Deck, I could not turn the images before me into meaningful information.

Not that I got much time to try. Sitting next to me was a cheerful man from Colorado who engaged me in conversation for most of the game. By the seventh-inning stretch, we had dissected the SABR Convention, the paper I gave at the Convention, female baseball fans, his wife, autograph seekers, memorabilia, the Middle Ages, the United States public education system, the youth of today, popular music, grammar, literature, New York City, airplane travel, Coors Field, baseball stadium tours, and climbing Everest, among other subjects. I realized I hadn't the faintest idea who was winning the game or what had happened. I had looked forward to seeing Nomar Garciaparra's at-bat tap dance, but I wasn't even sure he was playing. I didn't know why Maddux was no longer pitching for Atlanta. The game had passed before my eyes, and I had missed it. I tried-against the tide of conversation about reading, and the Rockies, and suitcases, and the relative merits of different ballpark snacks, to watch the last two and a half innings, in which the Braves' bullpen was airtight and their offence managed to bury the Red Sox. The Boston fans screamed and pounded on the metal signs behind us, and John and Ryan shouted "Go Sox" in increasingly hoarse voices. The players moved around before me like toys on an old mechanical game, and I was lost in the sounds that surrounded me.

We left, climbing down the stairs and through the concession area under the bleachers, too tired to bother to look at what was for sale at the stands the vendors were wearily closing. Back on the street, the city pressed in. Crowds flowed out of exits, heading in different directions as we made our way around barriers, fences, and parked cars. Within blocks we were passing lively cafes and bars, people spilling onto the street with their own Saturday night adventures. Back in the hotel room, I looked at my husband's scorecard, a pattern of letters, numbers, and images forming an untranslatable picture of the game I hadn't seen.

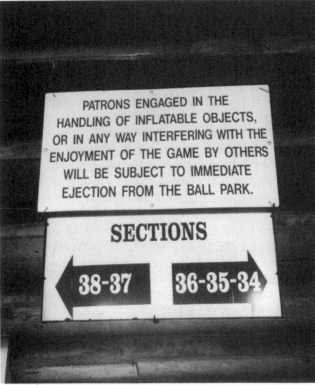

On Being Interviewed by NESN

John Zajc

Watching the game from the dugout seats allows you to see the players up close, especially the Red Sox players as they head to the on deck circle, or walk back from home plate after a strike out. These seats also make you a little easier to find when the broadcast team wants to find someone to interview.

Around the seventh inning, NESN on-field reporter Tom Caron and a man I assume was an engineer of some type dropped by the dugout seats looking for SABR President Claudia Perry who had thrown out the first pitch. They were unable to find her so they figured interviewing the Acting Executive Director of SABR would be a good alternative. They displaced Daniel Levine and James Bouffard, who were sitting with me, so that Tom could sit next to me to do the interview. The hope was that they would be gone in 5 to 10 minutes.

First, Tom explained that the interview would take place only after an out that did not need a replay, like a strikeout or a routine ground ball. He started reviewing the general outline of the interview and started searching for segues to and from the broadcast booth. While I was telling him about the more than 700 SABR members in Boston for our annual convention, and the 750 tickets sold to SABR members, and that we were hoping that as many as possible would participate in The Fenway Project, the NESN cameras were trying to find us. It was a bit comical with Tom listening in on his earpiece, occasionally waving his microphone and trying to direct the third base/left field roof cameraman to us. I told him that one of the other highlights would be the Luncheon the next day with Johnny Pesky and Dom DiMaggio. He asked more about SABR and what we do and I started to tell him about The Baseball Index. For awhile we were going to go with that as our main topic. We thought we'd be on imminently but then the game started to get interesting.

We sat through the top of the seventh; then the bottom of the seventh. Watching a game knowing you are going to be interviewed during a dull moment makes the game a little different. Over a half hour later, I finally made my NESN broadcast debut. I tried to concentrate on keeping my answer (which we rehearsed a couple of times) on point and to allow Tom to have his segues and think I did a good job, but I still have not actually seen a copy of the tape. I did get my jollies out of finishing my spiel about The Fenway Project with "and some are watching the game on New England Sports Network!"

It was really fun to do this, and I created my own special trivia (no, let's face it, it's minutiae) question, "What do John Zajc and Stephen King have in common?" Answer: Both were interviewed on NESN during the Red Sox-Braves game on June 28, 2002.

VIEW FROM THE PRESS BOX

Cecilia Tan

Since Major League Baseball's earliest beginnings there have been players and managers, umpires and owners. And there have been beat writers. There have been the men (and these days, women) who reported the scores, the locker room quotes, the clubhouse personalities, who created the myths or shattered the illusions. In the olden days before ESPN and MLB.com, when every major city had a dozen or more newspapers including morning and afternoon editions, teams were followed by packs of writers toting steno pads and manual typewriters. Nowadays though, even as television channels have proliferated into the thousands, many major metropolitan areas have been reduced to one daily paper.

But here in New England, we have always resisted certain kinds of change in the name of upholding our traditions. And baseball is, if nothing else, a game built on tradition. In other places, the beat writers have dwindled to fewer than a half dozen, but not here. The Boston Red Sox carry what might be the largest press contingent of any major league team. (The one team that might rival this claim is none other than the New York Yankees. Each team has so many reporters filling their press boxes that the two groups of writers face each other annually in exhibition baseball games. But rumor has it since Bob Klapisch, a former independent league pitcher, became a columnist for the *Bergen Record*, the New York press has been unbeatable.)

The *Boston Globe, Boston Herald, Quincy Patriot Ledger, Worcester Telegram & Gazette, Hartford Courant, Boston Metro*, and many others send representatives (sometimes more than one) to cover every angle of the Red Sox season. Add to their ranks the writers for Redsox.com, ESPN.com, sound bite seekers from local sports radio, TV crews, and statisticians, it makes for quite a gaggle around the dugout on a summer weekday afternoon.

On this particular day, the opponent is the Atlanta Braves. It is June 28, 2002 and Red Sox Nation is high on the team's incredibly hot April and May. The best start in forty years, some are saying. Best record in the league for a while there. First year with the new owners. "The Year To Be Here." The only blot on the season so far has been the team's dismal record in interleague play. Tonight the Sox take on the Braves for the final interleague series of the season. This is one of the many subplots running through the minds of the writers as they set about their work.

The writers have seen it all before, the highs and the lows, and regardless whether they are recording an epic, or an epic failure, their daily routine is the same. The beat writers are not historians. Each one's job is to produce about seven hundred words per day, encapsulating the day's events, a snapshot of one game, or one player, or one moment in a season. By three thirty in the afternoon, most of them have settled their laptop computers in the press box, checked their email, spoken to their editors, and have already finished their daily briefing from manager Grady Little. Now they are down on the field waiting. Most of the players are not even here yet—outside Johnny Damon is pulling up in his giant black SUV. Nomar Garciaparra, in an almost identical vehicle, pulls up behind him. They hand their keys to Red Sox employees who will add the trucks to the jigsaw puzzle of team cars crammed into the tiny triangle of a lot off Van Ness Street.

Mike Fine of the *Quincy Patriot Ledger* is among the throng of media members loitering on the warning track this afternoon. With nothing to do but wait for whatever story will come his way, he is chatting with the crew of a local television station. They talk about the previous night's dugout flood. A torrential downpour washed out the contest against Cleveland, and the press corps had to navigate shin-deep water in the clubhouse. Mike is a home-grown Bostonian who has worked in sports all his life. While studying journalism at Boston's Northeastern University, he took a student co-op job in the sports department of the *Boston Globe*. Six months

later, in 1968, he moved on to the *Patriot Ledger* and has been there ever since. After a few years writing about high school and college sports, he began covering the Red Sox full time in 1975. Now Mike only covers Red Sox home games and has Saturdays off, since the *Patriot Ledger* has no Sunday edition. When I ask him what he likes best about being a baseball writer he says he loves having his days to himself. "I don't do nine to five, no rush hour—today I went to the gym," he says. "And, it's fun."

At almost four o'clock Grady Little comes up the runway to the field, which is covered with a tarp thanks to the threat of more rain. He leans on a fungo bat like a cane and sniffs at the air, eyeing the tarp in a vaguely displeased way. The writers begin to fidget. Some of them are in seats in the shade, flouting Fenway's no smoking rule. Others are on the dugout bench. Some stand on the warning track. Everyone's eyes are on Grady. He doesn't say anything, but then goes down the tunnel toward the Red Sox clubhouse. Through long years of observation, each writer comes to the same conclusion: no batting practice today.

I find myself in a conversation with Michael Silverman, one of the *Boston Herald's* three full-time writers who cover the Red Sox, and one of four who are there to cover this particular game. One will handle the game recap, one will write on the home pitcher, one on the away pitcher, and one on whatever else emerges of note during the day. Silverman is there to do the home pitcher, John Burkett. He is carrying the traditional reporter's "steno" pad and a ballpoint pen in one hand. He seems sanguine about the prospect that batting practice has been called off. "I'm hoping to get a word with Manny, too," he says. Silverman always "knew I wanted to write for newspapers. And when I got into sports I wanted baseball. I was at the paper five or six years before getting the Red Sox beat." He started Sox coverage in 1995, and he shares one of the most valuable lessons of beat writing with me when my pen goes dry in the middle of interviewing him. "Very important. Always carry two pens," he says, as he pulls another ballpoint out of the breast pocket of his short-sleeve dress shirt and hands it to me.

This shirt is notable for one reason, which is the Fenway Park Press Box Dress Code. The dress code, which states that shirts with collars must be worn, is mostly adhered to. The press are in everything from dress shirts and suit jackets to polo shirts and promotional tees, though the majority are in button-downs with short sleeves. The style of shirt is secondary to the most important thing, which hangs hangs around their necks: the press pass. The regular beat writers have colorful I.D. tags on lanyards while others like me and radio station workers only there for the day have a cardboard tag on a string. There is one rule emblazoned on every one of them: No Autographs.

Some Red Sox personnel come out of the tunnel and begin to set up for infield practice. The tarp comes off, and players begin to drift out. The radio crew set up in the dugout grabs Tim Wakefield, a female reporter holds a microphone up to his mouth. I'm too far away to hear what he is saying. Some of the writers begin to drift back to the press box. "There's no story down here," one of them says to the other. "It's too early to eat," is his friend's reply. "Might as well stay here."

I drift over to one animated individual telling a funny story with hand gestures. It's Bill Ballou of the *Worcester Telegram and Gazette*. Ballou is a fixture in Boston sports media. He's not as high-profile as, say, Peter Gammons, but he has been around nearly as long and is heard often on WEEI Radio. Ballou started writing about sports when he was in high school. "I did my first story on football. They paid me one dollar per game, so for ten games a season I got ten dollars." After attending college at UMASS and writing for the *Collegian*, he decided to make it a living. He first hooked up with the Red Sox in 1987. Ballou seems to enjoy telling stories as much as writing them, so I ask him, what's the funniest thing he's ever seen happen in a press box? "About ten years ago, there was a guy, he must have been in his sixties. It was in the middle of this game in Kansas City. He was typing madly but everything was coming out numbers!" Was his num-lock key stuck? "Must have been. He got on the phone, right in the middle of the game, and

quit! You could hear him talking to his editor: it's all coming out numbers and I QUIT!"

The other writers around us have a good laugh about that one. One of them prods Ballou, "What about the time that guy fell into the screen?" He is talking about a game in 2000 at Yankee Stadium, when the Sox were in the Bronx for a Memorial Day Weekend series. Some drunkard fell from the upper deck right past the press box (on the mezzanine level there), onto the screen which protects the home plate seats from foul pops, and passed out. "It wasn't that funny while it was happening," Ballou says. "The guy could have been dead." Joe Torre pulled his players off the field and the game was suspended while the seriousness of the situation was evaluated. "But then he woke up and was promptly dragged away by New York's Finest, and then we had a pretty good laugh about it!" (Roger Angell reported in *A Pitcher's Story* that Joel Sherman of the *New York Post* had the last laugh, breaking up his fellow writers by commenting "'I thought it was Cashman,'—Yankee General Manager, fired at last and flung into the void by the Boss.")

"That's nothing compared to what I've seen in Fenway Park," Ballou continues. "I saw the Twins get beaten by a fan." He points to a column in the stands on the third base side. "See that pole that says number twenty nine on it?" The wire that suspends the backstop screen runs from the top of the pole toward home plate. "This was in 1988, during Morgan's Magic. I think the pitcher was Benzinger? Beringuerre? Well, this fan climbed up the pole, and shimmied down the wire! They did not stop the game, I don't know why, and the next thing you know, the pitcher has walked a couple of guys because he can't take his eyes off this fan!" The Twins, of course, were the reigning World Champions at the time. "Next thing you know, three-run home run." [Incidentally, the pitcher was Juan Berenguer. –Eds.]

He waxes nostalgic about the old press box at Fenway Park, before renovation. "I only got to be in it for a few years. It was like the rest of the park, cramped, uncomfortable... but I'll take being uncomfortable for being closer to the game." Ballou considers the current

Fenway press box to be one of the worst in the major leagues. "Near the top of the list because you are so far away. It has no disastrously bad features, it's just very far."

Manny Ramirez comes out of the clubhouse with his hair frizzed out to the max. Apparently he's taken his cornrows out. Several writers jot notes on their pads—you never know what colorful detail may add to a story later. Manny signs several dozen autographs for kids who are beginning to jam the area next to the dugout. He eyes the writers hovering nearby and then goes back to the clubhouse, patting Nomar Garciaparra on the back as he goes by. Nomar doesn't appear to be in a talking mood, either, and none of the writers approach him. It's getting close to five thirty now, and some of the Red Sox are taking an optional infield practice. Nomar jogs out to join them. The writers head upstairs in greater numbers. It's time for dinner.

To reach the press box level at Fenway Park, you have to go all the way to the top. They are the highest seats in the house, above the roof level. In addition to the main press box where the writers sit, there are broadcast booths for the various radio and television teams (home, away, Spanish language, etc.), and there is the Press Dining Room.

Contrary to popular belief, the press do not eat for free. No, they pay $7 a person to eat in the cafeteria. Accepting free food would be akin to graft and corruption, explains John Tomase, a writer for the *Lawrence Eagle-Tribune*. I chat with him as we look over the culinary options: there are several hot entrees being served up by cheerful concessions staff (fish and chips, burgers, shoestring fries, grilled vegetables, and more), a salad bar, soup, a deli sandwich bar, a large selection of desserts, even the makings for peanut butter and jelly. Tomase has been covering the Sox for five years. He began at the *Metro-West Daily News* and has been doing the Red Sox beat full time for the *Tribune* since 1999. "I only do a little travel," he says. "New York, Opening Day, the playoffs," he says wistfully. In the offseason he switches to covering the Celtics and Patriots. He is not as nostalgic about Fenway Park as some. "When I was a kid, the best thing was coming up the ramp and seeing all the green. Now, it's where I work, so it's lost its charm. I do like the atmosphere, though." And the food's good, at least in the press dining room.

Once the majority of folks—writers, media people, and other guests of the Red Sox—are done in the dining room, the staff break down the hot food stations and clean the tables. But the door remains open throughout the game. The soft serve ice cream machine and the popcorn machine are kept on, and a roller grill of hot dogs sizzles merrily.

In the press box, the seats are filling up. The Fenway press box is four tiers of seats, each row with a high, deep countertop desk. With all the computers it resembles NASA mission control. The "home" writers have assigned seats in the front row, the "away" writers in the second row. The third tier is a mish mosh of Boston-area and national media who do not have the seniority that the front row enjoy. The fourth row is for non-press visitors and guests. From the second and third rows, some craning of one's neck is necesssary to see home plate. From the fourth row, you may as well stand up. I take a seat in the third row. On my right is Katsushi Nagao, a reporter for the Japanese baseball magazine *Monthly Major League*. On my left is the rookie of the press box, *Boston Metro* staff writer Alex Speier.

Metro is a freebie newspaper handed out to commuters every morning at T stations and bus stops throughout Boston. As Speier puts it, "If *USA Today* is the McDonald's of newspapers, *Metro* is the drive-thru." I have actually met Speier once before, in 2001 in the press box of the Norwich Navigators, who were then the New York Yankees' Double-A affiliate. At the time the Red Sox did not recognize *Metro* as a publication and would not give them press credentials. So on that evening Speier decided to take in the Navigators versus the Trenton Thunder (who were then a Red Sox affiliate team). In 2002, however, the Red Sox, under new management, accredited *Metro* to report on all games. This is the twenty-four-year-old Speier's first year as a full-time baseball writer and he is loving it. "It's novel to me at this point," he says. "There's so much to know."

He points out many useful features to me, like the

storage lockers under the press box tiers. "There's archives of information on the Red Sox under there. Some of the lockers are for certain organizations. But there is all kinds of stuff." He's also the one who tips me off about the popcorn and ice cream machines.

"I used to sit in the bleachers," he tells me, pointing to the spot in the stands physically the furthest from where we sit now as possible. "Those seats that run from box 34-36, dead centerfield bleachers. On a weekend afternoon, you roast out there. You're sweating your brains out. It's not a trickle, it's a rainstorm. But I love the angles out there. It's better than the press box," he says. "It's like you're the dead center cam. You can identify every pitch. I also like the idea that you're stuck there without a lot of distractions. Most of the people in that section are season ticket holders. You're not out there to ride a ferris wheel. You're there to scrutinize what is going on in the game." You can see how being a baseball writer comes naturally to him.

The sun is setting behind us somewhere and the rain clouds are breaking up. Despite its difficult angle of vision to the field, the press box has a breathtaking view of the Boston skyline. Michael Silverman loves this view. "Sure Fenway has its

drawbacks. The clubhouse floods, the seats are antiquated, you see trash being carted around, and the press are in an isolation tank. But you also look around and you think 'Ted Williams sat here. Babe Ruth played here.' And then there are days when you sit in the press box with the sun setting behind you, reflecting off the skyline, and you think 'this is an amazing job and I'm lucky to have it.'"

"The theory is," says one writer who asked to remain nameless, "that this press box was the big 'fuck you' from the Yawkeys to the writers. When they renovated they could have done anything, built it anyway they wanted. But look at it. It's a glass box with terrible sight lines." With all the windows closed and sealed, even the announcement of the starting lineups is inaudible from inside. Of course, the writers do not need to write down the lineups. We have each been handed a pre-printed scorecard, a legal-size sheet of paper complete with scoreboxes, lineup and roster, freshly printed from somewhere in the media relations office. We also have available to us stacks and stacks of stats and information, including official releases from each team, from Major League baseball, notes on recent player performance, and bios and

UP AGAINST THE WALL, Y'ALL
Wynn Montgomery

It was the most perfect of baseball nights

As Fenway welcomed a horde of SABRites.

The pitching match-up was truly great-

A sure Hall-of-Famer versus his former teammate.

After eight, those starters (and several others) were through,

And each of the teams had scratched out just two.

Then, just on the verge of some "free baseball,"

Sheff doubled to left—off that world-famous wall.

It seemed that his effort might be for naught

'Cause both of the Jones boys weakly flied out.

But after a "ribbie" (game-winning?) by Vinny,

The Bravos found that they had heroes a-plenty.

After Darren walked, for his fifth time on base,

Blanco's bloop double plated the "coup de grace."

With a save in sight, Smoltzie turned out the lights,

And one former Bosox earned BRAGGing rights.

That ended the game, but the rivalry's not over.

Here's hoping they play again—in very late October!

information on players who are not in each team's pre-printed Media Guide, like the newly acquired Alan Embree (Sox) and Henry Blanco (Braves).

If you poke through memorabilia shops you will find that Media Guides of even ten years ago were not that large. They look almost like you could carry them in your back pocket, and I assume many writers did. But nowadays they are like small phone books, packed with information on a given club's roster, coaching staff, team history, minor league system, and much more. Each one is a hefty tome. Several people have dog-eared copies of the Red Sox media guide beside their laptops. A fresh box of the Braves' guide is delivered shortly before game time, and Guy Spina, the press box attendant, doles them out.

Guy has been a Red Sox employee for twenty eight years. "I've been working the press box since 1990," he tells me. His job includes distributing press material and also working the beverage machine during the game. Around the sixth inning, he puts out a platter of donuts. "I do whatever people need me to," he says by way of a job description. "You need anything, you ask me."

During the singing of the national anthem, everyone in the press box stands. Then, as the song finishes, and people take their seats, the senior writers in the front row begin flinging open the windows. It takes three or four men per window to get them open, but they do, sliding the large panes of glass upward to let the sound of the ballpark in.

As we prepare for the first pitch, I count the number of

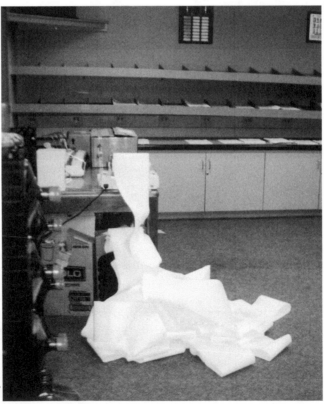

people present. There are forty seven people there, almost all of them typing. Four of us are women. There is me, a woman from ESPN.com, one from Sportsticker, and one who works in radio. None of us are beat writers in the traditional sense. I have been told that there was a time when the Fenway Park press box, like many of its counterparts throughout the leagues, was unassailable by women. I am happy to report that now there is even a Ladies Room up there.

The first pitch comes at 7:06 PM and it is seventy six degrees at game time. I know this because an announcer inside the press box tells us so. This is the same announcer who will inform us of the decisions of the official scorer (hit/error, wild pitch/passed ball, etc.). If you listen to radio broadcasts of baseball games you will sometimes be able to hear this voice. The announcer sits in the front row, next to the official scorer. Bruce Guindon is the scorer, but given that he was quite busy throughout the game, I did not have a chance to talk with him.

Since other contributors are reporting other details of the game, I will not recap the specifics of the plays. What I will tell you are some of the other sub-plots that the writers were mulling over in the early stages of the game. John Burkett had come to the Red Sox from the Braves, and credited Greg Maddux with helping revive his career. Now these two pitchers were opposing each other, but that story had been mined already since the two had faced each other in Atlanta a few weeks earlier. After two innings, though, Burkett was six up, six down, while Maddux, who got walloped with a line drive, gave up three hits in the same span and looked vulnerable. Burkett, too, had been a hot hand at the beginning of the year (7-0), but had since lost three straight. Would this be the game where he turned it all around, and stopped the Sox slide? The writers are poised to take whatever hops come their way, win or loss.

During the second inning, someone's cell phone rang in the second row. The tune was "Take Me Out To The Ball Game." Another one, from the first row, went off shortly thereafter. Same tune. For all that beat writing is a job, these people love baseball. At 8:38 PM a mouse ran through the press box, causing most of the second row to stir from their seats. The mouse made a quick exit and, terrified he would be misquoted, did not return.

Most writers kept score in the traditional way, with a pencil on the scoresheets we were provided. They would type occasionally on their laptops, but for the most part during the game the laptops were there for checking on stats and information. Everyone was connected to the Internet and it was interesting to see which sites the writers preferred. There are various sites now where you can follow a game pitch-by-pitch, and all of them were in use. Yahoo, ESPN.com, MLB.com Gameday, but the most popular was CBS Sportsline. Of course the interesting thing about following the pitch-by-pitch web cast of a game you are at live is that someone else in the same press box is the one sending that data out.

I watch over the shoulder of the guys who work for MLB.com. Mike Petraglia is entering the pitch by pitch data and he shows me how it works, how he can indicate where the pitch was, what kind of pitch, and so on. I comment that the poor angle of the press box might account for some of the discrepancies between what shows up on MLB.com and the radio play by play announcers, for example. He admits it is mostly guesswork based on the positioning of the catcher's glove, but the technology is still quite nifty. Petraglia and his cohort Ian Browne are among the youngest members of the press corps, as befits their station, I suppose, with the youngest medium. Unlike the newspaper writers,

they are reporting on the game live, as it happens, and will write stories that will appear on the site within minutes of being filed.

"I've always wanted to do baseball writing," says thirty-year-old Browne. "I started out working for CBS Sportsline and then went to MLB.com. I grew up in Boston and covering the Red Sox is great. Never a dull moment, plus since the team has been winning it's been very enjoyable." He doesn't mention the dismal interleague record. "I love the atmosphere here, the park is packed every night, even for a Tampa Bay weeknight in April." Browne travels to about seventy percent of all Red Sox games, and between he and Petraglia they have every game covered. I ask him how long he thinks he'll be a beat writer. "Forever. I can't see myself doing anything else. As long as someone keeps paying me." He loves being part of the "new media." "We can write more offbeat features. And we write the same stories [as traditional reporting] but our deadlines are different. After a game they might only have fifteen minutes to file a story to make tomorrow's paper, but we can take up to an hour. Also, we're not trying to fit into a hole in the paper. We have more freedom." Among the things MLB.com does well is preview upcoming games and series in more depth than the daily paper can. Browne's piece that ran on the site prior to the day's game is all about how interleague play, and the Braves in particular, have killed the Sox traditionally.

The game is nip and tuck out there. Another potential sub-plot: Grady Little has put Brian Daubach in as the starter at first base. In baseball parlance Tony Clark has "not been producing," so he is benched. Daubach goes 0-for-2 with a walk and is lifted in the eighth for pinch hitter Rickey Henderson, who walks and is erased on a double play.

One of the cardinal rules of baseball writers is "no cheering in the press box." There is, however, no rule against grumbling. Back at the soft serve ice cream machine between the sixth and seventh innings I overhear some of the writers trying to come up with a plausible explanation as to why the Braves seem to own the Red Sox number. "The Sox are 5-10 in interleague this year," the one says. "I know," answers the other. "10-16 versus Atlanta since '97." I wonder if they have read Ian Browne's piece at Redsox.com or if they are quoting from the many stat sheets we have been given. They are shaking their heads and not looking optimistic.

When the game ends, at 10:16 PM, it is 4-2 Braves and a subdued crowd files out of the park. About a third of the press corp stay at their laptops, while the rest file downstairs to the clubhouse and Grady Little's office for post-game sound bites. At ten thirty, the seating bowl of the park is deserted and the field lights go out. At eleven PM, the only sounds in the press box are that of typing and the whoosh of the ventilation system. Many of the writers have earphones attached to their tape recorders, as they transcribe nuggets from Grady Little or whatever players they spoke to downstairs. The room now resembles a classroom during a final exam. The writers are serious and studious, looking through the voluminous sheafs of game notes, team releases, and media guides. There is the occasional whine of a modem dialing as each story is filed. Some of them will be there for an hour or more, depending on their deadline and how easily their prose is flowing on this particular night. Here are some samples of what appeared in the press the next day.

Michael Silverman wrote not only the home pitcher story on John Burkett for the *Boston Herald*, he also turned in a piece on Sun Woo Kim. "Sunny Kim sounded a lot like Derek Lowe once did. And his words in the Red Sox clubhouse before last night's game with the Atlanta Braves are certain to be spoken by Casey Fossum in the future. Kim is the latest Red Sox pitcher to go from being a starter, to a reliever, and back to a starter." The Burkett story, although shorter, took him longer to write. "John Burkett knew he could not quibble much at all about how he threw last night at Fenway Park. Still, the fact that the Red Sox lost, 4-2, to the Atlanta Braves left the right-hander in a bit of a nit-picking mood.... What bugged Burkett most was an 0-2 cut fastball that he threw to Keith Lockhart in the fifth inning." Burkett ended up with a no-decision.

Boisterous Bill Ballou decided his story for the *Worceester Telegram* lay with the pitcher who took the loss, Tim Wakefield. "He probably should be in the starting rotation, and has done well as the closer when called upon. At age 35 though, Tim Wakefield finds himself working baseball's version of KP. He's a setup guy, and last night got set up for his third loss of the season." Ballou noted in his story that Wakefield's appearance was his 300th with the Red Sox, and only six other pitchers have appeared in more games for the team. "He has been in a Boston uniform since 1995, longer than anyone else on the current team, and is slowly creeping up the all-time ladder to join people like Mel Parnell and Bill Lee and Bob Stanley, and yes, Cy Young."

Ian Browne filed both a game recap and a pitcher story on Burkett. His optimism and hope for the Sox comes through if you read between the lines. "Vinny Castilla doesn't hit many balls softer than the looper that fell in front of Red Sox center fielder Johnny Damon in the top of the ninth inning Friday night," he wrote to open the recap, downplaying any failure on the part of the Red Sox. The headline on the pitcher story read "Strong Burkett performance wasted." "It went into the books as a no decision, not to mention a quality start. Quite simply, John Burkett gave the Red Sox a chance to win Friday night, going seven innings and limiting a hot Braves team to two earned runs."

John Tomase did not quite share Browne's optimism. He filed two stories with the *Eagle-Tribune*, one almost an opinion piece on John Burkett, and one column of "notes" including segments on Maddux, Sunny Kim's recall, and Nomar's love of World Cup soccer. "There is a debate raging among Red Sox fans," Tomase wrote regarding Burkett in the piece entitled "Time To Upgrade at No. 3." "Should the team aquire a hitter or a pitcher for the stretch run? Those in favor of the former cite Boston's .236 team batting average during a 6-7 streak entering last night. Those in favor of the latter say you can never have too much pitching. To each camp I throw out one name: John Burkett. The numbers say he's pitched well. But the numbers behind the numbers say something else." Tomase is point blank with his analysis. "At age 37, Burkett is what he is—a solid middle-of-the-rotation veteran who will probably win a couple more than he loses. If the Red Sox feel comfortable sending that to the mound in Game 3 of the divisional series or ALCS, more power to them. But it might say more for their chances if he's starting Game 4." Tomase noted in his other piece: "Strangest clubhouse sight: Rey Sanchez fastidiously using his fingers and a comb to remove Manny Ramirez' cornrows in favor of the Tony Clark, Bride of Frankenstein look."

"Sox still stymied by that 'other' league" read the headline on Mike Fine's piece in the *Patriot Ledger*. "As far as the Sox are concerned," he wrote, "the lack of respect accorded them by their interleague rivals has reached near-disastrous proportions after their 4-2 loss.... Coupled with the Yankees' 11-5 victory over the Mets, the defeat dropped Boston to one game behind New York in the AL East."

Fine's is one of the few pieces that mentions the drop into second place. With the hindsight of historians, of course, we can now look back at June 28, 2002 as part of what kept the Red Sox out of the postseason again. Hopes to win the East were beginning to wane, and the front runners for the Wild Card, then the Oakland A's, were sweeping interleague series' left and right. Ultimately, the slip into second place was the beginning of a long slide, as a team which overachieved in April and May (e.g. Burkett 7-0), underacheived in the second half. But none of the writers in the press box on June 28th could look forward to see that. They could only record what they saw and heard that day, seven hundred words at a time.

AN EVENING WITH MY TWO DARLINGS

Jay Walker

I was part of the crew from San Diego that organized and produced the initial report of this genre, *Facets of the Diamond*, and the only one here in attendance at Fenway. With a three-hour time difference to the left coast, most of my fellow reporters from that effort are either busy wrapping up their work weeks or fighting rush hour traffic, while I casually munch on a frank this beautiful summer evening. For *Facets*, my contribution was a marginally serious sabermetric effort on something called Win Expectancies. But now I'm on vacation, in the city where I attended college and lived for ten years, and headed to a game at Fenway for the first time in almost a decade. This morning in a visit to old Braves Field, I set eyes on the dormitory where my first college sweetie lived and as of this evening, San Diego's own Teddy Ballgame still lives. In short, my mood is kick back and enjoy. Plus there are many more SABR people here to cover this game than the group we had in San Diego. My initial thought is to take a pass on filing a report, but in recalling our plans for *Facets of the Diamond*, the notion was to report on anything at all about the game—big or small, substantive or off-beat. Okay, this time around we'll opt for the small and off-beat.

My seat in the cozy confines turns out to be a mere five rows away from the right centerfield outer wall, roughly 817 feet from home plate, with Dunkin' Donuts and Verizon Wireless signs hovering over me. Needing room to stretch due to a prior knee fracture, I'm on the aisle, with an empty seat to my left. For my report, I harbored some notions about documenting the obliteration of the batter's box as the game progressed, but a gaze into the far horizon shows this to be an impossibility. Momentarily stumped, I decide—what the heck—to document the doings of the second base ump for the evening. With some luck there could be a few juicy arguments and maybe even an ejection. The umps are announced just prior to the first pitch. Covering second base tonight will be Gary Darling.

TOP OF THE 1ST

I'm sure SABR's Umpires & Rules committee will correct any inaccuracies here, but basically a second base umpire in a four-umpire system will set up at one of four positions near the base prior to the pitch. With none on or with only a runner at third, he'll set up on the shallow outfield grass, about 12-15 feet past the infield. He'll usually shift towards RF for a lefty batter and to LF for a righty. This position allows him to run out to the outfield for possible catch/no catch calls and to get back to second base in plenty of time for a call if the batter tries for a double. Whenever there are runners on first and/or second, the umpire will position himself on the infield grass close to the base, again shifting to either the left or right. Besides being able to make calls at the base on batted balls, this also allows him to call stolen base and pick-off attempts. Got all that?

This game will have over 30 base runners before it is completed, and with a preponderance of right-handed hitters in the lineups, umpire Gary Darling will spend quite a bit of time positioned on the infield grass shifted towards the 1B side. However, with the Braves going down 1-2-3 in the first, he will spend this half inning on the outfield grass. After occupying the same spot while Rafael Furcal and Julio Franco go down, I was a little surprised to see Darling turn around and march five steps deeper when Gary Sheffield comes up.

BOTTOM OF THE 1ST

After singles by Carlos Baerga and Nomar Garciaparra, Darling has a routine call to begin his night as Baerga, apparently dreaming of far-off Caribbean beaches, is easily picked off.

Darling's next call would turn out to be his toughest call of the night, but with the little warm-up provided courtesy of Baerga, he's ready. Manny Ramirez grounds

to third and Garciaparra is forced at second on a close play. As the inning ends, the first cries of "Yankees Suck" are heard. Gee, and I thought they were playing the Braves.

TOP OF THE 2ND

My seat mate arrives and turns out to be one of the elusive SABR Super Babes. While in one sense a welcome development, this threatens to reduce relaxed concentration level even further as I strive to keep one Darling straight from the other.

BOTTOM OF THE 2ND

Shea Hillenbrand doubles to left center. Darling first has to move back to the outfield for a possible call, and when it's clear the ball will drop, hustle back to second. He gets into position about a second before making a reasonably close safe call. I would rank this as his second toughest call of the night, not so much in the call itself, but in the hustle and timing needed to get into position.

TOP OF THE 3RD

With runners on first and second, Keith Lockhart grounds into a 4-6-3 double play. From his position on the infield grass, Darling has to run back a few steps to be in position for the call.

BOTTOM OF THE 3RD

Jose Offerman walks and steals second, as Darling makes the call on a play that's not close. Later in the inning, Garciaparra singles and steals second without drawing a throw. Having lived in Boston for ten years when two Red Sox stolen bases in a week were big news, these two steals in a single inning send my system into temporary shock. Later examination of the play-by-play reveals no further Darling calls this half-inning, and thankfully for my system, no further Red Sox steals.

BOTTOM OF THE 5TH

Perhaps bored by a few innings of inactivity, Darling talks to 1B ump Paul Emmel between innings as the grounds crew works the infield.

TOP OF THE 7TH

Finally a little bit of bang-bang action for Darling, although nothing so dramatic as actually having to make a close call. After a ho-hum Gary Sheffield steal of second, Darling has to move quickly out of the way to avoid being hit by a sharp grounder off the bat of Andruw Jones.

BOTTOM OF THE 7TH

Another half inning of no calls for Darling, but at least we get a good example of hustling umpire teamwork. With runners on first and second, Baerga hits a sharp liner headed straight for the Green Monster. As third base ump Rob Drake heads down the left field foul line for a possible call, Darling beats it to third base for a possible play there while first base ump Paul Emmel runs in tandem with Baerga to cover any calls at second.

TOP OF THE 8TH

As the Braves threaten to break a 2-2 tie, the other darling (seat mate) and I are engrossed in a discussion of the final scene from *Casablanca*, finally agreeing that it was best that everyone did the right thing in the end. Of all the bleacher seats in all the ballparks in all the world, why did she have to sit next to mine....

For one brief, fleeting moment it looks like the other Darling (umpire) might actually have to make a call on the front end of a double play, but pitcher Rich Garces fumbles the ball and has to go for the solo out at first.

BOTTOM OF THE 8TH

Oh my gosh, Darling finally gets to make a call! It's on the front end of a double play off the bat of Jason Varitek. Undoubtedly pumped up, he goes over for a little chat with third base ump Rob Drake at the conclusion of the inning.

TOP OF THE 9TH

Gary Sheffield doubles off the wall, with Darling having to make a routine safe call as he pulls into second. Sheff would later score the tie-breaking run on a Vinny Castilla single.

At the end of the half inning, my seat mate gets up and disappears into the Boston night. Well kid, we'll always have Fenway.

BOTTOM OF THE 9TH

The Red Sox go down in order, preserving the 4-2 Atlanta lead, and now the other Darling also disappears, this time into the Red Sox dugout with his fellow umps.

CONCLUSION

So ends Gary Darling's night, at least from my perspective. And a pretty routine one it is at that—no heated arguments, no ejections. He did have one play where he had to hustle to get into position to make a call, another where he had to hustle for a possible call, and once he had to step nimbly to avoid being hit by a batted ball. My highly unofficial count shows eight calls for the evening—one force, two double plays, two safe calls on doubles, two steals and a pick-off. Only one of these I could call close.

On the way out, someone rewards me with my very own Yankees Suck sign. It will later be presented to my 14-year-old niece. As a ex-Bostonian and a caring uncle, I feel a strong sense of responsibility to see that she is instilled with the proper values in these impressionable years.

NUF CED MCGREEVEY DOES THE WAVE

R. J. Lesch

In the middle of the 8th inning, while Rich Garces warmed up on the mound, the Wave broke out at Fenway Park.

I was a little surprised by this. I always associated the Wave with football fans; when I've seen baseball fans do the Wave, I always figured they were casual fans, not serious about the game. This was certainly not true of the Boston fans, who clearly knew the players and who always seemed to know how many outs there were and what the count was on the batter. These were serious fans.

And yet here was the Wave, circling a park built in 1912. "Nuf Ced" McGreevey and "Honey Fitz" FitzGerald led the Royal Rooters in choruses of "Tessie" during the World Series against the Giants that year. What would they have thought? I put the question to Tom Simon, chair of the Deadball Era Committee: what would "Nuf Ced" have thought of the Wave?

"He probably would have loved it," said Tom as we exited the park. "He would have liked to see fans getting into the game."

The Fenway fans did that, in a big way. All around us they cheered Nomar, clapped when Garces got two strikes on Julio Franco, brawled (we counted three in the bleachers and saw a near-miss on a fourth when a fan irritated by a bouncing beach ball swatted the ball out of the stands) and chanted "Yankees Suck!" at a fellow wearing a Yankees shirt.

This tumult bypassed the SABR group in Section 43 of the bleachers. We sat filling out our scorecards and wisecracking with each other. Some rose to cheer and clap, but for the most part we were a quiet pocket in the bleacher chaos.

The Boston fans let us get away with it. The Wave originated in Section 42 and went clockwise through us and over to Section 1. The Wavers were led by a big, beefy guy

in a bright yellow tank top who was adamant that everyone participate in this mob activity. And yet when those of us in the upper-middle part of Section 43 remained seated, the big beefy guy in the yellow tank top didn't even so much as glower in our direction. He and his cronies directed their invective toward Section 1, on the other side of a fenced divide between bleachers and grandstand. Even when one of our group started chanting "Don't-do-the-Wave" back at them, they ignored us. Maybe they pitied our stunted social skills; maybe they decided we were beyond hope.

So we were left in peace to wonder whether five consecutive 4-3 plays (Boston batters, third through fifth inning) was unusual, to debate whether that Lockhart plate appearance in the sixth inning would be scored a hit or an error.

Of course we were detached. We are researchers. We were also, of course, mostly fans of other teams. The most excited I got, myself, was when news of a White Sox win appeared on the scoreboard. I stood to clap a couple of times but sat when I realized the folks behind me remained seated. I was only clapping to be a good guest, anyway. Had it been Mark Buehrle or Antonio Osuna on the mound, it might have been different, maybe.

Good guest or no, fan or no, I still can't bring myself to do the Wave. I learned recently that the Wave made its first national appearance at a baseball game back in 1981 (Yankees at Athletics, October 15, 1981). [The Wave originated with a professional cheer leader named Krazy George who began it at college football games but was employed by the A's in 1981.–Eds.] I still don't like it. It's still mob behavior, and in these times there's something scary about thirty-three thousand people doing the same thing on cue and bullying those who don't, even if those people are as otherwise alive and exuberant as the crowd in Fenway that night.

Tom's probably right, though. Nuf Ced McGreevey is almost certainly somewhere on high cheering Shea Hillenbrand and Johnny Damon and doing the Wave with his modern-day simpaticants. I hope he isn't wearing a bright yellow tank top, though, because that just isn't a good look for anybody.

Lyle Spatz

As the chairman of SABR's Baseball Records Committee, in addition to watching this game for sheer enjoyment, I paid special attention to see if any records would be tied, broken, or even approached. Of course, Rickey Henderson, playing for Boston this season, has the potential to extend any of the several career records he holds anytime he gets into a game. He did so in this one, when as an eighth-inning pinch-hitter for Brian Daubach he drew a leadoff walk against the new Braves pitcher, Mike Remlinger. That extended Henderson's career record for most base on balls, but he failed to extend his record for most career runs scored, when after Shea Hillenbrand fanned, he was erased at second as Jason Varitek grounded into a double play.

In the bottom of the third inning, Manny Ramirez made Boston's final out by grounding to second baseman Keith Lockhart. That started a string of five consecutive batters that Braves' pitcher Greg Maddux retired on ground balls to Lockhart, and eight overall. Lockhart got a ninth assist in the sixth inning, and at that point the major league record for most assists by a second baseman in a nine-inning game, which is 12 in both the NL and AL, seemed in danger of being broken, or at least tied. But Lockhart got no more the rest of the way, and after being pinch hit for, didn't even play the ninth inning. Mike Remlinger of Atlanta was the winner, with John Smoltz getting the save. It was Smoltz's 26th save of the season, a season in which he joined a select group of pitchers who have both won 20 games in a season (he won 24 in 1996) and also saved 20 in a season.

FRIDAY NIGHT BASEBALL

Lewis Trott

It's Friday night, it's hot, and it's summer. And that means Friday night baseball, although I'll be enjoying it from the couch on this Friday night and not grand old Fenway Park with fellow SABR members. And while there are no smells of hot dogs and beer at my house, no fellowship with SABR members, no grand view of the green monster, there is still the game. And this is what I saw.

The match-up for this weekend's series features the hometown Red Sox facing their "natural" inter-league rival, the Atlanta Braves. The Atlanta Braves have been dubbed "America's Team," not necessarily because of their outstanding record over the years, but because of the reach WTBS has as the Braves vehicle for broadcasting their games across the country. Because of WTBS, I watch the Braves as much as I do my beloved Baltimore Orioles, and therefore know as much about them as I do the Orioles. But despite my exposure to the Braves, their announcers make them a very hard team to root for.

One of the biggest differences between watching a game live and on television is the presence of television announcers. Announcers can either enhance a broadcast, do nothing for the quality of a broadcast, or make you wish they were on a word count throughout the games as many pitchers are on pitch counts. Of the Braves announcers, Pete VanWieren is the only one who enhances the broadcasts, and without mentioning any further names, there are two other announcers who really do nothing to improve what I'm watching. The final Braves announcer is why I hate the Braves (it has become a sort of rally cry for me—-"Come on boys... hate the Braves!"). He spends nine innings alternating between praising "America's Team" and brushing up on his comedic skills. On this night this stand-up informs the viewers that the Red Sox starting pitcher and former Brave, John Burkett, is 7-1 this season with his natural brown hair, and 0-2 with his dyed blonde look. No doubt the SABR members attending the game at Fenway are missing out on this type of valuable statistic.

The game itself turns out to be a good one, despite what I consider unsatisfactory result (i.e. a Braves win). I keep a scorebook on certain games at home (and all games I attend live) and I have kept a scorebook for this one. Keeping score at home forces me to focus on the game and be more attuned to every play. Without the scorebook, I take a little longer in the kitchen in between innings, read during innings, and forget what happened during the game by the next night. But the glory of keeping score is keeping a document of what happened, and being able to pick it up and remember even the most ordinary of plays.

Looking at my score sheet, I know that the game was tied 2-2 in the 7th inning. But in the top of the 8th, something interesting happened, that although did not result in any runs, I think lost the game for the Red Sox. Alan Embree relieved John Burkett to start the 8th, and immediately got Vinny Castilla to ground out to Nomar Garciaparra at shortstop. But then Embree walked both Darren Bragg and Henry Blanco, the 7th and 8th batters in the lineup. The Red Sox went to their bullpen once again and brought on Rich Garces, who got Matt Franco to ground out to the pitcher for the second out. Garces then walked Rafael Furcal, but was able to get out of the bases loaded jam by retiring Julio Franco on a grounder to second.

At times like this in a ballgame it is often said that in this case, the walks did not hurt the Red Sox. But looking at the score sheet, maybe they did. Leading off the ninth for the Braves was Gary Sheffield who doubled off Tim Wakefield. Two outs later he scored on a Vinny Castilla single. Without the walks given up in the previous inning, Sheffield would not have led off the inning, and Castilla, the first out in the 8th inning, would not have had the RBI chance in the 9th.

The Braves would go on to score once more and the final would be 4-2 Braves. Without my score sheet

handy, I might have gone right along with the announcers assessment that those walks in the 8th inning turned out to be harmless.

Game 2 in the series is a FOX network game of the week. Not only does that give me a reprieve from the WTBS announcing crew, but it gives the broadcast a truly New England flavor with Jerry Remy and his distinct Bostonian twang. The game is another close, exciting game with the Braves once again prevailing 2-1. I remember Jerry Remy from his playing days as a Boston second baseman (I do not recall his days with the Angels though) and I was curious as to how his statistics stacked up against one of the Braves announcers who is also a former player, Joe Simpson. Thanks to *Total Baseball*, I learn that although Simpson only played in 607 games compared to Remy's 1,154, he actually out homered Remy 9-7. Remy outdoes Simpson in all other major offensive categories and played ten years in the big leagues, one more than Simpson.

Sitting on the couch as opposed to in the stands affords me the opportunity to look up such valuable numbers like those comparing Remy and Simpson. But what I miss the most about being in the stands is what others around me have to say (and I don't mean "Hey beer man!"). Knowledge gleaned from others more insightful and studious than I is always welcomed and even anticipated. Sometimes watching a game on television provides me with some kernel of information that I find valuable, but most often it's rehashed opinion and excessive verbiage designed to prevent dead air.

On Sunday, the broadcast returns to WTBS and thankfully Pete VanWieren rescues his colleagues from their on-air dreadfulness. VanWieren can be counted on for the insightfulness I appreciate from knowledgeable announcers. He even stated during Friday night's broadcast that he had addressed the SABR convention earlier that day, the first time I have ever heard SABR mentioned during a televised game. During this broadcast, he relates the history of the old Boston Braves with the Red Sox, and how the Red Sox were sometimes forced to play their games at Braves Field on Sunday's because baseball was forbidden on Sunday at Fenway Park.

Later on in the broadcast, VanWieren's less astute, sometimes partner, Skip Caray, informs me that Red Sox reliever, Ugueth Urtain Urbina, is the only major leaguer to have the initials U.U.U. Unfortunately this oddity does not help him too much this afternoon and he gives up three runs in the tenth inning and the Braves sweep the Red Sox with a 7-3 win. During the Braves half of the tenth, Skip laments, "Win, win, win, that's all we seem to do." I don't know about Caray, but however much it pains me to admit it, the Braves do seem to win quite a lot lately. I don't know if being at the game would have lessened the pain of seeing them win another game, but I would have been spared the critical commentary which Caray provided.

With the weekend series completed, I can finally get some work done that was neglected because I think weekends were made for watching baseball and not housework. I try to compare watching a game in person and watching it on television, and realize there is no comparison. Being at the ballpark is almost being a part of the game. Fouls balls fly your way, the same wind that blows your hair around, blows dirt off the mound, and although they are sometimes picked up on television, insults yelled at the umpires become part of sensorial receptions in my mind as well as that of the umps. Perhaps the one advantage of watching from the couch is there is no traffic to beat, no train to catch, or miles to walk. I am already home and there's just enough time to get ready for the Yankees and Mets on Sunday Night Baseball.

IN AND OUT

Mark Pattison

Interesting to see OPS—On-base percentage Plus Slugging percentage—shown among the stats on the center-field jumbo scoreboard, even including a pregame explanation. Also interesting to see the pitchers' ERA go down with every out recorded. I can't rightly say I've seen that anywhere before.

Even though SABR enjoyed a luxury of riches by having member Joseph Mancuso sing The Star-Spangled Banner before the game and SABR President Claudia Perry tossing a ceremonial first pitch, I still kept looking to see SABR acknowledged among the groups at the game, if only to take a picture of the sign as it flashed on the scoreboard. I never saw it, and I never heard anybody else in our section exclaim that they saw it. You'd think that with 750 tickets sold we might get a mention. [The author must have missed it because a message did appear.–Eds.]

It must take a postseason game to taunt Braves left fielder Chipper Jones as "Larrr-ryyyyy."

It's awfully tough finding the "official" program for sale inside Fenway. I'm glad I bought the "unofficial" program sold outside the park before I went in. While on that thought, there were darn few concession stands in the upper areas of the park. I guess this is where teams want to have their stands nowadays, so customers don't have to miss any of the action while they're waiting in line. The handful of concession stands with some sightline to the field were clogged like an old man's arteries. It took me ten minutes to get a Designated Driver-sized Sprite from one booth—and this was a half-hour before the first pitch. While I'm ranting, the Bosox are comparatively stingy, offering just one free Designated Driver drink. At Camden Yards in Baltimore, where I see most of my games, I can get two tickets—

and the concession stands stock lemonade. Ah, well, but the vendors are out in full force—at least through the sixth inning. Still, I wonder why they don't work until the game's over, what with their captive audience, and why none of them appear to be hawking programs?

I wondered whether that line drive went off Braves starter Greg Maddux's foot. I thought it had hit the mound in front of his foot. My notions were disabused when I saw the trainer coming out. My verdict: If it hit, it must not have hurt for him to stay in the game and pitch five innings.

$5.75 for a big bag of peanuts? No way, José! Given the prices of ballpark concessions, I'll eat my food outside the stadium, thank you. Not that the prices outside are much of a bargain. Five bucks for a quarter-pound hot dog garnished with veggies at one stand, and six bucks for a chicken teriyaki sandwich at the Sausage King stand. I don't think I've ever seen chicken teriyaki or steak tips (these days, better steak tips than stock tips) offered for sale inside or outside any other ballpark, so I thought I'd try one. My chicken teriyaki tasted a little dry. Still, I couldn't resist taking a picture of the Sausage King stand, which features a pig wearing a crown. I'm always amused by food merchants who use animals in their advertising. It's almost as if the animals are saying, "Please! Come help me be the instrument of my own demise!"

Nice coordinated marketing touch in having Fleet Bank sponsor the two signboards showing how fast each pitch is thrown. Better Fleet Bank, I suppose, than Fleet enemas.

Call me slow on the uptake, but I don't think I really knew before that a backwards "K" stood for a called strike three. I assumed that Pedro-maniacs and their ilk supporting other pitchers were either drunk or didn't care.

Some of us took perverse delight in Red Sox second baseman Carlos Baerga's base running goof at second base in the first inning. There were a few hoots and hollers, a few inspired nicknames like "Bye-Bye Baerga" and "Careless Baerga." At which point a Red Sox fan who is a SABR member started admonishing us along

the lines of "like *you've* never made a mistake" and "he *tripped*." In her case, "Red Sox fan" is the noun, and "SABR member" is the adjective.

Jose Offerman, for all the derision he gets, manufactured a run the old-fashioned way by walking, stealing second, taking third on a groundout to the right side of the infield, and scoring on Nomar Garciaparra's single. Still, I wouldn't want him on my team—fantasy or reality.

Something else I don't think I've ever noticed before at Fenway is the flashing John Hancock sign above the center-field scoreboard when Boston scores. It's a nice touch. But in the only two other games I've seen at Fenway, I've sat in the bleachers, which makes it a bit harder to see. Another nice touch is seeing the Hood Milk bottle behind right field splash, although I still don't really know what prompts the milk to spill. But I'm not going to cry over it. [The Hood Milk bottle splashes on every strikeout by Red Sox pitchers and every home run.—Eds.]

You'd expect the hand-operated scoreboard in left field at Fenway to be slow on the uptake, but I didn't expect to see the big scoreboard above the bleachers get caught in errors. Atlanta's #28 was not Cory Aldridge, as the big board said on at least two occasions, but Darren Bragg. By Bragg's third trip to the plate, they had fixed the goof.

For some reason, I seem to be taking a lot more notes during the Atlanta halves of the inning than the Boston halves.

Another SABR friend sitting close by got beers for himself and his wife. At $4.75 each, it's a typical ballpark price. What wasn't so typical, he told us when he got back, was when the vendor took the two quarters my friend expected as change, dropped them into a tip box and said, "Thank you."

The sound system sounds terrible under Section 27. I heard some kind of Beatles song before the game, and some salsa-ish tune between innings at one point. The only song I could really make out was The Who's "Boris the Spider," which complemented the bass rumblings under Section 27 well. I thought, "What an inspired choice!"—even if the between-innings songs were picked out in advance by the nearby Virgin Megastore. But it wasn't until after the game that I had learned that John Entwhistle, The Who's bass player and composer-vocalist on "Boris the Spider," had died the night before.

I don't care who hears it. Tony Clark is a bum, and the Tigers were smart to have ditched him. He can't even hit his weight. My theory is that Clark doesn't get hot until his team is effectively out of contention. For Detroit, that's Memorial Day. But for the Red Sox, that won't happen until about September 28.

$44 for a ticket?! That's the most I've ever paid for a ballgame. I hope I never have to pay that much again. (Maybe I should just shut up. When my wife joined me in Boston to take in all three games of the Tigers-Red Sox series, we had to pay $60 each for two of the games.)

Part of our time, we must admit, was spent coming up with Chris Berman-style nicknames. Our best efforts included "Rafael Furcal Me in the Morning" and "My Cousin Vinny Castilla."

I wonder what the significance of the 514-foot sign is beyond the Green Monster, since Ted Williams hit one "only" 502 feet. I have my doubts that Manny Ramirez' light-tower shot was just 501 feet, because if it were any longer it would crush the myth about Terrible Ted.

It's true, it's true! There are plenty of seats at Fenway that face away from home plate. If the new owners renovate the park as they say they will, this is one of the things they can fix. Personally, I'm glad there is a Save Fenway Park organization out there. I hope it achieves greater success than the Tiger Stadium Fan Club, although the latter made things quite interesting in the Motor City for several years. But I digress. Fenway is worth saving, but it shouldn't have to be at the cost of booting the vendors out of Yawkey Way. If you ask me, that's not the Yawkey way.

There are times I go to a ballpark and repeat Samuel F. Morse's first telegraph message: "What hath God wrought?" I look at all of the carnival atmosphere pervading every ballgame—before, during and after—and it makes me wonder. For instance, from my seat I could count 37 separate advertising or promotional signs from AT&T, behind home plate counterclockwise to the Citizens Bank sign beyond left field. And some of those signs flashed different advertisers. There's so much corporate sponsorship in the game today it's detracting from fans' enjoyment of play.

During an idle moment in this interleague "natural" rivalry game, I came up with the lamest such rivalries: Detroit vs. Pittsburgh; Seattle vs. Colorado; San Diego and Arizona vs. anybody. And this year the scheduling solons couldn't find space to pit Cincinnati vs. Cleveland? I'm still suspicious of interleague play; the word "interleague" doesn't register with my spell-check program, so you know it's something foreign.

It's obvious that Bostonians and New Englanders have a deep affection for their Sox, even after they lost in the ninth inning. While the "Yankees Suck" mini-industry outside the park treads the line of good taste, the "Jeter Swallows" T-shirts definitely cross that line.

Kudos to the Red Sox for repeatedly encouraging fans to use private buses or public transportation to and from Fenway. There was trouble on the tracks at the Fenway station on the Green Line subway before the game was over. That meant a madhouse at the Kenmore station for well more than 40 minutes after the game was over. Even though the last pitch was thrown at 10:16 PM, it took me until 11:58 PM for my subway, my change of subway, my bus and my four-block walk to my in-laws' home in Somerville. That tends to put a damper on things.

Richard Cohen

I decided to walk from the Park Plaza Hotel to Fenway rather than take the Green Line in order to get a taste of Newbury Street. The sidewalk cafes were tempting, but I was determined to have my dinner outside the ball park. The landscape changed abruptly as I passed the Kenmore Square T Station exit. The calls of ticket scalpers and the feeling it had suddenly become congested told me I was now in the Fenway neighborhood. On a single street outside the park was the congestion and pregame buzz I had been hoping to savor. Sausage, chicken or steak tip sandwiches were the fare from most of the street vendors. I was a little disappointed in the lack of variety having, I remembered, a shish-kabob sandwich the last time I had been at Fenway several years ago. Nonetheless, I did not suffer as I people-watched while consuming my steaktip/peppers/onions barbecue sandwich.

I picked up an emergency supply of pistachio nuts for the game and got frisked on the way in, not knowing that my fanny pack was not allowed (the security people decided it qualified as a purse and let me pass). The ticket taker gave me his card so he could give me a Fenway tour next time I was in town. I did not want to leave my seat once the game started, so I made a bathroom stop before finding my seat.

The seats for my party were rows 1 and 2, seats 1-3, section 42, exactly in right center field. Directly in front of us was a walkway, which was a problem only on occasion with vendors and sauntering fans. Bordering the walkway was a short fence at eye level and with square openings just big enough to allow a baseball to pass through. This served to keep fans from intruding into the Red Sox bullpen which was just beyond. Through the fence, we had a great view of the main stands, of the Green Monster, and of the right and center fielders. It was a little hard to tell the shortstop from the third baseman or the shortstop from the second baseman from our perspective.

My family arrived as the National Anthem started.

Sitting on my right was my wife Margie. On her right was her brother, Richard. In the three seats behind us were Richard's wife Linda, and two of their four children: David, age 10, and Jeremy, 7. Richard's family lives about 40 minutes south of Boston on a good driving day, and staying at their home is always a wonderful albeit tiring few days. During the course of the game I did my best to lean back in order to give pointers and answer questions asked by David. Jeremy just took it all in fascinated by loud vendors with wads of dollar bills in their hands. Margie and I had to readjust to the upside-down perspective compared to our usual seats which are between first base and third base at the minor league park we usually attend in Syracuse, and this was an opportunity to view a game from a different perspective. Several fly balls and a wonderful shoestring catch in front of us by right fielder Trot Nixon gave us both an appreciation of outfield play we did not have previously.

The privilege of sitting next to a gentleman named Bill Gould turned out to be a special treat. Bill is a fellow SABR member who traveled from Stanford, California to attend the annual meeting in Boston. He has been rooting for his Red Sox for 53 years, most of his adult life. As often happens when baseball fans sit near one another—especially those keeping score as we were—a relationship developed. His turn of phrase and his earnestness about the game were eerily similar to those of my late father and my most vivid memory of this game came from something Bill said in the eighth inning.

The Red Sox were threatening to take the lead with a two-out bases-loaded rally, and the Fenway fans were on their feet cheering across and around that beautiful field of green grass. Immediately in front of us we could hear the wonderful sound of not just one but two balls as they were caught by the bullpen catchers and then see the balls cross our field of view as they were tossed back to the warming up pitchers. There was a cooling breeze blowing over us on this clear night which was meant for baseball. Bill turned to me and said, "I wish I could freeze this moment. It's perfect."

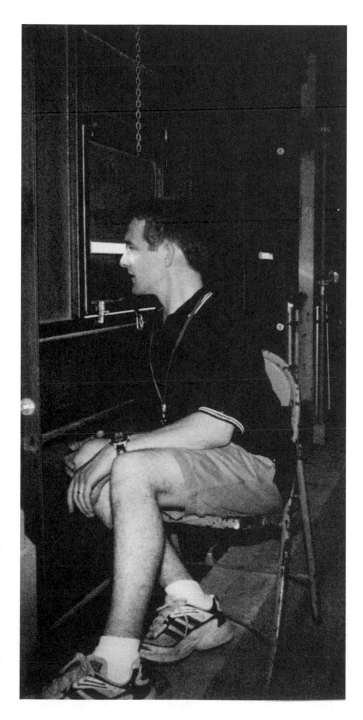

INSIDE THE MONSTER

Eric Enders

Eighty-one times a year, sometimes more, Rich Maloney and Chris Elias spend four hours together in a dark, long, narrow room, perhaps five feet wide by 40 feet deep, with a sloping ceiling just high enough to walk under. It is, to be sure, an unusual place to report for work, but Rich and Chris have two of the best jobs in baseball. They are the men who work behind Fenway Park's hand-operated scoreboard.

Both in their early thirties, they have been doing this together for twelve years—not long enough to witness the ecstasy of Fisk or the heartbreak of Buckner, but long enough to give them perhaps the most unique perspective on America's oldest ballpark. Not only do they handle the scoreboard, but they also supervise the informal wall of honor that their "office" has become. The back wall of the room—the mass of concrete that separates them from Lansdowne Street—is strewn with many of the names that also dot baseball record books. For years, it has been a tradition for players to come back to this secret room behind the big green wall and sign their names on the concrete.

Of course, all the names are signed in chalk, so they don't last more than a few years. Still, this is the one place where the ghosts of Fenway—or at least of recent Fenway—are most plainly visible. "There's some stuff up there from '92, '93," Rich says when asked about the wall's oldest signatures. "They're mostly chalk, but some guys have done it with rocks, even markers."

There is Derek Lowe, who signed the wall on April 27, 2002, the day he pitched a no-hitter here. "Larry Walker's in here, Jeff Bagwell's in here," Rich says, pointing to names scrawled in white. "Tim Wakefield, Jeromy Burnitz, Mike Piazza. Chuck Knoblauch's up top there. And you can barely see Luis González. He's a really good guy. Darren Holmes, he signed it back in '91 or '92 when he was with Milwaukee. See where it says 'Temple of Doom' underneath there? That's Holmes, Crim, and Bosio. Milwaukee thought they had the best bullpen in baseball that year, so they called themselves the Temple of Doom." And immortalized themselves in chalk on a slab of concrete.

"This is kind of like a shrine," Rich says of the signature wall—but if so, it may be the only shrine where one of the major icons was willfully destroyed. On July 13, 1999, Tony Gwynn visited Fenway Park for the first and only time, and signed the wall to commemorate the occasion. Soon afterward, the Red Sox front office needed to put a electronic control box on the wall, and they placed the box—you guessed it—right over Gwynn's signature. "Tony Gwynn was probably one of the nicest guys, too," Rich says. "He came here for the '99 All-Star Game because he'd always wanted to see Fenway, and he came back here to hang out with us, telling stories and stuff. They were looking around for him because they were getting ready to take the National League team photo, and they couldn't find Tony Gwynn. He was back here with us."

Of course, not everyone was as polite as Gwynn. "See David Wells there? Right above his name he wrote 'Fenway Sucks,'" Rich says, pointing to a large white smudge on the wall where a partial letter 'F' is still visible. "ESPN the Magazine did an article about us, and they took a shot of that. The guys at the Red Sox got a little bit perturbed, so we wiped it off."

Working outside of the public eye behind the big green wall, Rich and Chris are able to do many things other Red Sox employees cannot—like, say, kicking up their shoes and turning up Stevie Ray Vaughan on the radio while the national anthem plays outside. This is their time to relax: Once the action begins, they cannot afford to miss anything. With the game about to start, the two prepare for work, with Chris sitting at the end of the scoreboard nearest to center field, and Rich occupying the end nearest the foul line. "I always sit here," Rich says, pointing to a metal folding chair beside a tiny opening in the wall. This opening, about an inch tall and

ten inches wide, is what allows a viewer to watch the game from inside the wall, as if peering out from behind Venetian blinds. There are several of these little slits along the bottom of the Green Monster. Rich's job during the game is to sit here and change the runs, hits, errors, and inning-by-inning score as needed, hanging the big, green, aluminum numerals from hooks. "You know the Fisk home run in '75? This is where the camera was," he says, pointing to another opening in the wall, this one the size of a man's head. "This is the slot they were looking through. If the game's on national TV, or on the local Fox affiliate, they'll put a camera in here."

Of course, the most famous moment in Fenway's long history involves this particular hole in the wall—and a rat. According to legend, NBC cameraman Lou Gerard was stationed inside the Green Monster during the 1975 World Series when he saw "a rat the size of a cat" coming toward him as Carlton Fisk strode to the plate. Not wanting to provoke the rat, Gerard kept his camera trained on Fisk after the swing, rather than turning it quickly to follow the flight of the ball as he normally would have. As a result, the memorable image of Fisk waving his home run fair was preserved for posterity—something that never would have happened if not for the fearsome rodent. "I wasn't here at the time, but I wouldn't be surprised if it was true," Rich says. "We're actually below ground level—Lansdowne Street is about three or four feet above the ground in this room. We've never really had any rat problems, but we've seen some evidence they've left behind."

Talking with these men, I am reminded of the only other time I've been inside a hand-operated scoreboard. It was in Cuba, where the rural Western province of Pinar del Rio has a manual scoreboard in its 12,000-seat ballpark. There the board is operated by two elderly men named Rolando Castillo and Julio Hernández. Like Rich and Chris, they operate the board with the familiarity of an old married couple; they've been working together for 35 years. But unlike Rich and Chris, who work on the ground floor, the Cubans do their jobs from high up inside the tall scoreboard, peering out on the world like

Quasimodo in his bell tower. Like the Bostonians, Castillo and Hernández peer out at the game through holes in the scoreboard, and they too have a radio going at all times. But in Cuba, instead of the classic rock tunes heard inside the Green Monster, the radio is blaring the broadcast of the game—just in case Castillo and Hernández miss anything. There are other differences too. Instead of hanging signs on hooks, at each turn of events the Cubans crank a heavy steel handle that rotates the proper numeral into place. All four scoreboard operators I have met—two in Boston and two in Cuba—are painfully aware of how rare and precious their jobs are. In both Cuban and American baseball, most ballparks have long since begun operating their scoreboards with electricity instead of human beings. "It is a curse upon us," the Cubans say of the electronic scoreboard.

Back at Fenway, the crowd suddenly roars to life, drowning out our conversation, and a loud metallic bang over our heads announces that Shea Hillenbrand has hit a double off the wall. We scurry to the little openings in time to see Chipper Jones throwing the ball back to the infield. Jones is playing his first game as a left fielder at Fenway, which means he will likely soon join Rich and Chris's circle of close personal friends— the guys with whom they converse through the small openings in the wall. "It's kind of like a club," Rich says. "A lot of the left fielders come back here and shoot the breeze with us. Albert Belle was great. My personal favorite was Mike Greenwell, though. He spent more time back here than anyone, and he was a genuinely good guy. Anytime there was a pitching change, he'd come back here and talk NASCAR with us."

A pitch to Jason Varitek is called a strike. It doesn't matter, for balls and strikes are tallied electronically from the control room upstairs in the press box. Down here in the trenches (literally), Rich and Chris control only the manually operated parts of the scoreboard: runs, hits, errors, the inning-by-inning score, and the American League out-of-town scores. On a table sits an old telephone, "the big phone," they call it, on which the front office calls down the out-of-town scores to be posted between innings. "If we're in a pennant race or

something, they might call the Yankee scores down in the middle of an inning," Chris says, "but otherwise it's in between innings." The phone is set on the loudest possible ring, for the metal wall makes the crowd noise seem even more intense in here than outside.

The scoreboard we are sitting behind reflects not only the scores, but also pitching changes in each out-of-town game. On the wall behind Chris are hooks on which hang dozens of heavy rectangular metal plates. The plates are white on dark green, hand painted (by whom, nobody knows), and contain the uniform numbers of every pitcher in the league—even the retired 42, which is still worn by Mariano Rivera. Chris asks me if I want to be in charge of changing the numbers for a while. He doesn't have to ask twice.

Like most people with unspeakably cool jobs, Rich and Chris more or less stumbled into their positions. "I didn't even know this job existed," Rich says. "I was in college, and I wrote a letter to the Red Sox PR department, got called in for an interview, and this was the job I got." Asked whether scoreboard operators are generously compensated, Chris offers a coy response. "It's a labor of love," he says. "You get some pocket change, but it's really not about the dough." Indeed, this is merely a second job for these men, both of whom perform more mundane tasks during the daytime. Rich works for a printing company, and Chris is a concert promoter, selling luxury boxes for performances at the Fleet Center and other venues. And while they both love their unique moonlighting job, they admit that being sequestered in a tiny dark space for hours at a time with only one other person is not always their idea of a good time. "At first I would have done it for free," Rich says. "But eventually it becomes a job. You know, some Tuesday or Wednesday night games during the summer, playing a crap team, you'd rather be somewhere else. But you take the good with the bad."

Included in "the bad" is losing many of the simple pleasures most fans take for granted—like, say, the ability to go use the restroom whenever you need to. "You know, it's funny, I haven't watched a Red Sox game from the stands in 12 years," Chris says. "But I have been to a couple of World Series games in New York. And it's fun, you know, because you forget what it's like after a while." For more than a decade, these two men have been watching baseball games only through an inch-high hole in a metal wall. It is, both literally and figuratively, a narrow view of the game. But it's a view nobody else has, and for that they are grateful.

A BALLPARK FAN'S THOUGHTS ON FENWAY

Steve Bennett

My first visit to storied Fenway Park can be summarized in three words: Fenway must go!

This bit of heresy comes from someone who grew up at Comiskey Park, loved his only visit to Tiger Stadium, and still enjoys seeing games at Wrigley Field. I choose to think of it this way: Sleeping eight to a room on a dirt floor in a log cabin is intimate, but I wouldn't want to do it; cramming 33,000 into a space better suited for 22,000 is intimate, as well, and I sure as hell don't want to do it again. Fenway must go!

Age alone does not confer status, beauty, grace, or wisdom. Sometimes, though, the masses can be gulled into thinking so, as in the rehabilitation of Richard Nixon's image as he settled into his forced retirement. (It was even suggested in some circles that Nixon should be Commissioner of Baseball. Though baseball's ruling elite never tapped the former President to be their Commissioner, they did eventually embrace the notion of appointing a liar and a stonewaller possessed with an amazing disregard for protecting the very institution he was hired to serve. Perhaps if we wait long enough, all bad ideas find their time.) And so it goes with Fenway: It is old; not exactly beautiful; certainly not graceful or wise; and totally undeserving of the status it has misappropriated.

Let's take a look at what makes Fenway Fenway and what would be lost if the old dame were euthanized. For starters, no new memories would be added to the field where Ruth, Williams, and Buckner tread. Perhaps in a city that embraces its history as Boston does, Fenway could be retained as a living museum. The field and the left field wall could be preserved in a city park. Generations of New England high schoolers could take aim at the Monstah. Fiscally impractical? Probably. It's still worth exploring in some fashion. If the field can be saved, then all the accrued layers of history can be preserved, even if major leaguers are no longer performing there. So what else might be lost? Proximity to the field for a maximum number of fans? Sure, it would almost certainly be diminished, but good design and engineering could still put a lot of fans right next to the action. And beyond that, nothing would be lost. Nothing. Everything else that is good about Fenway could be transferred to the new park. Fenway must go!

To be sure, Fenway Park has character. From the Green Monster to the Pesky Pole, it oozes charm from every outdated and decrepit pore. Character, however, can be achieved in a new stadium, whether by contrivance or dictated by the outside constraints of urban geography.

What would be gained by leaving Fenway to the visiting pilgrims? Let's start with seats wide enough to accommodate 21st-century, Big Mac-infused uber-butts. If Fenway Park were run by an airline, a lot of people would have to purchase two seats just to sit down. Of course that wouldn't really help because the armrests don't retract. Then let's move on to leg room. In Fenway the leg room I had could only be measured in negative integers. Only an Arthur Andersen accountant could claim otherwise. I had to sit with my legs splayed in order to keep the seat in front of me from digging more than a half inch into my knees. It was a painful experience. The lean Babe Ruth who played for the Red Sox could not have sat comfortably at Fenway. Perhaps that's the source of the curse of the Bambino.

The weather on the night I attended was almost perfect for baseball. A gentle breeze was blowing, and the temperature was in the 70's. Where I sat, down the left field line in section 27 under the overhang, conditions could not have been more stifling. The air was stagnant. Surely a new park could design this little bit of "character" away.

One of the crassest parts of the new stadium experience (it has nothing to do with the stadium being new, but everything to do with the crassness of management) is the constant blare of noise otherwise packaged as "entertainment." Blessedly, this was not the case at Fenway. Instead we were exposed to the other extreme, a sound system so bad that I didn't know a song was performed for the seventh inning stretch. Did they play "God Bless America," "Take Me Out to the Ballgame," both, or neither? I have no idea. No one around me knew. None of the fans sang. The answer is a better sound system used judiciously.

Boston fans are a rabid bunch. I don't know if they are that way because a deep-rooted love of the Red Sox is in the New England DNA that gets passed from one generation to the next, or if the hardscrabble lot of enduring games at Fenway has toughened them to the point of blind fanaticism. I think these people deserve better, even if many of them don't yet realize it. They deserve wide and comfortable seats with adequate leg room and cup holders. They deserve aisles that can handle the necessary traffic rather than choke it. They deserve a sound system that can be heard in every part of the stadium. They deserve natural ventilation. They deserve more and better food choices. They deserve more accommodating restrooms. They deserve to stay close to the action. They deserve a signature design that instantly screams, "Boston Red Sox!" when viewed on TV or in photos. They deserve a field upon which new memories can be sketched, even (dare I say it?) memories of a World Series championship, something few Bostonians currently possess. And they deserve to have the best of Fenway Park preserved as a park so anyone can scoop up grounders where Joe Cronin did or field caroms off the wall just like Yaz did. When it comes down to it, that's the only real argument for keeping Fenway: many of the game's greatest stars have dazzled us on that very ground. The best solution, then, is to save it as a public park, but get the Red Sox and their fans into something better. Fenway must go!

AT THE FEN

Gene Carney

I heard about The Fenway Project on the SABR email list, and was instantly intrigued. I believe the idea was Bill Nowlin's. Bill has authored a number of books, including *Ted Williams: A Tribute*, with Jim Prime (Masters Press, 1997), and Bill hoped The Fenway Project might produce one more.

If The Fenway Project works, it could spawn a whole series of books. Here is the plot: (a) annual national SABR convention, usually in city with major league franchise; (b) part of convention is attendance at a ball game (or more, if other parks are within reach); (c) why not ask the several hundred SABR members who attend to write about it? This will produce a kaleidoscope of viewpoints from some of the most rabid and informed fans, on the planet. There will be stat-rats and record experts, literary folks and fans with a long history with one or both of the teams on the diamond—just about any brand of fan you can imagine.

This year, the SABR national convention was in Boston; as luck would have it, the Braves were in town. Bill had opened The Fenway Project up to include SABR members who heard the game on radio or watched it on TV, so, thanks to TBS, I was able to participate. I don't think it was the most exciting game I've ever seen, but here is how I responded to the invitation.

It felt like a homework assignment, and watching a baseball game should not have that feel. But I liked the randomness of the thing—I will watch very few games from beginning to end on television, so doing this (for a good cause) was fun anyway.

Not being a close follower of the Braves nor the Red Sox, I wasn't sure if this was the first time that the Braves had played in Beantown since they left for Milwaukee, after the 1952 season. I soon learned that it was not;

Atlanta's Braves were 9-3 at the Fen going into this June 28 contest. Ah, well, maybe something else would make the night historic.

That's one of the things I love about baseball—you never know. In any game, fans can witness something that either never happened before, or hasn't happened since ... (race to record books)... 1909! And only three times since 1888!

But this was not that kind of night. For a while, it looked like maybe Keith Lockhart, the visitors' second baseman, might set a new record for assists in a game—he got two in the first and third innings, three in the fourth (in the middle of a streak of five straight 4-3's), and when the first Boston hitter bounced one his way to open the sixth, he had ten. But that was it, and Lockhart was pulled before the game ended, anyway.

This was my first close look at these two teams this season. Of course I knew that they were both doing very well in 2002. I am a NL fan, but I almost always root against the Braves, and for the Sox. Hey, I'm from Pittsburgh, and we've had a thing against the Braves since the early nineties, and we like under- dogs.

Few of these Braves were around back then—Glavine and Smoltsie were; but I recognized most of them, because I do tune in TBS from time to time, even when not on assignment. There was Julio Franco at first, where my memory still sees Sid Bream and Fred McGriff and Andres Galarraga (I still look up the spelling, it's just a blind spot);

Gary Sheffield at DH (which I like), forever in memory as the former Padre whose trade caused lawsuits in San Diego; the smug but talented Jones boys; Vinny Castilla. And on the hill, Greg Maddux, the ex-Cub Factor, once an unhittable ace, reduced to damn tough humanity.

For the home team, I was pleased to get my first long look at Johnny Damon; he came into the game at .322 but swallowed an 0-fer in the leadoff spot. Carlos Baerga fared better this night, and I was glad to hear he is indeed having a good summer; once a sure-Hall-of-Famer, he had hard times, and I'd lost touch. Nomar, Manny (back from injury, but still not right) and Trot Nixon, a fellow I caught on his way up, down in Durham.

I kept score of the game, which the Braves won 4-2, and my main recollection is that it was mostly dull—if you like offense. Maddux and Burkett dueled well, then Greg had to leave after five; Burkett lasted seven. It went into the ninth tied 2-2, then the Braves squeezed two across with two out. The hero was Castilla, who was working hard to avoid an 0-for-5 (but his ball hit in the sixth, snagged by Nixon in right, rated the only star in my scorebook.)

The Braves win- ning outburst came against Tim Wakefield, who was described by one of the announcers as a "nemesis." And that took me back to 1992, when Wakefield dominated the Braves twice in the NL Playoffs. When Doug Drabek ran out of gas in Game Seven, more than a few Buc fans called for Wakefield to come in and deliver one more inning. But manager Leyland went with Stan Belinda, who (overachieving, I

think) got a couple outs before Francisco Cabrera's hit scored Sid Bream—Barry Bonds' throw being just late, just off the mark. Of course it all came back when Wakefield was called in to hold the Braves at bay.

But the Braves hit him this night—as they might have done in 1992. Who knows? I forgave Jim Leyland a little bit after the game (the Sox went quietly in the home half.) It is not easy to forgive. Holding grudges, plotting revenge—these are easy. The home team lost. "If they don't win, it's a shame." But it's not a tragedy. There will always be tomorrow, and maybe something will happen in ten years that will take me back to this game. You never know.

LET FENWAY REST

Andrew Zinner

My first glimpse of Fenway Park was like most everyone's, I suppose. When I emerged from the subway and began walking across the tracks, baseball's oldest living ballpark appeared as I expected her to look. An aged, overworked collection of walls and bleachers wedged between the bustling, narrow streets of an old city.

Such an inelegant setting for a rare gem, I thought. Of course, the Fens was there long before the freeway that snaked along its outfield wall. Still, it would have been nice had it lived in the Common.

Enough about that. As I continued walking to the park, my focus turned to the Boston Beer Works, a local brewery across the street from the park. I had been looking forward to this stop since I'd read about the beer on the Internet several weeks earlier.

And I was not disappointed. As I nudged my way through the pre-game throng toward the bar, I was reminded of the Cubby-Bear Lounge, a Chicago landmark across the street from Wrigley Field. A warm feeling washed over me. I was in my element, with good beer and baseball talk all around me.

After a couple cold libations, it was on to the game. I walked around to the back of the park because I had an outfield seat. I pity those who don't take this walk, past the vendors' stands and hungry fans wolfing down hot dogs, peanuts and an amazing variety of other affordable fare. This was a classic pre-game baseball scene. So unlike the huge, sterile, impersonal parking lots that surround the new stadiums of today.

This is the way I remember my first game at Wrigley Field many years ago. So many people, so much history seeping out of the park. In Chicago it was Jenkins, Banks, Williams. Here I can feel Tiant, Yaz, Pudge, George "Boomer" Scott.

I soon arrived at my gate, and was surprised by the

heightened level of security. Indeed, we all got frisked before heading inside. No doubt the guards were looking as much for contraband food and drink as they were for guns or bombs. One must buy concessions at inflated prices, after all. It, too, is part of the game.

With a Sam Adams Lite stand just inside my entrance, I quickly had my desired concession. A couple, in fact.

I was surprised by the fine shape of the park's blood and guts. The posts were freshly painted and the rest rooms readily available and clean. Sure, this was before the game, but it was clear the park was being treated with the pride it deserved.

I walked around the concourse for a while. It, too, was like Wrigley. Dark, tight, a place to take care of business and move on. So much different than Bank One Ballpark in my adopted Phoenix. There fans mingled, lounged about, and agonized over the many fast-food selections that ringed the seats. Still, real fans don't go to a ball park to eat. They go to watch baseball.

The magic moment had at last arrived. Up the stairs and there it was. The Green Monster. The Pesky Pole. The classic depths of right-center field. I touched the Pole, took a deep breath, turned, and headed heading to my seat in left-center.

If only my night had ended there. I was in Row 3, near the end of the longest and tightest line of cramped seats I had ever seen. The row, incredibly, was a dead-end. It had no aisle at the other end. My pre-game euphoria was destroyed by the harsh reality of a classic park that had, sadly but inevitably, become obsolete.

I quickly assessed my situation. I drank lots of water, as well as several beers, before the game. And I've got an active bladder. To get to where I now stood would require me to step on at least 40 pairs of feet. No way am I sitting there, I decided. These people are nuts, I thought. Don't they go to the bathroom?

I grabbed a seat on the aisle, a couple rows above the view-blocking bar. If I had to move, I'd stand. Or leave.

Against all odds, I sat in that seat all night long. Still, I was shocked at the disregard for fan comfort in this cramped bleacher. These were nothing like the storied

bleacher seats at Wrigley. Sure, Wrigley's "seats" were just numbers painted on long benches. But I could see, and enjoy, the game there. And I could breathe.

I recall little about the game itself. Much of my remaining time was spent gazing at the many features of the park, trying to change my mind. Maybe the seats in the grandstands were better. That little upper deck along the right field line looked pretty good. Maybe I just sat in the wrong part of the park, I thought.

I am, after all, a baseball purist. I hated to see old Comiskey Park torn down. Heck, I even came to like the Kingdome. The designated hitter drives me crazy. And what happened to pitchers who finished what they started?

But I knew I was only fooling myself. This is different. This park is too small. There aren't enough seats to survive in today's baseball economics. Yet there are too many to allow for even minimal comfort.

There was no room to expand. Sure, I suppose another deck could be added along the right field line, but that would add only a few thousand seats. And at what cost, I thought? It wasn't worth it. It was too late. The yacht was sinking. There was no need to worry about the deck chairs.

Fenway Park needs to retire. She's too tired and too old. She has outlived her usefulness. She's beyond improvement. She's done.

The long-suffering fans of Boston deserve more. They should have room to move, clear views of the game, bright, safe, wide entrances and concourses. And the price of tickets cannot be raised forever. Boston needs some low-priced sections, like those at a big, new park.

There, I said it. Boston needs a new ballpark. The sooner the better.

Save Fenway if it must be saved. Pamper it and polish it. Turn it into a museum. Charge admission to adoring fans, who can leisurely stroll the open spaces. Let them see the clubhouses, sit in the dugouts and press box. Teach the young fans baseball history. Let the old-timers reminisce. Keep the tradition alive.

But do not ignore the obvious. Embrace today and tomorrow. Build a new park, and let Fenway Park rest.

Q & A WITH RYAN

John T. Saccoman and Ryan M. Saccoman

Ryan is a seven-year-old Mets fan. He has been to numerous major and minor league baseball games in his young life, but this was his (and Dad's) first time at Fenway Park. Dad interviewed son for The Fenway Project.

J: Tonight we're going to see Atlanta play against the Red Sox. Who would you like to see win?

R: Red Sox. Because we are in Boston, and that's the home team.

J: The Mets are fighting Atlanta for their division, so your rooting for Boston to beat Atlanta actually helps your Mets.

R: I know.

J: Did you bring your baseball mitt?

R: Yep. If a ball comes near us, I'll try to catch it.

J: So maybe you'll get a souvenir. Do you know where we are sitting?

R: Almost by the front?

J: In right field. (Actually, the seats were two or three rows from the very top of the bleachers in straightaway right center—about as far away as one could get from home plate.)

R: Somebody could hit a home run by us.

J: What is the Green Monster?

R: It's a big tall wall and it's green.

J: What do you like best about going to Mets games?

R: Well, last time they had the Fan Fest before the game.

J: And sometimes what do they let you do after the games?

R: Run the bases. Only the kids.

J: You like getting on the field.

R: I ran around the bases with Natalie and Julia. (Friends who also went to the game.) There was a lot of people. And I got a free jersey. (All kids did.)

J: What do you like best about going to the baseball games?

R: Running the bases.

J: I don't think they are going to let you on the field at Fenway Park after the game tonight. Are you going to be okay with that?

R: Yeah.

J: We are here in Boston at the convention for the Society for American Baseball Research. Why, specifically, am I here?

R: You are going to talk about Gil Hodges and that you want him to be in the Hall of Fame.

J: You want to know something interesting? The Atlanta Braves, playing the Red Sox, used to play in Boston, too.

R: How?

J: You know how in New York, we have the New York Yankees and the New York Mets? And in Chicago, there's the White Sox and the Cubs?

R: (Ryan nods enthusiastically)

J: In Boston, there were the Boston Braves and the Boston Red Sox.

R: Oh? Boston Braves! How'd they go to Atlanta?

J: First they went to Milwaukee for twelve years or so, and then they moved from Milwaukee to Atlanta. But they used to be in Boston, and some of the people at the conference are talking about the Boston Braves.

R: Oh, like you're doing Gil Hodges, they're talking about that.

J: Now, the other question I wanted to ask you is who are some of your other favorite players in baseball?

R: Nomar (Garciaparra), Robin Ventura.

J: He plays third base just like you.

R: Bobby Valentine.

J: The Mets manager?

R: Yes. And Derek Jeter. I do not like [the pitcher] who hit Mike Piazza. (With a ball, and nearly with a bat.)

J: Roger Clemens.

R: Do you?

J: No. And he's not very popular here in Boston, either. He used to play for the Red Sox, but he left.

R: Why did he leave?

J: Because he wanted to be paid more money, so he left Boston. When he comes here to pitch for the Yankees, the fans boo him, like they do in Shea Stadium.

R: Why?

J: Because they don't like him. He left their team.

J: Now Ryan wants to interview me.

R: Who do you want tonight?

J: I want the Red Sox to win. It helps the Mets if Atlanta loses. The Mets can move up.

PART II: THE GAME (AT FENWAY PARK)

J: We're here outside of Fenway Park. What do you think?

R: It's good!

J: We're here with our friends (Angela, Bob, and Geno) and Mom. Fenway Park looks different from Shea Stadium, doesn't it?

R: Some parts are the same.

J: But we're here in fair territory, so if someone hits it to you, it's a home run. There aren't many seats like this at Shea Stadium. What do you think of the Green Monster? Pretty high up, isn't it?

R: Different from Shea Stadium.

J: John Burkett is pitching for the Red Sox. He won't hit because this is the American League. Pitchers don't hit.

R: Why not?

J: The American League has a rule that the pitchers don't hit, because they usually don't do well anyway. It's called the DH: designated hitter.

R: Where is Nomar?

J: He's over there at shortstop for the Red Sox. Number 5. At second base there is Carlos Baerga. He used to play for the Mets.

R: Why do the Braves have that axe?

J: That's a tomahawk. That's for the Braves: they represent Native Americans, who sometimes used tomahawks.

J: Pitching for the Braves is Greg Maddux, probably the best pitcher in baseball. I wrote an article about him once. Maddux doesn't throw real hard, but he fools them. That was 86 miles per hour.

R: How does he fool them?

J: He changes speeds and he can put the ball in a good location, right on the plate where they think it's going to be a ball, but at the last second it's a strike. He's very good at that.

R: There's not going to be a ball that comes to us.

J: There might. A left handed batter might hit it this far.

(Later)

J: Looks like Greg Maddux might be hurt, Ryan, by that hit by Baerga. They're checking him out.

R: Who's that?

J: The trainer is checking him out.

(A while later: Garciaparra up)

J: There's Nomar, Ryan.

R: Nomar's gonna hit a homer.

J: He got a base hit, Ryan! Baerga's going to second.

R: He is good.

(Fans boo)

R: What happened?

J: Baerga got picked off of second. Maddux threw to second and got him out. Now there are two outs. Deuces wild.

R: What's that mean?

J: A deuce is a two. Two balls, two strikes, two outs. Twos all over the place.

R: What are bleachers?

J: These are the seats in the outfield, and there is no overhang. See over there, by third base, there is some overhang. But there is none here, so you would get "bleached" by the sun, like clothes. They have these at Yankee stadium too.

R: A guy was selling tickets, and he said "bleachers."

R: Why do they put that fence over there behind home plate?

J: They are trying to protect the fans because a lot of foul balls are hit back there, and they don't want them dodging fouls all the time.

R: So they don't have to waste baseballs?

J: That too, but a lot of time they won't put them back in the game with a little cut on them.

J: There is a very famous home run hit in this park by Carlton Fisk. It was Game 6 of the World Series in 1975, and in extra innings, he hit a home run over the Green Monster, into the net, I think. He was moving his arms hoping the ball wouldn't go foul. I have a tape of it I'll show you some time.

R: Did he hit the Cherry Coke [sign]?

J: I don't think the sign was there.

R: The Green Monster doesn't look so big.

J: It doesn't look big? Look at the man standing at the base of the wall. Look how high it goes. Remember the wall at Shea Stadium? I jumped up and touched the top of it. You couldn't jump up and touch the top of that. You have to hit it that high to be a home run.

(A while later: a cheer goes up from the crowd)

J: See that? Hillenbrand hit it off the Green Monster. He got a double. When the wall is high like that, you might not get a home run, but you can hit it off the wall and get a double.

R: What are they doing?

J: The concession guy is throwing peanuts to the people who want them when they are far away.

R: Is that a double?

J: It was a single. Bragg walked, and then Franco hit the single, and Bragg went to third. That's a good play, to take the extra base.

R: They scored a run?

J: Yes. Bragg was on third, and he scored when Lockhart grounded into the double play.

R: Why did they throw to second and back to first?

J: If they went to first first, they would have to tag the guy at second, and that's hard to do sometimes. All they have to do if they get the out at second first is tag the base, because he is forced.

(A while later: playing game announcers)

R: Baerga's up, runner on third, one out, third inning at the bottom. (sic) Atlanta's winning, 1 to nothing.

J: Here's the pitch...

R: Ball!

R: Here's the pitch...

R: Oooo, good swing!

R: Strrrrrrike!

R: And the pitch...

R: Foul ball. One and two, one out.

R: Both teams have no errors.

R: Nice swing.

J: Strikes him out. Now who's up?

R: Nomar Garciaparra! The fans are cheering.

J: Here it is...

R: Base hit!

J: They called it a hit. Not an error. Nomar on first, two outs, Manny Ramirez up.

J: And the count is one and one.

R: The fans are clapping.

J: There he goes: Nomar steals second! Three and one count, runner on second.

J: Three and one count to Brian Daubach, two outs, Ramirez on first.

R: Walks him.

J: That is uncharacteristic of Maddux to give up the walk there. They're talking to him now.

(A while later: after an unsuccessful trip to see Bosox mascot Wally, the Green Monster)

J: Okay, we went under the stands to the store, and what did you get?

R: A Red Sox pin, with an American flag.

J: What else?

R: A Nomar shirt, and French fries.

J: Top of the seventh inning. Good game so far, huh, Ryan?

R: Do they have the seventh inning stretch?

J: They will after this half inning.

R: So it's three balls, one strike, top of the seventh.

J: Gary Sheffield walks, bringing up Chipper Jones.

J: Aces wild: one ball, one strike, one out one on.

J: Chipper Jones is an excellent hitter.

R: That is why he makes Looney Tunes. (Reference to animator Chuck Jones. This is like having Phil Rizzuto as your broadcast partner)

J: Key pitch here. Center fielder has it.

J: One ball, two strikes on Andruw Jones.

R: He spells Andrew a different way.

J: He is from Curaçao. He's out.

R: It's the seventh-inning stretch.

J: Right now the Yankees are beating the Mets 8 to 5 in the seventh inning.

R: It's bad.

J: The Red Sox gotta win.

R: C'mon, Red Sox!

J: Chris Hammond is now pitching for the Braves. Bottom of the seventh.

R: What's WEEI mean? That weird "Weei" it says under "Fenway Park?"

J: That is W-E-E-I, the radio station that broadcasts the Red Sox games.

J: Three and one count. He walks, it brings up the top of the order. First and second, one out.

R: If they hit a home run, it will be three runs, and it will be 4-2. C'mon!

J: Pops it up. Castilla catches it. Two outs.

J: It's off the Green Monster! Left fielder can't get it. Second and third, tied it up!

R: It was a nice play. Here's the replay (on the score-board). When they started screaming, I thought it would be a home run!

R: Nomar!

J: Everyone's excited Nomar's up.

R: Yep.

(A while later: playing game announcers)

J: Two balls and no strikes. He's gotta throw a good

pitch or there will be three balls on him. Nomar is gonna look for the ball in a certain spot, and if it's there, he's gonna crush it.

R: You mean hit it!

J: Three and oh.

R: Yep.

J: They'll bring in Darren Holmes to face Manny [Ramirez].

R: Let's get a ball!

J: There it is: the unintentional intentional walk.

R: They walked him!

J: The bases are loaded with Sox.

R: This is a fun day!

J: They are gonna wait to the last minute to change pitchers. They are going to bring in the guy warming up in the bullpen in front of us here.

R: Manny be good! Let's hit a home run. We'll get four runs! We'll have six!

J: What do they call a homerun with the bases loaded?

R: Grand Slam!

J: A lotta people standing up around the park, Ryan.

R: Why are they standing up?

J: They are excited.

R: (Joining the chant) Man-ny! Man-ny! Man-ny!

R: Why are they booing?

J: Because the pitcher threw it over his head. But he's not trying to hit him. If he does, Manny goes to first, all the runners move up, and the Red Sox take the lead.

R: But if he swings, he won't.

J: Big cut. One and one. You think Manny's trying to hit a home run?

R: Yes. That was a good swing.

J: He only has nine homers, but he has a lot of power.

J: Long foul. One ball two strikes. On the roof.

R: What do you mean "on the roof?"

J: He hit it on the first base side over there. See the light? It went on the roof up there on top of the stands.

R: He did? Cool!

J: Pretty far, huh?

R: Yeah. (Joining the chant) Man-ny! Man-ny! Man-ny!

J: (Ramirez hits a shot) Ry! Ry! Oh, Chipper Jones catches it on the warning track.

R: All those persons on base for nothing!

J: So it's the top of the eighth inning, tied two-two, one out, and the count is one and one on Darren Bragg.

R: We have two errors.

J: That's right. We missed a few errors when we were under the stands.

R: Why are they booing?

J: They thought that pitch was a strike, but he called it a ball. One and oh, runner on first, one out.

R: Boo!

J: Two and oh to Henry Blanco. Alan Embree pitching, and the Red Sox have "El Guapo" (Rich Garces) warming up.

J: There's a fight in the stands. Five policemen are there, and some security.

R: Why are they fighting?

J: I don't know. Probably drinking too much alcohol. I don't believe they are SABR members.

J: Lost him. First and second, one out.

R: Top of the eighth.

J: And the police have brought the fighters out.

R: They got rid of them?

J: Yeah, they brought them out of the stadium.

J: And now the Red Sox are bringing in Rich Garces to face the righty pinch hitter Wes Helms.

R: Why are they cheering?

J: They like this guy.

R: Is he good?

J: He's an okay reliever.

(Ryan walks down to the bullpen and watches the rest of the game standing there. Not wanting to get in the vision of other fans, we terminated the inteview.)

EPILOGUE: ONE YEAR LATER

J: Ryan, do you remember the game we went to at Fenway Park in Boston last year?

R: Yes, I do. We saw the Boston Red Sox versus Atlanta Braves.

J: What do you remember about Fenway Park?

R: Well, I remember the wall called the Green Monster in left field. It was tall! Shea Stadium has the Big Apple that comes up when the Mets hit a home run. Fenway Park is a little smaller.

J: That is true. Did you feel closer to the action at Fenway?

R: We sat at the top, so we mostly saw everything, but we weren't very close to what they were doing.

J: What is your favorite place to see a game?

R: I like them all, but Shea Stadium is mostly what I see.

J: They are talking about building a new field for the Mets. We recently saw a game at Coors Field. Would you rather the new Mets Stadium look like Coors Field, Fenway Park, or Shea Stadium?

R: I want them to stay at Shea Stadium, but Coors Field is good too.

J: Shea Stadium is like home to me, but if I had a choice, I'd pick Fenway.

R: Fenway is a little too small for a lot of people to go.

J: You have done some interesting baseball things in the last year. What did you do at school?

R: We did this report at school on a person's biography. We had to read the book and make a[n oral] report on it. You had to memorize it and then dress up as the person.

J: Whose biography did you choose?

R: I chose Jackie Robinson. I know what you are going to say next, what did he do in his life? He was born in Cairo, Georgia, and he was the first black man to play in the major leagues.

J: What team did he play for?

R: The Brooklyn Dodgers.

J: What was his happiest day?

R: He had courage, and his happiest day was when the Dodgers won the World Series in 1955.

J: Any other thoughts about Fenway Park? Are you glad you went?

R: I am glad I went to Fenway Park. We had never been to Boston together. Can I ask you questions?

J: Sure.

R: So how did you like Fenway Park?

J: I liked it very much. I wanted to see it before they do something stupid like tear it down. They don't insult your intelligence by telling the fans when to cheer, and they give good, up-to date stats for each player. And the Green Monster was pretty cool.

R: What is your favorite place to see a game?

J: Anywhere, as long as I'm next to you.

UP ON THE ROOF

F.X. Flinn

It's the last half of the eighth inning, and Tanner Maguire has a serious case of rotating ad hypnosis. He's fixated on a 10-inch TV monitor across the room that brings the game-as-broadcast into his part of the Fenway control room. In his left hand is a stopwatch, and each time the regular broadcast shows the ad behind home plate, Tanner fires up the stopwatch and times the appearance of the ad on the screen. At the end of the half inning, he'll record the number of seconds the ad appeared on a clipboard, and then he'll call up the ad for the next half inning. The ad rotator behind the plate is his to command on behalf of his employer, A&C Sports Marketing.

Tanner is one of about a dozen people working in the control room at Fenway Park. There's the public address announcer, the scoreboard controller, the special effects driver, the musical director, two guys from Major League Baseball, three Red Sox video department employees, the organist, two interns who provide back-up assistance, and Danny Kischel, the director. Other Red Sox employees and vendors turn up from time to time during the game to take a gander at operations or check on plans for particular moments in the game.

Tony Rose and Ellen Teitel are the principle drivers of the scoreboard tonight. Earlier in the day they down-loaded the team rosters from the MLB office in New York, and today it was mostly correct—one of the ballplayers had changed his uniform number. This is a big change from the past, when the roster database used by the scoreboard had to be constructed manually for each series. Still, MLB doesn't always have the rosters right either; the vagaries of teams reporting transactions makes roster tracking a chore (note to Rotisserie players: teams provide the active rosters to the umps, press, and control room a few hours before the game. If the press doesn't report a change, it's usually because a note about the change was left off the roster list). Ellen generates the scores onto the boards as they come in and as events in the game require.

The public address announcer, Ed Brickley, shares the catbird seats in the control room with Rose. The two of them sit at the windows of the control room, which sits on the Fenway roof at the first-base end of the structure that houses the press boxes and Red Sox offices. Close behind them are walls about five feet high and a small stairway down to their aerie. Ascending the stairs into the front half of the control room, we find Tanner to our right with one of the interns, and Ellen to our left, with Danny Kischel taking a seat at a workstation behind Ellen. This smallish 'room' has crane-your-necks views of action on the field, but an outstanding unobstructed view of the scoreboard through the glass wall.

This view is important because the scoreboard is the focus of the control room team, one of the three methods the Red Sox use to communicate to the fans, the other two being the PA announcer and the organist. The organist (tonight it is Ray Totaro), sits in what must be the smallest room in Fenway, a room within a room, just wide enough to hold the keyboards and just tall enough to allow Ray to sit on a piano bench and play. This may also be Boston's tiniest workplace, but since it is built into the front half of the control room, on the right when your back is to the field (and just above where Tanner is sitting documenting the TV time the rotating ads are getting), it has a window that looks down over the PA announcer and scoreboard operator, giving Totaro one of Fenway's best seats. Seeing all, he can respond with a little arpeggio or chord, emphasizing the dramatic and the silly with a direct, immediate musical language. Ray's desire to deliver musically things people can take home with them shines through when his rousing "Take Me Out to the Ballgame" produces smiles everywhere the TV cameras look.

Amy Toby has taken on a similar task tonight. She's running the piped-in recorded music using a Click Effects machine. Ellen runs the Hood Milk Bottle with a low-tech switchbox. The milk bottle has a routine all fans are familiar with, but it does have its random moments that come as the operator's mood strikes, or as voices in the booth beg her to use the effect.

Danny sits at his desk like the captain of an aircraft carrier, the big windows giving him a view of the distant horizon but precious little of what happens on the field. He's got a "bug free" feed of the game on instead —the raw video without any of the text displays, superimposed ads, or other ephemera known to the entertainment trade as bugs. But early in the game, he's looking through a massive binder containing hundreds of CDs. The great mod (or was he a rocker?) bassist, John Entwhistle, the musical pillar of The Who, has passed away on this very day and Danny is determined to play "Boris the Spider" in tribute. He quickly finds their early album *Meaty, Beaty Big and Bouncy* and the track is queued up to be played during the first-inning changeover.

Two interns, Darren Gordon and Josh Silverstein, hang out waiting for Danny or Tony or anyone else to give them something to do. Today Josh has already spent six hours getting the player head shots ready for the scoreboard and Darren has been out running errands. The sweet part of the internship gig happens now, as they stand like ensigns on the flagship watching the admirals and captains command and, not for nothing, take in a ballgame.

Behind the group in the forward control room is another equally large group of people in the back, where there are no windows, and each of them is paying rapt attention to one or more monitors. These are jobs for technically adept twenty-somethings with good eyesight (not one of them is wearing glasses). Working clockwise around a room chock-a-bloc with television monitors, computer displays, racks full of video devices and computers, we find a three-person team coordinating the video feeds to the scoreboard and two employees of Major League Baseball: one is compiling a video database of the game (SABR researchers of 2102, take note); the other is operating the then-unpublicized and now-notorious Ques-Tec strike zone evaluator.

For the gang of three running the video component of the scoreboard, their job is quickly described the same way pilots describe theirs: hours of boredom punctuated by moments of sheer terror. In this case, the routine of delivering player photographs and stats, ads and "pump up" effects to the scoreboard is interrupted by the need to rapidly deploy replays of the action. This year, the new ownership has funded some slick new video equipment that lets the Red Sox control room capture, edit and playback their own replays, which means that when there is a play that deserves it, the operators have to swing into action and produce a clip in a matter of 30 seconds or so.

Glenn Schwartz, who is on the replays tonight, can mark the stream of the game at any point, return to that point, and then mark an endpoint. This clip is then transferred to "switcher" Christine Wychorski's control, and she generates the video to the scoreboard. Christine is working alongside Stephanie Vincent tonight, showing her the ropes. Stephanie stays on top of moving the head shots of the players to the scoreboard when they come to bat. As plays develop on the field, there is much animated conversation at the board. "This is going up! [will be a replay]… Okay, get ready… wow, did you see that? Okay here is the clip… Got it!... Okay there it is…. Listen to the crowd…. play it again…. play it again." The three-headed, six-handed team gracefully produces a TV show within a show for the crowd. In a quiet moment between innings they rave about the resources the new ownership has provided their department.

Proceeding to the very

depths of the control room we find the crown jewels of future baseball research being mined. Who among SABRen does not lust for access to a database from which might be retrieved a video record of such banalities as Tinker to Evers to Chance or Merkle's Boner, or Pesky's Slumber, or the Babe's Called Shot? Who among SABRen doesn't lust for a chance to, say, pull up all Ken Keltner's fielding chances during 1941? But these a trivial examples for students of the physics of the game, who might actually give their eyeteeth for access to a database which provides a 4 point tracked location and time value in 4 dimensions for each pitch thrown in a particular game by, say, Walter Johnson or Satchel Paige.

Well.

This is the data MLB is collecting in the control room bowels of ballparks today. One's mind drifts back to Bud Selig's promise at the Milwaukee convention to make MLB research assets more available to SABR researchers working through the SABR office, and what this promise will mean to SABRen in two or five or twenty or fifty or a thousand years. It is as if a great window on the past is opened, and we living now are the first of those who will be able to waive back to our descendants, cheering them on, validating their obsession with our existence.

Tonight the MLB Tape Retrieval Program Stadium Logger is Errol Hudson, sitting with the bug-free feed and entering free-form commentary on each play in a Microsoft Access database application from Nesbit Systems. What is really needed here is someone from Project Scoresheet marking the conclusion of each play in Scoresheet format and preparing

Wynn Montgomery

Positives (SABRites)

* *Did the SABRite-laden RF bleachers set a Major League record for scorebooks per capita?*

* *I experienced a microcosm of baseball fandom, sitting between a 70ish Michigander who sees 20 or so Tiger games every year and a young North Carolinian who was seeing his first Major League game.*

Negatives (Non-SABRites, I'm sure!)

* *"The Wave" in Fenway? If it isn't illegal, it is certainly sacrilegious.*

* *Even if it is true that "Yankees Suck," how is that relevant at a Braves-Red Sox game?*

the video for searching against that database. That would be a considerable value-add to this MLB effort; one wonders why or how baseball could go to the considerable expense of building such a data collection system without making it searchable in a highly atomic fashion—something the use of Project Scoresheet notation would radically simplify. As it stands, the free form commentary doesn't begin to do justice to the video data being captured.

Finally, in the deepest corner of the control room, hunched over a laptop and small black and white TV, is Derek Gagne, operating the Ques-Tec umpire evaluation system. Each time a pitch is thrown, four cameras pick up on the ball and through a triangulation algorithm produce four sets of ball positions at four different points in time. The cameras are positioned at each dugout and on the roof above first and third base. The data collected for each pitch tracks velocity changes and movement changes enroute to determining where in space the ball traversed the area between the batters boxes.

Quite aside from the umpire evaluations, this will be a rich trove for future researchers interested in questions about pitch movement, the effect of weather conditions on pitch movement, the velocity differentials between pitches of similar types, all of it sliced and diced by pitcher, situation and result.

For the umps, though, the system works by determining the position in space where the pitch crossed the plate and comparing the Ques-Tec "call" with the actual call. Strike zone calibration for each pitch of the game is done after the game is over; during the game, the operator records the result of each pitch in an Access database. Once the game ends, Derek replays each called pitch (as distinct from warm-ups, hits, fouls, and the like), choosing one of the dugout angles to see the hitter face-on. The operator performs the "human element" that umpires in the summer of 2003 will decry as "inconsistent" when he positions a super-imposed horizontal line at the "bottom of the batter's front knee" and "two ball diameters" above the "belt buckle." These lines tell the system where the top and bottom of the strike zone is located; the system already knows where the edges of the plate are. It isn't rocket science and the difference between what one operator might choose and another wouldn't amount to more than a quarter of the ball's diameter. Derek takes this part of his job very seriously and works intently to get it right. I watch him do 20 pitches and never disagree with his positions. The result of the analysis is then stored with the rest of the record of the pitch, and these results are then dispatched to MLB headquarters. Derek has no way of knowing what the system reports. [The park also has one other umpire evaluator, Kevin Connor, who views the game from down in the seats.—Eds.]

Having thoroughly explored the control room, one might now imagine turning around and heading back toward the field, into the upper control room, where Tanner sits now, late in the ballgame, one hand clenching a stopwatch, eyes glued to the television 12 feet away, waiting to mark the time the ads appear on screen during the Red Sox half of the eighth. A look around the room shows each person in turn with the same intense concentration on the task at hand; the hubbub of the early part of the game giving way to the quiet of the devoted yet weary worker. They all have real jobs to do, no less for the fact that they do them up on Fenway's roof while the Old Towne team toils below.

THE INNER SANCTUM

Jim Prime

For a lifelong Red Sox fan, it was an experience of a lifetime. Bill "Spaceman" Lee once said that Fenway Park is a shrine, you should enter it as you would enter a church. If that is so, and I believe it is, walking into the Red Sox dressing room is akin to scaling Mount Olympus and having an opportunity to observe the Pantheon of gods at rest between miracles. The fact that these miracles would soon be performed just a 5-3 throw away (if you are scoring at home), made me feel even more blessed. After all, working their wonders for 33,000 paying worshippers was one thing, but how many actually got to see these immortals being mortal?

I was fortunate to have two views of the dressing room—before the game and after. I'm sure there are two versions of the "after" dressing room, as well. The one I witnessed—after a loss to the Atlanta Braves—was a very different place from the one I had witnessed some 3 hours and 10 minutes earlier.

As with a climb up Mount Olympus, one must earn one's visit to the Red Sox' inner sanctum. In this case the challenge involves a treacherous trek through a Dickensian alley leading from the Red Sox dugout. The alley features a urinal just out of the view of TV cameras and, on this sodden day at least, rough planks to keep feet from getting soaked by the residual rainfall of the night before. Still, it is hard not to think of the legendary Red Sox players who have emerged from this brief, dingy purgatory to the verdant Elysian Fields beyond.

With the trepidation of the transgressor, I approach the dressing room door. I pause. Taking several deep breaths, I enter. Just inside the locker room door, guarding the entrance like baseball's version of St. Peter at the golden gate, sits sprightly, saintly Johnny Pesky.

Appropriately every player, coming and going, has to pass Mr. Red Sox. Very few are spared his bawdy benedictions. Fewer still fail to return them. When veteran second baseman Carlos Baerga passes, Pesky says: "There he goes, the heart and soul of the Boston Red Sox." Baerga stops in front of the seated Pesky, bends low and kisses him on his knee before exiting for the field. Pope Pesky the Benevolent has bestowed his blessing.

It is a large room with players' cubicles around its circumference. The coaches lockers are on my right. Dewey Evans, a former rightfield god glances up at the intruder. Manager Grady Little nods his welcome. I looked around and see Nomar, Ted Williams' chosen disciple, next to his friend Lou Merloni's. On the far side is Pedro Martinez. A card game is in full bustle, with Rickey Henderson the most vocal player. Music of the generation fills the room, and I wonder if the music of the sixties helped inspire Carl Yastrzemski to his 1967 Impossible Dream, or if Ted listened to Sinatra before homering in his last at bat.

After several minutes, Nomar rises from his place and walks toward the door en route to the field. He makes eye contact with the intruder. I stick out my hand and introduce myself as the guy who had interviewed him once on the phone. To my surprise and delight, he remembers me. This 27-year-old millionaire remembers the guy from Nova Scotia who once called to ask him questions about Ted Williams. He flashes a friendly smile designed to extricate himself from further chitchat, nods to Pesky and is gone, soon to reappear on the field to similar adoration from younger hero-worshippers and autograph seekers. After all, what is an autograph but an attempt to gain a measure of immortality by association? After a memorable conversation with Johnny Pesky, whom I had met before, I leave the inner sanctum.

In the roughly 3 hours and 10 minutes that elapsed between my two visits, the Boston Red Sox lost a baseball game to the visiting Atlanta Braves.

It was an ugly, unnecessary loss. Going into the contest, both teams were leading their divisions. After the game, the Red Sox were looking up at the—wait for it—first-place New York Yankees. Their record in interleague play had fallen to a dismal 5-11. Knuckleballing reliever Tim Wakefield took the loss. With the score knotted at 2-2, Wakefield took the mound in the top of the ninth inning. Braves DH Gary Sheffield, hitless to that point in the game, doubled. Wakefield settled down retiring the next two batters, but third baseman Vinny Castilla singled, scoring Sheffield. Former Red Sox Darren Bragg then walked and catcher Henry Blanco doubled to plate the second run of the inning. The Red Sox went quietly in the bottom of the ninth in the 4-2 defeat. Wakefield was wearing the goat's horns.

After the game, the locker room was a somber place. The pall that had been cast by this loss was palpable. The gods were angry. One god had fallen from grace, if only for a short while. There was no music. No card games. No muffled laughter and no nods of greeting. Resentful glances greeted interlopers. Cadres of beat reporters were gathered tentatively around Tim Wakefield and Jason Varitek. Players were economical with their answers to questions. Reporters seemed to treat the Red Sox with kid gloves, a fact I mentioned to a reporter from the *Boston Herald*. His reasonable response was that unlike the columnists—the Shaughnessys and Ryans—the working press did not have the luxury of criticizing and provoking and cajoling. They had to have access to these temperamental gods day after day. A reporter who was denied access to players was of limited use to his or her employer. Was this the way it had been when Ted Williams held court? I wondered. Did reporters allow for his moods after tough losses? I doubted it.

Wakefield and Varitek faced the music. "Timmy did a good job," insisted the gallant Varitek. "Balls just fell in. He threw a lot of balls that were moving extremely well." Especially as they crossed home plate, I thought. But of course, I didn't say anything.

The gods were in no mood.

PART THREE:
EXTRA INNINGS

ATLANTA 48-30 vs. BOSTON 46-28 at FENWAY PARK   Date FRIDAY NIGHT JUNE 28, 2002

MGR G B COX 30
1B 17 G HUBBARD 5 N YOST

Atlanta		1	2	3	4	5	6	7	8	9	AB	R	H	RBI
1 FURCAL	6										4		1	
23 J FRANCO	3										5		2	
11 SHEFFIELD	DH										4	1	1	
10 C JONES	9-51 7										5			
24 A JONES	8										4		1	
19 CASTILLA	5										5	1	1	1
28 BRAGG	9										2	2	2	
20 BLANCO	2										4		2	1
MADDUX LOCKHART											3		1	
18 W HELMS	Pit 4													
4 M FRANCO														
2 J GARCIA	4										36	4	11	3

19:06

E- ATL 1   BOS 11
CASTILLA BAERGA
GARCIAPARRA

DP- ATL 1   BOS 1

LOB- ATL 14 BOS 8

2B- HILLENBRAND BAERGA
SHEFFIELD BLANCO

3B-

HR-

SB- OFFERMAN
GARCIAPARRA
SHEFFIELD

Pitching Summary		INN. ENT.	IP	H	R	ER	BB	SO	NP		
31 MADDUX 7-2			5	3	1	0	1	4	74/43		CS-
49 GRYBOSKI 2-1 .44		6	1				2	0	18/5	18/8 19/10	
36 C HAMMOND 2-1		7	4/3	2	1	1	2		18/11		S-
40 D HOLMES 1.65		7	1/3						4/3	4/3	
51 REMLINGER W 4-0		8	1				1	1	10/5	10/5 10/9	
29 SMOLTZ SAVE 26		9	1					1	11/10		SF-

MGR J G LITTLE
51 T HARPER 39 CUBZABA

Boston		1	2	3	4	5	6	7	8	9	AB	R	H	RBI
18 J DAMON	8										5			
10 BAERGA	4										4		2	1
5 GARCIAPARRA	6										3		1	
24 M RAMIREZ	7										3			
23 DAUBACH	3										2	0		
35 R HENDERSON											0			
22 T CLARK											0			
29 HILLENBRAND	5										4		1	
33 VARITEK	2										4	1	1	

HBP-

WP-

PB-

Balk-

Notes:
76° W ENE AT 8 MPH

STRAT-O-MATIC RECREATION

Dick Dahl

The 1,000-or-so Major League players who live inside my computer are a great bunch of guys. They play for free, yet they never complain. And I mean never. I've summoned these fellows onto the field to play games at 5 o'clock in the morning, and I've yet to hear a whimper or a whine. So on Saturday, June 29, 2002, when I called upon 42 of them to replay (more or less) the previous night's Braves-Red Sox game at Fenway Park, they did so as cheerfully as always.

They are, of course, ballplayer simulations—in this case, part of the 2001 edition of the Strat-O-Matic computer-baseball game. I've been a Strat devotee for many years, stretching back to the days when their only baseball-simulation product was a board game, which I loved. But when they came out with the computer game—I bought my first one in 1994—there was no turning back. The board game was great, but it had certain drawbacks. Employing a set of three dice and hundreds of player cards, each containing a maze of numbers and symbols, the board game produced amazingly lifelike results.

But playing the game properly required at least an hour of initial study—meaning that playing the game with someone who wasn't familiar with it was more trouble than it was worth. I did have one Strat-playing friend, but much to my disappointment, I found that playing against him was often unpleasant because he was quicker at identifying the dice/card result than I was. Too often, just as I was sliding my index finger down my batter's card in hopeful anticipation that he'd just gotten a hit, my friend was punching the air with his fist and whooping in celebration of the fact that my guy had, in fact, just whiffed. Annoying.

So for the most part, I opted to play Strat against

myself—a slightly bizarre activity, I must confess. I actually would manage two teams simultaneously, making decisions for Team A based on what I thought the manager of Team B (myself) would do. And vice versa. It was disturbing behavior, and therefore enjoyable in its own perverse way. But of course that isn't how baseball is meant to be played.

That all changed when I bought my first Strat computer game. No longer did I have to live with the dark secret that I played Strat against myself because with the new game I could now match wits against the computer. The computerized Strat includes a virtual manager named Hal, who, like the players, is available day and night for a spirited run. Furthermore, the computerized Strat greatly opened opportunities for friendly games with baseball-loving guests willing to give the game a shot because the burying of all the hieroglyphics within a game that is now point-and-click meant that a newcomer could get up to speed in 10 minutes. The computer game also meant no more annoying opponents with faster eyes than mine because now the result was immediately evident on the screen.

I've updated my game with new annual versions several times since, and there have been a variety of little tweaks to make the game more lifelike. But the cheesy look of the game has remained about the same. You get a black-and-white photo backdrop of whatever big-league park you want (color ones are available, but cost extra) and the players are mere names (accompanied by various numbers that bespeak his abilities) occupying their positions on the field and in the batters box. Plays are described in an often cornballish play-by-play text function and the ball is a moving blip. Your average teenage computer gamer would howl in derision at Strat's archaic effects. But a true baseball fan shouldn't care about the absence of glitz because in terms of pure result, this is a game that is very much like the real thing.

Meanwhile, I've saved the best for last: Computer Strat has an automatic statistics function. That is, if you have created a league and are playing a schedule, the statistics from each game automatically get shipped to a statistical center that breaks information down into vast minutiae, player by player and team by team. It even provides ongoing lists of the top 10 players in various categories, just like newspapers do. Over the years, I've created quite a variety of my own leagues. Usually, they're small leagues of 8 to 12 teams playing a short schedule of 40 to 60 games. Usually, I'll select players to stock each team's large 40-man roster randomly and then cull it down to 25. I'll pick one team—prior to the random draft—as mine, just to give myself something to root for. Then I manage my team, against Hal, each game it plays. In all the other games, Hal manages both teams, a task that he can accomplish by effectively splitting himself into two beings—a trick that I'd always failed to master when I played against myself with the board game. In those dual-Hal games, I just watch, a scout in the stands taking notes that might help me when I play either of these teams down the road.

Over the course of a season, just like in baseball, strange things happen. A number-five starter throws a no-hitter. A .250 hitter goes on a tear. During the last season I played, late this past winter, I pegged my team, the Boston Body Snatchers (home park: Fenway) as a good bet to finish in the upper tier of its six-team division. Barry Zito was my ace. The core of my lineup seemed solid, with Bret Boone, Jeff Bagwell, Bobby Abreu, Rondell White, Frank Catalanotto, and Brian Jordan. While I guessed that I lacked the stuff to compete with the mighty Worcester Warriors (home field: Camden Yards), I also saw that my team had no glaring weaknesses. Inexplicably, however, the Body Snatchers stumbled badly out of the box, losing repeatedly. Distraught, I tried everything. I diddled with the lineup, brought up minor leaguers, swung a deal for Rafael Furcal. Nothing helped. Then, with a record of 8 and 20, everything changed. My Snatchers reeled off an 11-game winning streak. Then they won 13 out of the final 21 games to finish above .500 at 32-28, alone in third place, right where I thought they should be all along.

BRAVES VS. RED SOX, 6/28/02

It is impossible to create an exact simulation of the

June 28 game at Fenway Park, won by the Braves, 4-2, because the players I have available in my computer are 2001 versions. In addition, some guys on the rosters the night of June 28 either didn't play in the bigs in 2001 or had only a cup of September coffee, thus producing statistically skewed results that render them useless in a simulation. I did my best, though, and I think I came pretty close. In order to approximate the June 28 rosters, I had to delete some players from the 2001 rosters and add others by copying and pasting them from the rosters they occupied then. Counting the heads of those who didn't play in the majors last year or who played too little, I came up with four per side. So I would play the simulation with 21 per team. For the Red Sox, that meant the absence of that night's starting second baseman, Carlos Baerga, who was out of baseball last year; relief pitcher Chris Haney and utility man Bryant Nelson, who were in the minors; and Willie Banks, who pitched just 11 innings (0.84 E.R.A.) last year. For the Braves, it meant the loss of first baseman Matt Franco and relief pitcher Kevin Gryboski, who were in the minors last year; and two 2001 late-season call-ups, infielder Jesse Garcia (5 at-bats, .200 average) and pitcher Tim Spooneybarger (4 innings pitched. 2.25 E.R.A.).

In terms of the 20 players comprising the starting lineups, however, only one player was missing: Baerga. Which meant that I had to replace the Sox' top hitter for the month of June with Lou Merloni, a net gain for the Braves. But in assessing all the differences between the 2001 simulations I used and the real 2002 guys who played the night of June 28, I conclude that neither side enjoyed a significant replay advantage. For the Braves, the differences between the starting 10's 2001 stats and the 2002 numbers they brought to Fenway Park on June 28 were remarkably tiny. The Greg Maddux who started on the hill that night with an E.R.A. of 3.20 was very close to the guy who finished 2001 at 17-11, 3.05. The Red Sox simulation, on the other hand, was more of a mixed bag. The John Burkett who would pitch in my computer was an upgrade from the guy who pitched June 28 in Fenway. Last year, his E.R.A. was 3.04, and he

entered the game on June 28 at 4.04. The simulated Sox also would enjoy the truly lethal threat of a healthy Manny Ramirez who on the night of June 28, freshly returned from a long hiatus on the DL, was still feeling his way back. The Burkett/Ramirez upgrade, however, was countered by several other factors. In addition to the loss of Baerga, my computer replay would also include playing with the 2001 versions of Johnny Damon, Shea Hillenbrand, and Nomar Garciaparra, all lesser players than the ones in the June 28 lineup. In the bullpen, my replay Sox would have a much better Rich Garces and a much worse Allan Embree. The Braves, meanwhile, would feel the acute absence of Gryboski, who had emerged as their top right-handed setup guy, and, to a lesser extent, Spooneybarger. But with the 2001 versions of Darren Holmes, Kerry Ligtenberg, Mike Remlinger, and John Smoltz all healthy for this single game divorced from the rigors and pitcher-fatigue levels of a regular schedule, I figured the Braves should enjoy their usual top-notch relief help.

After I assembled the rosters, it dawned on me that I really should replay the game twice: once with Hal managing both teams and again with me managing the Sox against Hal. So that's what I did. Following are the results:

Game One, Hal managing both teams. Red Sox 3, Braves 0.

They say that if you're going to get to Greg Maddux, like many great pitchers, you've got to get him early. In this game, the Red Sox proved the wisdom of that adage, bunching four of their six hits off Maddux into the second inning, when they scored the game's only runs. In the other seven innings, they did almost nothing with him. With one out in the second, Brian Daubach singled to right. Hillenbrand also went to right for a single, advancing Daubach to third. Jason Varitek followed with a long double to the triangle in deep center to knock in Daubach, with Hillenbrand stopping at third. Trot Nixon popped out, but Jose Offerman followed with a seeing-eye bouncer through the right side for two runs.

Burkett, meanwhile, was Maddux' equal, shutting

down the Braves on six hits over six innings. He did wobble in the sixth, giving up three hits, but fortune was on his side. First, Furcal swung and missed on a hit and run and Keith Lockhart, who had led off with a single, ended up a dead duck at second. Furcal and Julio Franco followed with singles to keep the threat alive, but Burkett got Gary Sheffield to pop up and then Garciaparra ended the inning by ranging far to his right and making one of his patented plays from the hole to throw out Chipper Jones. Sensing that Burkett had gone far enough, Hal turned to Tim Wakefield, who closed out the shutout with a one-hit three-inning save. I was very surprised that Hal didn't call in Ugueth Urbina in the ninth. With two on and two out in the ninth, Wakefield fanned the tying run, Vinny Castilla, to end the game.

Interesting side note: the normally efficient Maddux racked up an astonishing 137-pitch count over his eight innings. In part, this high number was the result of four Braves errors and in part because even though he was deep into the fatigue zone, he was still retiring Sox hitters with his usual efficiency. So Hal apparently saw no reason to yank him.

Braves	AB	R	H	RBI
Furcal SS	4	0	2	0
J. Franco 1B	4	0	2	0
Sheffield DH	4	0	0	0
C. Jones LF	4	0	0	0
A. Jones CF	4	0	0	0
Castilla 3B	4	0	0	0
Bragg RF	3	0	2	0
Blanco C	3	0	0	0
Lockhart 2B	3	0	1	0
TOTALS	33	0	7	0

Red Sox	AB	R	H	RBI
Damon CF	3	0	1	0
Merloni 2B	4	0	0	0
Garciaparra SS	4	0	0	0
Ramirez LF	4	0	0	0
Daubach 1B	3	1	1	0
Hillenbrand 3B	4	1	1	0
Varitek C	3	1	1	1
Nixon RF	3	0	1	0
Offerman DH	3	0	1	2
TOTALS	31	3	6	3

		R	H	E
Atlanta	000 000 000	0	7	4
Boston	030 000 00X	3	6	1

2B-Furcal, Bragg, Varitek. E-Hillenbrand, Furcal 2, Lockhart, Blanco. Strikeouts-Furcal, Franco, Sheffield, A. Jones, Castilla, Blanco, Lockhart, Damon, Merloni 3, Ramirez 2, Hillenbrand, Varitek, Nixon. Walks-Damon, Daubach. SB-Damon, Nixon. CS-Lockhart. LOB-Braves 6, Red Sox 6.

Braves	IP	H	R	ER	SO	BB	#P
Maddux (L)	8	6	3	3	9	2	137

Red Sox	IP	H	R	ER	SO	BB	#P
Burkett (W)	6	6	0	0	5	0	91
Wakefield (S)	3	1	0	0	2	0	42

Game Two, me managing the Sox against the Braves and Hal. Braves 2, Red Sox 0.

The third match of the troika proved to be the weirdest of the bunch. In one sense, it was pretty much like the first two: a low-scoring game featuring strong performances by Burkett and Maddux. But perhaps because the weather turned foul for this one, creating slippery conditions, a couple of injuries hurt the Sox' chances. Castilla's home run into the screen above the Monster gave the Braves a 1-0 lead in the second. Then, in the third, Garciaparra came up lame after grounding out. Looking at my roster, I saw that the only other shortstop I had available was second baseman Merloni, and the only second baseman I had to replace Merloni was my DH, Offerman. Which meant no more DH and Burkett batting in Garciaparra's vacated three-hole. Other than the dinger to Castilla, Burkett had coasted through six innings on two other harmless hits and two walks. So in the bottom of the sixth, with Burkett due to lead off, I opted to let him bat. A puny hitter, Burkett managed to hit the ball fair, a popup to second. No doubt it was a combination of the mud and his thrill at hitting a fair ball, but just like Nomar, Burkett pulled something on the way to first. He couldn't go on. I turned to Embree, who pitched a 1-2-3 seventh, but in the eighth I called for Garces, who experienced a bit of trouble. Furcal singled, stole both second and third, and scored on a double into the right-center gap by Franco. Meanwhile, my Sox squandered several opportunities. In the second, they loaded the bases with two outs, but Offerman flied out to end the threat. In the seventh, trailing by a run, Nixon doubled with two outs and Hal called for the lefty Mike Remlinger to pitch to Offerman, who again failed, looking at strike three. In the eighth, Daubach had a shot with two on and two out, but Hal turned to John Smoltz, who came on to fan him. Smoltz followed with a 1-2-3 ninth for the save.

Braves	AB	R	H	RBI
Furcal SS	5	1	1	0
J. Franco 1B	4	0	2	1
Sheffield DH	3	0	1	0
C. Jones LF	4	0	0	0
A. Jones CF	4	0	0	0
Castilla 3B	4	1	1	1
Bragg RF	4	0	0	0
Blanco C	3	0	0	0
Lockhart 2B	3	0	1	0
TOTALS	34	2	6	2

Red Sox	AB	R	H	RBI
Damon CF	4	0	0	0
Merloni 2B	4	0	0	0
Garciaparra SS	2	0	0	0
Burkett P	1	0	0	0
Embree P	0	0	0	0
PH Clark (8th)	0	0	0	0
Garces P	0	0	0	0
Wakefield P	0	0	0	0
Ramirez LF	4	0	1	0
Daubach 1B	4	0	1	0
Hillenbrand 3B	4	0	0	0
Varitek C	4	0	1	0
Nixon RF	3	0	2	0
Offerman DH	3	0	0	0
TOTALS	33	0	5	0

		R	H	E
Braves	010 000 010	2	6	0
Red Sox	000 000 000	0	5	1

2B-J. Franco, Sheffield, Nixon. HR-Castilla. E-Hillenbrand. Strikeouts-J. Franco, C. Jones, A. Jones 2, Castilla, Bragg 3, Blanco, Damon 2, Ramirez, Daubach, Varitek 2, Offerman. Walks-Blanco, Lockhart, Clark, Daubach, Nixon. HBP-Sheffield. Stolen bases-Furcal 2. LOB-Braves 8, Red Sox 8.

Braves	IP	H	R	ER	SO	BB	#P
Maddux (W)	6.2	4	0	0	3	2	100
Remlinger	1	1	0	0	2	1	22
Smoltz (S)	1.1	0	0	0	2	0	11

Red Sox	IP	H	R	ER	SO	BB	#P
Burkett (L)	6	3	1	1	5	2	83
Embree	1	0	0	0	0	0	13
Garces	1	2	1	1	2	0	26
Wakefield	1	0	0	0	1	0	11

CITY SERIES RESULTS

Compiled by Phil Bergen

1954
in Milwaukee, Braves (Spahn) 3-1
in Boston, Sox 5-1
Opening day note, Braves Field now officially renamed Boston University Field.

1953
4/9, in Milw. Red Sox 3-0 (2-inning game, rain)
4/11 @ Fenway, Red Sox 4-1
    WP: Skinny Brown, LP: Bob Buhl, A: 9,000
"Braves receive more applause than Sox."
"Those still faithful to the Braves raised louder applause than did the supporters of the winning Red Sox."
4/12 @ Fenway, Braves 4-1
    WP: Jim Wilson, LP: Herschel Freeman, A: 8500, HR: Walker Cooper, Pafko

1952
4/10 @ Braves, Braves 5-4
    WP: Warren Spahn, LP: Bill Wight, A: 5800, HR: Vern Stephens ,Ted Williams: 0/3
4/12 @ Fenway, Red Sox 12-7
    WP: Bill Henry, LP: Vern Bickford, A: 8100, HR: Ted Williams (2), Sammy White, Sam Jethroe
4/13 @ Fenway, Red Sox 2-1
    WP: Rae Scarborough, LP: Jim Wilson, A: 3800, HR: Faye Throneberry

1951
4/13 @ Braves, Red Sox 12-8
    WP: Chuck Stobbs, LP: George Estock, A: 4500, HR: Sid Gordon, Ted Williams: 1/3
4/14 @ Braves, Red Sox 15-8
    WP: Rae Scarborough, LP: Warren Spahn, A: 7100, HR: Ted Williams 3/5 6 RBIs Spahn: 8 runs, 2.1 IP
4/15 @ Fenway, Red Sox 6-3
    WP: Maurice McDermott, LP: Max Surkont, A: 7500, HR: Lou Boudreau, Vern Stephens, Sam Jethroe (4 hits), Ted Williams: 2/4

1950
4/14 @ Braves, postponed, cold weather
4/15 @ Braves, Braves 4-1 (7 inn.)
    WP: Warren Spahn, LP: Joe Dobson

1949
4/16 @ Fenway, Red Sox 3-1
    WP: Chuck Stobbs, LP: Ernie Johnson, A: 14,200

4/14 @ Braves, Red Sox 6-2
    WP: Ellis Kinder, LP: Johnny Sain, A: 7000, HR: Johnny Pesky, Tommy Holmes, Ted Williams: 1/4
4/16 @ Fenway, Red Sox 5-2
    WP: Mel Parnell, LP: Bill Voiselle, A: 17,246, HR: Tom O'Brien, Vern Stephens, Phil Masi, Ted Williams: 0/3
4/17 @ Fenway, Red Sox 4-3
    WP: Chuck Stobbs, LP: Johnny Antonelli, A: 8100, Ted Williams: 1/4

1948
4/16 @ Braves, Red Sox 19-6
    WP: Joe Dobson, LP: Johnny Sain, A: 12,000, HR: Ted Williams 3/5, Sox had 24 hits Torgeson- Hitchcock fight
4/17 @ Fenway, Red Sox 2-1
    WP: Earl Johnson, LP: Johnny Beasley, A: 16,300, Ted Williams: 1/3
4/18 @ Fenway, Braves 3-2
    WP: Warren Spahn, LP: Maurice McDermott, A: 26,663, Ted Williams: 0/3

1947
4/11 @ Braves, Red Sox 3-0
    WP: Tex Hughson, LP: Red Barrett, A: 14,665, Ted Williams: 2/4
4/12 @ Fenway, Red Sox 2-0
    WP: Mel Parnell, LP: Ed Wright, A: 18,700, Parnell retires 17 in a row
4/13 @ Fenway, tie, 7-7 16 innings
    Boo Ferris, Warren Spahn, A: 30,884, HR: Ted Williams 1/4, Rudy York, Earl Torgeson, 5 hits. Walt Lanfranconi relief heroics.

1946
4/12 @ Fenway, Red Sox 11-5
    WP: Boo Ferriss, LP: Ed Wright, A: 8800, HR: Ted Williams (2, GS), 7 RBI, 3/4
4/13 @ Fenway, Braves 7-3
    WP: Bill Lee, LP: Jim Bagby, A: 7300, Ted Williams: 1/3
4/14 @ Braves, Red Sox 19-5
    WP: Mike Ryba, LP: Bill Posedel, A: 34,000 (over 1500 turned away), Ted Williams: 2/4, Bobby Doerr 4/5, 7 RBI

1945
4/11 @ Braves, Braves 3-1

    WP: Al Javery, LP: Rex Cecil, A: 4227, HR: Tommy Holmes

1945
4/12 @ Braves, Braves 12-11
    WP: Ben Cardoni, LP: Red Barrett, HR: Tommy Holmes, Chuck Workman, Jack Tobin, Geo. Metkovich 8 errors, 15 walks
4/13, Cancelled, FDR death
4/15 @ Fenway, Red Sox 6-5
    WP: Pinky Woods, LP: Johnny Hutchings, A: 13,000
"Negro players to have tryout at Yawkey Yard" AM 4/16

1944
4/14 @ Braves, Red Sox 6-5
    WP: Clem Hauseman, LP: Ben Cardoni, Holmes 5 hits
4/15 @ Fenway, Red Sox 3-2
    WP: Vic Johnson, LP: Jim Tobin
4/16, RAIN

1943
4/17 @ Braves, RAIN
4/18 @ Fenway, Red Sox 5-3
    WP: Joe Dobson, LP: Nate Andrews, A: 10,010, HR: Bobby Doerr, Stengel hit by cab
4/19 @ Fenway, Braves 6-1
    WP: Lou Tost, LP: Norman Brown, A: 3,500, 1 game of doubleheader. Second game called after two innings, "excessive cold"

1942
4/11, RAIN
4/12 @ Fenway, Braves 7-5
    WP: Johnny Sain, LP: Charlie Wagner, A: 8,700, Ted Williams: 1/3, Johnny Pesky four errors

1941
4/11 @ Natl. L. Field
Red Sox 11, Bees 6
    WP: Dick Errickson, LP: Wes Ferrell, A: 7,700, HR: Sibby Sisti, Ted Williams: DNP
4/13 @ Fenway, Bees 10-3
    WP: Manny Salvo, LP: Mickey Harris, A: 10,990, HR: (Bees) Babe Dahlgren, Max West Ted Williams: DNP

1940
4/13 @ Fenway, BAD WEATHER
4/14 @ Natl. L. Field, Bees 7-3
    WP: Nick Strincevich, LP: Mickey Harris, A: 9,900, HR: Max West, Ted Williams: 1/4, single

1939
4/15 @ Natl. L. Field, Bees 7-1
 WP: Lou Fette, LP: Joe Heving, A: 6100, Ted Williams: rookie, bats 6th, RF, 0/3
4/16 @ Fenway, Red Sox 1-0
 WP: Woody Rich, CG, 5 hit, LP: Tom Early, A: 15,000, Ted Williams: 1/3 RF

1938
4/16 @ Fenway, Bees 6-2
 WP: Jim Turner, LP: Fritz Ostermuller, A: 8,400
4/17 @ Natl. L. Field, Red Sox 2-1
 WP: Emerson Dickman, LP: Ira Hutchinson, A: 10,120

1937
4/17 @ Bees Park(at the hive), Red Sox 7-5
 WP: Jack Wilson, LP: Johnny Babich, A: 6,100, HR: Mike Higgins, Vince DiMaggio
4/18 @ Fenway, Red Sox 10-8
 WP: Doc Bowers, LP: Jim Turner, A: 11,100, HR: Vince DiMaggio, Wally Berger, Fabian Gaffke

1936
4/10 @ revamped Allston ballyard RAIN
4/11, RAIN
4/12 @ Fenway, Bees 8-4
 WP: Jim (Tiny) Chaplin, LP: Jim Henry, A: 6,500

1935
4/12-13 RAIN
4/15 @ Fenway, Braves 3-2
 WP: Ben Cantwell, LP: Geo. "Lefty" Hochette, A: 11,000, Babe Ruth, 1B, 0/3, E

1934
4/13 @ Braves, Braves 4-3 (10 inn)
 WP: Ed Brandt, LP: Herb Pennock, A: 4,000, HR: Carl Reynolds
4/14 @ Braves, Red Sox 8-2
 WP: Rube Walberg, LP: Ben Cantwell, A: 2,000, HR: Carl Reynolds, Joe Mowry, Wally Berger (B)
4/15 @ Braves, Red Sox 11-3
 WP: Johnny Welch, LP: Huck Betts, A: 12,000, HR: Carl Reynolds, Bill Werber

1933
4/8 @ Fenway, Red Sox 7-0
 WP: Ivy Paul Andrews, LP: Ben Cantwell, A: 2,500
4/9 @ Braves, Braves 4-2

WP: Fred Frankhouse, CG, LP: Gordon Rhodes, A: 6,000, HR: Smead Jolley

1932
4/9 @ Fenway, Braves 2-1
 WP: Huck Betts, LP: Denny MacFayden, A: 2,300
4/10 @ Braves, Red Sox 4-1
 WP: Jack Russell, LP: Bruce Cunningham, A: 7,500

1931
4/11 @ Fenway, Red Sox 7-2
 WP: Ed Durham, LP: Bill McAfee, A: 11,000, HR: Earl Webb, "record crowd"
4/12 @ Braves, Red Sox 6-0
 WP: Denny MacFayden, LP: Socks Seybold, A: 12,000

1930
4/12 @ Fenway, Braves 4-3 (11)
 WP: Ben Cantwell, LP: Red Ruffing, A: 8,000
4/13 @ Braves, Braves 4-1
 WP: Bob Smith, LP: Ed Morris, A: 2,800

1929
4/13 @ Fenway RAIN
4/14 @ Braves, Braves 4-0
 WP: Socks Seybold, LP: Milt Gaston, A: 5,000
1st Sunday games in Boston. Freezing cold, oil stove used in dugout.

1928 NO GAMES

1927
4/8 @ Fenway, Red Sox 13-2
 WP: Slim Harris, LP: Bob Smith, A: 2,500
4/9 @ Fenway, Braves 6-5
 WP: Art Mills, LP: Tony Wilzer, A: 1,000

1926
4/8 @ Fenway, RAIN
4/9 @ Fenway, Red Sox 6-1
 WP: Howard Ehmke, LP: Rube Benton, A: 5,000, HR: Phil Todt

1925
4/11 @ Braves, Braves 4-3
 WP: Johnny Cooney, LP: Jack Quinn (spitter), A: 12,000
4/13, COLD

1916
4/10 Harvard 1, Red Sox 0 @ Fenway, Sox beat BC next day 9-1.

1913
Red Sox beat Harvard 4-2

1912
4/9 Sox beat Harvard 2-0 to christen Fenway Park, while Braves practice at SE Grounds

1910
Sox beat Harvard 4-1, Doves beat Providence Grays 8-1

1907
10/7 @Huntington, Americans 4-1
 WP: Cy Young, LP: Gus Dorner, A: 3,800
10/8, RAIN
10/9 @ South End, Americans 4-2 (11)
 WP: Fred Burchell, LP: Sam Frock
10/10 @Huntington, Americans 2-1
 WP: Cy Morgan, LP: Irving Young, A: 3,600
Americans 5-4
 WP: Cy Young, LP: Sam Frock
10/11 @South End, Americans 6-4
 WP: Joe Harris, LP: Ernie Lindamann, A: 1,500, HR: Bill Carrigan
10/12 @Huntington, Americans 5-4
 WP: Ralph Glaze, LP: Jake Boultes, A: 5,000
Tie 3-3 (10)

1905
10/9 @Huntington, Nationals 5-2
 WP: Vic Willis, LP: Bill Dineen, A: 7,100
10/10 @Huntington, Americans 3-1
 WP: Cy Young, LP: Irving Young, A: 7,900
10/11 @Huntington, Americans 5-1
 WP: Harris, LP: Wilhelm
10/12 @Huntington, Americans 12-0
 WP: Winter, LP: Chick Fraser, A: 3,000
10/13 @Huntington, Americans 6-2
 WP: Jesse Tannehill, LP: Vic Willis, A: 1,750
10/14 @Huntington , Americans 8-2
 WP: Gibson, LP: Irving Young, A: 5,000;
2nd game, Americans 4-3, WP: Harris, LP: Chick Fraser, HR: Fred Parent, Bob Unglaub

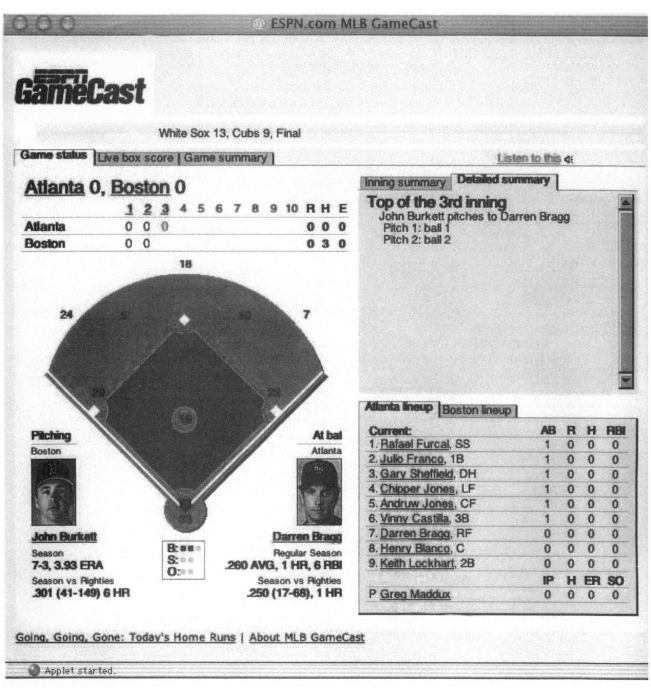

INTERNET GAMECASTS

Ken Carpenter

As part of the Fenway Project, I volunteered to "watch" the game on the Internet. I quickly realized I am addicted to the sound of baseball—trying to follow a game via a text report is very difficult and, frankly, pretty boring. (I was also distracted quite a bit because I am a Cleveland Indians season-ticket holder, and they traded their ace, Bartolo Colon, the night before, so I was glued to the television—watching and listening to the Tribe game vs. Arizona to get additional news and reaction about the trade.)

At my computer, I decided to sample various "game casts" online. I concentrated on three services—ESPN.com, MLB.com and CNNSI.com. I have a high-speed cable modem Internet connection at home. With this connection, all three services delivered information within seconds of the live television broadcast; MLB.com was the fastest, CNNSI.com the slowest, but all three were acceptable and virtually "live."

Overall, the three services were very competent about delivering the detail of the game in a separate, "pop-up" browser window to give the game info. I'd pick MLB.com as the best in this area, because it allowed me to see more information in one glance, including an in-game box score. MLB.com also had the most visual elements—at 9:04 PM, I could "see" Boston's Shea Hillenbrand batting against Kevin Gryboski with one out in the bottom of the sixth inning. Both players' mug shots were shown in color. A centerfield "view" showed an illustration of a right-handed batter; pitch locations popped up in and around a strike zone. Hillenbrand took the first pitch low for a ball, then put the second ball in play—he grounded into a force to end the inning. The screen immediately updated to show Gary Sheffield would be leading off the top of the seventh against John Burkett.

Both ESPN.com and MLB.com showed defensive players in a field diagram, but MLB.com's was superior, conforming to the park dimensions, and listing the defenders and runners by name (ESPN.com showed numbers only, which were of no use to me. CNNSI.com also showed a field, but its "little men" were not identified.)

CNNSI.com's old-fashioned scoreboard design was the coolest looking of the three, but the site offered far less than the other two services. (At the time it was also the only one of the gamecasts to show advertising in the game window—by 2003 all three did.) I noted when Chris Hammond came in to pitch for the Braves in the bottom of the seventh that MLB.com had his photo, ESPN.com did not.

All three services use a Java application in their game-cast windows, so you can't copy the game log or pitch-by-pitch information. ESPN.com does offer logs and pitch-by-pitch detail on another page within its baseball scoreboard section, and from there I copied it (see pitch-by-pitch at the bottom of this report). I could not find an importable version of the pitch-by-pitch detail anywhere on MLB.com. That's not to say it isn't there somewhere, but if an active, computer-savvy user can't find it, then there is a problem.

Darren Holmes, color picture included on MLB.com, came in for Atlanta, and induced Manny Ramirez to fly out, ending the seventh. Alan Embree started the eighth for Boston, but his photo still had him in a Padres' cap.

One unique feature of MLB.com is its "on the benches" tab, which shows a list of the players who aren't in the game, with their stats—a nice touch.

I will say that if you don't have access to television, and don't want to pay the additional fees to access the live audio or video feeds on MLB.com, then the online "game casts" can quench your thirst for "live" information.

I hope you can stay awake for the whole game, though!

Game Log | Pitch-by-Pitch
ATLANTA 1ST
John Burkett pitches to Rafael Furcal
Pitch 1: strike 1 (looking)
Pitch 2: ball 1
Pitch 3: ball 2
Pitch 4: in play
R Furcal fouled out to third.
John Burkett pitches to Julio Franco
Pitch 1: strike 1 (looking)
Pitch 2: strike 2 (looking)
Pitch 3: ball 1
Pitch 4: ball 2
Pitch 5: strike 3 (swinging)
J Franco struck out swinging.
John Burkett pitches to Gary Sheffield
Pitch 1: strike 1 (looking)
Pitch 2: ball 1
Pitch 3: ball 2
Pitch 4: ball 3
Pitch 5: strike 2 (swinging)
Pitch 6: strike 3 (swinging)
G Sheffield struck out swinging.
0 runs, 0 hits, 0 errors
Atlanta 0, Boston 0

BOSTON 1ST
Greg Maddux pitches to Johnny Damon
Pitch 1: ball 1
Pitch 2: strike 1 (foul)
Pitch 3: strike 2 (foul)
Pitch 4: foul
Pitch 5: foul
Pitch 6: foul
Pitch 7: ball 2
Pitch 8: in play
J Damon grounded out to second.
Greg Maddux pitches to Carlos Baerga
Pitch 1: ball 1
Pitch 2: strike 1 (foul)
Pitch 3: in play
C Baerga singled to left center.
Greg Maddux pitches to Nomar Garciaparra
Pitch 1: ball 1
Pitch 2: in play
N Garciaparra singled to left, C Baerga to second.
Greg Maddux pitches to Manny Ramirez
Pitch 1: ball 1
C Baerga picked off second.
Pitch 2: strike 1 (looking)

Pitch 3: strike 2 (looking)
Pitch 4: ball 2
Pitch 5: foul
Pitch 6: in play
M Ramirez grounded into fielder's choice to third, N Garciaparra out at second.
0 runs, 2 hits, 0 errors
Atlanta 0, Boston 0

ATLANTA 2ND
John Burkett pitches to Chipper Jones
Pitch 1: strike 1 (looking)
Pitch 2: strike 2 (swinging)
Pitch 3: ball 1
Pitch 4: strike 3 (swinging)
C Jones struck out swinging.
John Burkett pitches to Andruw Jones
Pitch 1: strike 1 (looking)
Pitch 2: ball 1
Pitch 3: strike 2 (foul)
Pitch 4: foul
Pitch 5: in play
A Jones flied out to right.
John Burkett pitches to Vinny Castilla
Pitch 1: in play
V Castilla popped out to first.
0 runs, 0 hits, 0 errors
Atlanta 0, Boston 0

BOSTON 2ND
Greg Maddux pitches to Brian Daubach
Pitch 1: in play
B Daubach grounded out to shortstop.
Greg Maddux pitches to Shea Hillenbrand
Pitch 1: ball 1
Pitch 2: ball 2
Pitch 3: in play
S Hillenbrand doubled to left.
Greg Maddux pitches to Jason Varitek
Pitch 1: strike 1 (looking)
Pitch 2: strike 2 (foul)
Pitch 3: strike 3 (looking)
J Varitek struck out looking.
Greg Maddux pitches to Trot Nixon
Pitch 1: ball 1
Pitch 2: strike 1 (swinging)
Pitch 3: ball 2
Pitch 4: strike 2 (foul)
Pitch 5: in play
T Nixon grounded out to second.

0 runs, 1 hit, 0 errors
Atlanta 0, Boston 0

ATLANTA 3RD
John Burkett pitches to Darren Bragg
Pitch 1: ball 1
Pitch 2: ball 2
Pitch 3: ball 3
Pitch 4: ball 4
D Bragg walked.
John Burkett pitches to Henry Blanco
Pitch 1: ball 1
Pitch 2: strike 1 (looking)
Pitch 3: ball 2
Pitch 4: in play
H Blanco singled to right, D Bragg to third.
John Burkett pitches to Keith Lockhart
Pitch 1: ball 1
Pitch 2: ball 2
Pitch 3: strike 1 (swinging)
Pitch 4: in play
K Lockhart grounded into double play, second to short-stop to first, D Bragg scored, H Blanco out at second.
John Burkett pitches to Rafael Furcal
Pitch 1: strike 1 (looking)
Pitch 2: ball 1
Pitch 3: in play
R Furcal grounded out to second.
1 run, 1 hit, 0 errors
Atlanta 1, Boston 0

BOSTON 3RD
Greg Maddux pitches to Jose Offerman
Pitch 1: ball 1
Pitch 2: ball 2
Pitch 3: strike 1 (looking)
Pitch 4: ball 3
Pitch 5: strike 2 (foul)
Pitch 6: ball 4
J Offerman walked.
Greg Maddux pitches to Johnny Damon
Pitch 1: ball 1
Pitch 2: strike 1 (swinging)
Pitch 3: ball 2
Pitch 4: ball 3
J Offerman stole second.
Pitch 5: strike 2 (looking)
Pitch 6: foul
Pitch 7: in play
J Damon grounded out to second, J Offerman to third.

Greg Maddux pitches to Carlos Baerga
Pitch 1: strike 1 (looking)
Pitch 2: ball 1
Pitch 3: strike 2 (foul)
Pitch 4: strike 3 (swinging)
C Baerga struck out swinging.
Greg Maddux pitches to Nomar Garciaparra
Pitch 1: in play
N Garciaparra reached on infield single to third, J Offerman scored.
Greg Maddux pitches to Manny Ramirez
Pitch 1: ball 1
Pitch 2: strike 1 (looking)
Pitch 3: ball 2
Pitch 4: ball 3
N Garciaparra stole second.
Pitch 5: strike 2 (looking)
Pitch 6: in play
M Ramirez grounded out to second.
1 run, 0 hits, 1 error
Atlanta 1, Boston 1

ATLANTA 4TH
John Burkett pitches to Julio Franco
Pitch 1: in play
J Franco singled to center.
John Burkett pitches to Gary Sheffield
Pitch 1: ball 1
Pitch 2: ball 2
Pitch 3: strike 1 (foul)
Pitch 4: in play
G Sheffield lined out to third.
John Burkett pitches to Chipper Jones
Pitch 1: strike 1 (foul)
Pitch 2: ball 1
Pitch 3: strike 2 (foul)
Pitch 4: ball 2
Pitch 5: strike 3 (swinging)
C Jones struck out swinging.
John Burkett pitches to Andruw Jones
Pitch 1: ball 1
Pitch 2: strike 1 (swinging)
Pitch 3: ball 2
Pitch 4: ball 3
Pitch 5: ball 4
A Jones walked, J Franco to second.
John Burkett pitches to Vinny Castilla
Pitch 1: ball 1
Pitch 2: ball 2
Pitch 3: ball 3

Pitch 4: strike 1 (looking)
Pitch 5: in play
V Castilla flied out to center.
0 runs, 1 hit, 0 errors
Atlanta 1, Boston 1

BOSTON 4TH
Greg Maddux pitches to Brian Daubach
Pitch 1: strike 1 (looking)
Pitch 2: in play
B Daubach grounded out to second.
Greg Maddux pitches to Shea Hillenbrand
Pitch 1: ball 1
Pitch 2: strike 1 (looking)
Pitch 3: strike 2 (swinging)
Pitch 4: foul
Pitch 5: in play
S Hillenbrand grounded out to second.
Greg Maddux pitches to Jason Varitek
Pitch 1: in play
J Varitek grounded out to second.
0 runs, 0 hits, 0 errors
Atlanta 1, Boston 1

ATLANTA 5TH
John Burkett pitches to Darren Bragg
Pitch 1: strike 1 (looking)
Pitch 2: strike 2 (foul)
Pitch 3: in play
D Bragg reached on infield single to second. D Bragg to second on throwing error by second baseman C Baerga.
John Burkett pitches to Henry Blanco
Pitch 1: ball 1
Pitch 2: strike 1 (looking)
Pitch 3: strike 2 (looking)
Pitch 4: ball 2
Pitch 5: in play
H Blanco grounded out to shortstop.
John Burkett pitches to Keith Lockhart
Pitch 1: strike 1 (foul)
Pitch 2: strike 2 (swinging)
Pitch 3: in play
K Lockhart singled to center, D Bragg scored.
John Burkett pitches to Rafael Furcal
Pitch 1: strike 1 (looking)
Pitch 2: in play
R Furcal reached on bunt single to first, K Lockhart to second.
John Burkett pitches to Julio Franco
Pitch 1: in play

J Franco singled to left, K Lockhart to third, R Furcal to second.
John Burkett pitches to Gary Sheffield
Pitch 1: strike 1 (looking)
Pitch 2: strike 2 (looking)
Pitch 3: ball 1
Pitch 4: foul
Pitch 5: in play
G Sheffield flied out to shallow left.
John Burkett pitches to Chipper Jones
Pitch 1: ball 1
Pitch 2: in play
C Jones flied out to left.
1 run, 4 hits, 1 error
Atlanta 2, Boston 1

BOSTON 5TH
Greg Maddux pitches to Trot Nixon
Pitch 1: strike 1 (looking)
Pitch 2: ball 1
Pitch 3: in play
T Nixon grounded out to second.
Greg Maddux pitches to Jose Offerman
Pitch 1: strike 1 (looking)
Pitch 2: ball 1
Pitch 3: strike 2 (foul)
Pitch 4: foul
Pitch 5: ball 2
Pitch 6: strike 3 (looking)
J Offerman struck out looking.
Greg Maddux pitches to Johnny Damon
Pitch 1: strike 1 (looking)
Pitch 2: ball 1
Pitch 3: strike 2 (foul)
Pitch 4: strike 3 (looking)
J Damon struck out looking.
0 runs, 0 hits, 0 errors
Atlanta 2, Boston 1

ATLANTA 6TH
John Burkett pitches to Andruw Jones
Pitch 1: ball 1
Pitch 2: in play
A Jones singled to center.
John Burkett pitches to Vinny Castilla
Pitch 1: in play
V Castilla flied out to right.
John Burkett pitches to Darren Bragg
Pitch 1: in play
D Bragg singled to right center, A Jones to second.

John Burkett pitches to Henry Blanco
Pitch 1: ball 1
Pitch 2: strike 1 (looking)
Pitch 3: strike 2 (looking)
Pitch 4: ball 2
Pitch 5: foul
Pitch 6: in play
H Blanco flied out to right.
John Burkett pitches to Keith Lockhart
Pitch 1: in play
K Lockhart safe at first on throwing error by shortstop N
Garciaparra, A Jones to third, D Bragg to second.
John Burkett pitches to Rafael Furcal
Pitch 1: ball 1
Pitch 2: in play
R Furcal grounded out to second.
0 runs, 2 hits, 1 error
Atlanta 2, Boston 1

BOSTON 6TH
Greg Maddux pitches to Carlos Baerga
K Gryboski relieved G Maddux.
Pitch 1: strike 1 (looking)
Pitch 2: ball 1
Pitch 3: ball 2
Pitch 4: in play
C Baerga grounded out to second.
K Gryboski pitches to Nomar Garciaparra
Pitch 1: ball 1
Pitch 2: ball 2
Pitch 3: in play
N Garciaparra grounded out to shortstop.
K Gryboski pitches to Manny Ramirez
Pitch 1: ball 1
Pitch 2: ball 2
Pitch 3: ball 3
Pitch 4: ball 4
M Ramirez walked.
K Gryboski pitches to Brian Daubach
Pitch 1: strike 1 (foul)
Pitch 2: ball 1
Pitch 3: ball 2
Pitch 4: ball 3
Pitch 5: ball 4
B Daubach walked, M Ramirez to second.
K Gryboski pitches to Shea Hillenbrand
Pitch 1: ball 1
Pitch 2: in play
S Hillenbrand grounded into fielder's choice to third, M
Ramirez out at third, B Daubach to second.

0 runs, 0 hits, 0 errors
Atlanta 2, Boston 1

ATLANTA 7TH
John Burkett pitches to Julio Franco
Pitch 1: in play
J Franco grounded out to second.
John Burkett pitches to Gary Sheffield
Pitch 1: strike 1 (foul)
Pitch 2: ball 1
Pitch 3: ball 2
Pitch 4: ball 3
Pitch 5: ball 4
G Sheffield walked.
John Burkett pitches to Chipper Jones
Pitch 1: strike 1 (looking)
Pitch 2: ball 1
Pitch 3: ball 2
Pitch 4: strike 2 (foul)
Pitch 5: foul
Pitch 6: in play
C Jones flied out to right center.
John Burkett pitches to Andruw Jones
Pitch 1: strike 1 (looking)
G Sheffield stole second.
Pitch 2: ball 1
Pitch 3: strike 2 (looking)
Pitch 4: in play
A Jones grounded out to second.
0 runs, 0 hits, 0 errors
Atlanta 2, Boston 1

BOSTON 7TH
K Gryboski pitches to Jason Varitek
C Hammond relieved K Gryboski.
Pitch 1: in play
J Varitek singled to left.
C Hammond pitches to Trot Nixon
Pitch 1: strike 1 (bunted foul)
Pitch 2: strike 2 (bunted foul)
Pitch 3: strike 3 (swinging)
T Nixon struck out swinging.
C Hammond pitches to Jose Offerman
Pitch 1: strike 1 (looking)
Pitch 2: ball 1
Pitch 3: ball 2
Pitch 4: ball 3
Pitch 5: strike 2 (looking)
Pitch 6: ball 4
J Offerman walked, J Varitek to second.

C Hammond pitches to Johnny Damon
Pitch 1: strike 1 (swinging)
Pitch 2: strike 2 (swinging)
Pitch 3: in play
J Damon fouled out to left.
C Hammond pitches to Carlos Baerga
Pitch 1: strike 1 (looking)
Pitch 2: in play
   C Baerga doubled to deep left, J Varitek scored, J Offerman to third.
C Hammond pitches to Nomar Garciaparra
Pitch 1: ball 1
Pitch 2: ball 2
Pitch 3: ball 3
Pitch 4: ball 4 (intentional ball)
N Garciaparra intentionally walked.
C Hammond pitches to Manny Ramirez
D Holmes relieved C Hammond.
Pitch 1: ball 1
Pitch 2: strike 1 (swinging)
Pitch 3: strike 2 (foul)
Pitch 4: in play
M Ramirez flied out to left.
1 runs, 2 hits, 0 errors
Atlanta 2, Boston 2

ATLANTA 8TH
A Embree relieved J Burkett.
Alan Embree pitches to Vinny Castilla
Pitch 1: ball 1
Pitch 2: strike 1 (swinging)
Pitch 3: ball 2
Pitch 4: strike 2 (foul)
Pitch 5: in play
V Castilla grounded out to shortstop.
Alan Embree pitches to Darren Bragg
Pitch 1: strike 1 (looking)
Pitch 2: ball 1
Pitch 3: ball 2
Pitch 4: ball 3
Pitch 5: strike 2 (looking)
Pitch 6: ball 4
D Bragg walked.
Alan Embree pitches to Henry Blanco
Pitch 1: ball 1
Pitch 2: ball 2
Pitch 3: ball 3
Pitch 4: strike 1 (looking)
Pitch 5: ball 4
H Blanco walked, D Bragg to second.

W Helms hit for K Lockhart.
Alan Embree pitches to Matt Franco
R Garces relieved A Embree.
M Franco hit for W Helms.
Pitch 1: ball 1
Pitch 2: in play
   M Franco grounded out to pitcher, D Bragg to third, H Blanco to second.
Rich Garces pitches to Rafael Furcal
Pitch 1: strike 1 (looking)
Pitch 2: ball 1
Pitch 3: strike 2 (foul)
Pitch 4: ball 2
Pitch 5: ball 3
Pitch 6: ball 4
R Furcal walked.
Rich Garces pitches to Julio Franco
Pitch 1: ball 1
Pitch 2: strike 1 (swinging)
Pitch 3: strike 2 (looking)
Pitch 4: foul
Pitch 5: in play
J Franco grounded out to second.
0 runs, 0 hits, 0 errors
Atlanta 2, Boston 2

BOSTON 8TH
J Garcia at second base.
M Remlinger relieved D Holmes.
R Henderson hit for B Daubach.
Mike Remlinger pitches to Rickey Henderson
Pitch 1: ball 1
Pitch 2: ball 2
Pitch 3: ball 3
Pitch 4: ball 4
R Henderson walked.
Mike Remlinger pitches to Shea Hillenbrand
Pitch 1: strike 1 (looking)
Pitch 2: strike 2 (foul)
Pitch 3: foul
Pitch 4: strike 3 (looking)
S Hillenbrand struck out looking.
Mike Remlinger pitches to Jason Varitek
Pitch 1: ball 1
Pitch 2: in play
J Varitek grounded into double play, shortstop to first, R Henderson out at second.
0 runs, 0 hits, 0 errors
Atlanta 2, Boston 2

ATLANTA 9TH
T Clark at first base.
T Wakefield relieved R Garces.
Tim Wakefield pitches to Gary Sheffield
Pitch 1: ball 1
Pitch 2: in play
G Sheffield doubled to left.
Tim Wakefield pitches to Chipper Jones
Pitch 1: ball 1
Pitch 2: in play
C Jones flied out to center.
Tim Wakefield pitches to Andruw Jones
Pitch 1: strike 1 (looking)
Pitch 2: ball 1
Pitch 3: in play
A Jones flied out to left center.
Tim Wakefield pitches to Vinny Castilla
Pitch 1: in play
V Castilla singled to shallow center, G Sheffield scored.
Tim Wakefield pitches to Darren Bragg
Pitch 1: ball 1
Pitch 2: ball 2
Pitch 3: ball 3
Pitch 4: strike 1 (looking)
Pitch 5: ball 4
D Bragg walked, V Castilla to second.
Tim Wakefield pitches to Henry Blanco
Pitch 1: ball 1
Pitch 2: strike 1 (looking)
Pitch 3: in play
 H Blanco singled to shallow right, V Castilla scored, D
Bragg to third. H Blanco to second advancing on throw.
Tim Wakefield pitches to Jesse Garcia
Pitch 1: strike 1 (looking)
Pitch 2: strike 2 (foul)
Pitch 3: strike 3 (looking)
J Garcia struck out looking.
2 runs, 3 hits, 0 errors
Atlanta 4, Boston 2

BOSTON 9TH
J Smoltz relieved M Remlinger.
John Smoltz pitches to Trot Nixon
Pitch 1: in play
T Nixon grounded out to shortstop.
John Smoltz pitches to Jose Offerman
Pitch 1: strike 1 (looking)
Pitch 2: in play
J Offerman grounded out to second.
John Smoltz pitches to Johnny Damon

Pitch 1: strike 1 (looking)
Pitch 2: ball 1
Pitch 3: strike 2 (looking)
Pitch 4: foul
Pitch 5: foul
Pitch 6: foul
Pitch 7: strike 3 (swinging)
J Damon struck out swinging.
0 runs, 0 hits, 0 errors
Atlanta 4, Boston 2

CONTRIBUTORS

Jean Hastings Ardell grew up in New York City, where she rooted for the New York Yankees. She got over it, and now works as a baseball researcher and freelance writer in Corona del Mar, California. Her book about women in baseball is forthcoming from Southern Illinois University Press.

Phil Bergen works for the Massachusetts Historical Commission, involved in the preservation of historic buildings. His mother took him to Ladies Day at Braves Field, and to the Kenmore Hotel to obtain autographs of the 1952 Pittsburgh Pirates in the coffee shop. Ralph Kiner took room service.

Steve Bennett was born a White Sox fan. As a 5-year-old, he simulated games in the backyard, playing all the roles. The Sox always won. Steve learned then that life doesn't imitate art. He lives in Grinnell, Iowa with his wife and two children. His son, Will, hopes to pitch for the Sox.

Bob Brady grew up as a fan of the Boston Braves and Boston Red Sox and remains true to both to this day. In his free time, you can find him either seated in Section 26 at Fenway Park or working on the next newsletter for the Boston Braves Historical Association. Bob has been a SABR member since 1991.

Steve W. Brooks grew up in Seattle, Washington rooting for the Mariners. He's a writer for a Mariners magazine that is sold outside of Safeco Field. This is his first year as a SABR member, but many more are sure to follow. Plans to move to Boston in two years.

Bob Buege grew up worshipping the Milwaukee Braves and has never stopped. He has written *The Milwaukee Braves: A Baseball Eulogy* and *Eddie Matthews and the National Pastime.* A SABR member since 1988, Bob teaches at UW-Milwaukee and is presently writing the definitive history of Pine Bluff, Wisconsin.

Anne Campbell, high school classmate of SABR stalwart Skip McAfee, was thrilled to attend the ballgame with Skip and her son and grandson. Anne has been one of those "hopeful" Red Sox fans since moving to Boston in 1970. Although Dwight Evans is her all time favorite player, Trot Nixon is doing a good job as a right field replacement.

Jeff Campbell lives in Washington, DC. He grew up listening to Houston Astros games on the radio in Shreveport, LA. Jeff has been a member of SABR since 1997 and that same year formed the Songs and Poetry committee. He also produces the baseball song compilations, "Diamond Cuts," to benefit his organization Hungry for Music.

Jim Campbell, an Army major from Old Town, Maine, hasn't had many opportunities to go to Fenway in recent years, but he toured the park with his Boy Scout troop and attended many games with his father and brothers while growing up in Boston. And he ate many slices of Yaz bread, the bread of choice for all Sox fans in that era.

Jimmy Campbell, age 10, was very excited to attend his first major league baseball game, coming from Maine for the event. Although he sported a Nomar T-shirt, Trot Nixon made some spectacular catches and he wished he'd waited until after the game to get his T-shirt.

Gene Carney has been writing baseball since 1989. A SABR member since 1991, Carney has edited "Notes from the Shadows of Cooperstown" under his pen name Two Finger since March 1993 and an on-line version since March 1999. Visit "Notes" at www.baseball1.com/carney/ His writing credits include "Romancing the Horsehide," the play (now a musical) "Mornings After," and a variety of fiction, essays, reviews, humor and baseball history.

Ken Carpenter is a copy editor at the Orlando (Fla.) *Sentinel,* but retains his season tickets for the Cleveland Indians at Jacobs Field. He will add four new major-league baseball stadiums to his career list of 33—Milwaukee, Cincinnati, Pittsburgh and Detroit—during a two-week tour in July.

R. Chamberlain holds a bachelor degree in English literature with an emphasis on creative writing and poetry from the University of Cincinnati. Currently, he lives in Cleveland, works in the SABR office, and is finishing his masters from the E.W. Scripps School of Journalism at Ohio University.

Randall Chandler started his journey through the baseball world when he was eight years old. Growing up in West Tennessee and following the St. Louis Cardinals, he now lives in Germantown, Tennessee and has been practicing pharmacy for the last thirty-four years. A SABR member since 1986, he enjoys book collecting, reading, and baseball statistics.

Will Christensen is general manager of BaseballTruth.com and a life-long baseball fan. He has been a member of SABR off and on since 1989 and is working on his first book, on minor-league history.

Rich Cohen is a family doctor in Hamilton, New York, home of Hooks Wiltse. Invigorated by the 1975 World Series, Rich became a volunteer umpire for the local "little league" program, and umpiring has been under his skin since. He was lead author of "Life Expectancy of Major League Baseball Umpires" which appeared in *The Physician and Sports Medicine* in June 2000.

When Dick Dahl isn't playing Strat-O-Matic baseball or rooting for the hometown Boston Red Sox, he makes his living as a freelance writer. His work has appeared in the *Boston Globe Magazine* and *The Nation*. He considers baseball too daunting a subject, so he generally writes about law and politics.

Frank D'Urso, Jr. actually remembers the Impossible Dream year even though he was only three years old at the time. His dad, Frank D'Urso, Sr., worked as a soda jerk for the Boston Braves before they moved away. His newborn son, Frank D'Urso III is looking forward to this thing called "baseball."

Eric Enders is a baseball writer and historian whose books include *Ballparks: Then and Now* and *100 Years of the World Series*. A lifelong Dodger fan, he has traveled to 26 major league ballparks and countless minor league and amateur ones. He specializes in African-American baseball history, particularly the integration era. Originally from El Paso, Texas, he now lives in Cooperstown, New York.

Joe Favano grew up in Southwestern Connecticut as a fan of both the Yankees and Mets (yes, there are a few of us around). A member of SABR's Ballpark Committee, he helped start the Committee's Ballpark Photo Collection and continues to add to the collection.

F. X. Flinn, whose baseball career ended at age 12 after hitting just .287 as the first string catcher for the Bishops of the St. Hugh–St. Elizabeth Little League in Huntington NY in 1966, was named 'Midwife of Rotisserie League Baseball' by the Founding Fathers of Rotiball in recognition of his role in getting Bantam to publish the first roti-book. He is also to blame for the Rotiball position 'middle infielder.'

Michael Freiman is a math major at the University of Pennsylvania. He has been a baseball fan since 1993, when he discovered John Kruk, Mitch Williams and *Total Baseball*. He is interested in the statistical analysis of baseball and has done research on the mathematics of hitting streaks.

Roy Gedat moved to Boston in '75 just in time to see the Bosox blow the World Series against the Reds. Sox fans still believe they won the seventh game started by Bill Lee. The day after Mr. Lee spoke to students at BU and was not the least bit sad about the result. "I took off work to watch the Bucky Dent game and got beer thrown on me in the bleachers during the Yanks/Sox Boston Massacre series," Gedat explained. "Those were only a couple of highlights for this displaced Yankee fan living in New England."

Rich Gibson rediscovered his love of baseball after moving to Cincinnati in 1989. His interest in baseball was further strengthened when he met and eventually married lifelong baseball fan, Lynne. Both are diehard Reds fans, but also enjoy attending minor league games. Rich has been a member of SABR since 1996.

Irv Goldfarb, though born in the Bronx, is a longtime Met fan/Yankee hater. After almost ten years at ESPN, he now works as a unit manager for the ABC Television network. Irv, whose area of interest is the Negro Leagues, has been a SABR member since 1999. Every summer he and his brother make the journey to different ballparks around the country.

Rich Klein grew up in Northern New Jersey and is that rare combination of an Astros and Yankees fan. He now lives in Dallas and works for Beckett.Com as one of the Editors of the *Beckett Almanac of Baseball Cards and Collectibles*.

Francis Kinlaw was born in Detroit and, after moving to North Carolina at the age of nine, became the only fan of the Detroit Tigers in Laurinburg, North Carolina. He has been a SABR member since 1983 and has contributed to four convention publications. He resides in Greensboro, North Carolina.

R. J. Lesch lives in Des Moines, Iowa, with his wife, Christee. He has been a member of SABR since 1998 and is a founding member of the Field of Dreams (Iowa) chapter of SABR. He is an avid fencer, sabre being his weapon of choice. This is confusing to his friends and family.

Glenn LeDoux is a graphic designer from New York City. He loves his wife Elizabeth, and wears a glove when he writes about himself in third-person.

Daniel Levine was a baseball fanatic long before becoming an Internet consultant/developer. He has been a SABR member since 1997, and currently lives in Houston, with his wife, Marian, and daughter, Morgan, who, at age three, insists that "Jeff Bagwell stands silly."

Howard Luloff has attended every SABR National Convention since 1986. He has been a SABR member since 1984. He enjoys visiting different ballparks, playing vintage baseball and serving as public address announcer for various high school and College of St. Catherine athletic events. He lives in St. Louis Park, MN.

Joseph Mancuso is an Electrical Engineer turned Audio Engineer/Producer and Independent Musician originally from Staten Island, New York. He is a songwriter and performer in Ann Arbor, Michigan where he attended college and now lives with his family. He owes his interest in baseball research largely to his father, Peter Mancuso. More information about his work is available online at *www.josephmancuso.com*.

Peter Mancuso is a SABR member since 1999. A Brooklyn Dodger fan growing up in a NY Giant household and NY Yankee neighborhood on Staten Island left him deflated after 1957. The discovery of really old (19th-century) baseball players of his native place has brought baseball back into his life.

Lawr Michaels is a writer and analys who lives in El Cerrito, CA. He works in Telecommunications, covers the Athletics in the STATS, Inc. Scouting Notebook, and runs www.CREATiVESPORTS.com

Wynn Montgomery is an avid Atlanta Braves fan who also loves minor league and college baseball. He is a member of SABR's Magnolia Chapter and is revisiting his youth by working on a biography of Willard Nixon, 1950s BoSox pitcher and the only Major Leaguer he knew personally.

Andy Moye listens to baseball on the radio in his home on the river near Columbus, GA. While his playing years are past, he still umpires and does the research for vintage base ball games played at Westville—a living history village in southwest Georgia.

Around 1997, Bill Nowlin began writing about Boston baseball and Ted Williams, and hasn't let up since, having completed several books (often with frequent co-author Jim Prime) and scores of articles. He is also a founder of Rounder Records. Music and baseball—keeps him busy.

Paul Parker is currently team historian for the Colorado Rockies. Born and raised in Brooklyn, New York, he has served with the Rockies from their inception, working in ticketing and merchandising, with the speakers' bureau and in historical and community projects. He lives in Boulder, Colorado with his wife Ruth, daughter Rebecca (13) and son Marcus (10).

Detroit native and D.C. resident Mark Pattison, a SABR member since 2000, is media editor at Catholic News Service, co-author (with David Raglin) of *Detroit Tigers Lists and More: Runs, Hits, and Eras* and writes song parodies in his spare time. He also gets his oil changed every 3,000 miles.

Joining SABR in 1993, Fred Peltz continued his love of baseball. He previously was a minor league player and member of a championship Army team in Japan with Dave Bristol. A native Californian, he called upon his avocation of photography to record his first visit to Fenway Park.

Claudia Perry is a former president of the Society for

American Baseball Reaearch. A longtime newspaper writer, she works for the *Star-Ledger* in Newark, New Jersey writing about radio among other things. A former *Jeopardy!* champion, she retains an inexplicable allegiance to the Houston Astros, but always roots for the Red Sox against the Yankees.

Bobby Plapinger has been selling used, rare & out of print baseball books out of Ashland, Oregon for over 15 years. In case it's not apparent, he's a lifelong Mets fan, though proximity and quality have drawn him towards the Mariners in recent decades.

Jim Prime has written several books on the Boston Red Sox, including *Ted Wiliams' Hit List*, which he coauthored with the late Teddy Ballgame himself, and *The Little Red (Sox) Book*, in which Jim teamed up with Bill "Spaceman" Lee to literally change Red Sox history. Jim compiled *Tales from the Red Sox Dugout*, and co-authored *Fenway Saved, Ted Williams: The Pursuit of Perfection* and *More Tales From the Red Sox Dugout*. He lives in Nova Scotia.

Denis Repp lives in Pittsburgh, where he spends his summers tracking the play-by-play of Pirate games for MLB.com. He has never met a ballpark hot dog he didn't like.

Susan Riggs was born and raised near Farmville, VA. She played fast-pitch softball in high school and was an avid fan of Early Wynn and the 1959 White Sox. She spent a year in St. Louis where she attended many Cardinals' games. Her husband Dave is a SABR member and they currently reside in Williamsburg, VA.

John T. Saccoman is an Associate Professor of Mathematics and Computer Science at Seton Hall University in New Jersey. His father grew up as a New York Yankees fan and his mother as a Brooklyn Dodgers fan, so he, of course(?), is a die-hard Mets fan. This has been passed along to...

Ryan Saccoman, a nine-year old Mets fan (seven at the time of the Fenway Project). His long-suffering mother, Mary Saccoman, accompanies the guys on their ballpark odysseys.

Anthony Salazar has a hard time not bleeding Dodger Blue. However, ten years in the Pacific Northwest has cemented his

heart for the Seattle Mariners. He has enjoyed his SABR membership since 1998, specializing in areas of Latinos in baseball. Going to ballgames will always be a multi-dimensional pastime for him.

Jim Sandoval was born and raised in Southern California and migrated to Alabama. He somehow became a lifelong fan of the Cincinnati Reds. He has begun writing a book on the 1919 Reds. When he realized as a utility infielder for a small college team that professional baseball was not an option, he actually began to go to class. He is currently a history teacher and freelance baseball writer.

Lyle Spatz is the chairman of the Society for American Baseball Research's Baseball Records Committee, a post he has held since 1991. He is the author of *New York Yankee Openers-1903-1996; Yankees Coming, Yankees Going: New York Yankee Player Transactions, 1903-1999;* and a co-author of *The Midsummer Classic: The Complete History of Baseball's All-Star Game.* He is currently at work on a biography of Bill Dahlen.

Michael Spatz just graduated his freshman year at Howard High School. Introduced to SABR by his grandparents, Michael is 14 years old, has two loving parents, a fabulous sister, and an adorable dog. During his free time, Michael likes to play chess, surf the internet, and of course, watch baseball.

Steve Steinberg is a baseball historian whose articles have appeared in *Nine* and *The National Pastime*. He's just completed a book on New York Yankee manager Miller Huggins and is finishing a historical memoir of once-famous spitball pitcher Urban Shocker. He lives in Seattle with his wife and three children.

Allen Tait discovered baseball as an eight-year-old with a very patient dad who explained his favorite player was still in the game even though he was out in the first inning. A SABR member since 1976, proudly old school; outdoors, real grass and dirty uniforms.

Cecilia Tan was born a Yankees fan in New York City. She moved to Boston in 1991 and says "if the Yankees are my childhood sweetheart, then the Red Sox are my annoying housemate." She has written for *Yankees Magazine, Mudville, Baseball*

Ink, and elsewhere, and is currently at work on a book about the 50 greatest Yankees games of all time, due from J. Wiley and Sons in Spring 2005.

Stew Thornley has been a SABR member since 1979 and current serves as the organization's vice president. He is one of the founders of the Halsey Hall SABR Chapter in Minnesota and an author of numerous books on sports history. In Stew's spare time, he's managed to visit the graves of every single member of baseball's Hall of Fame.

Zack Triscuit has been stepping up to the plate since he was six years old, but only three years ago did he find such fellow hardball fanatics like himself in SABR. Zack is a sophomore at Boston University in 2003/2004 where a quick peek up from the books during his hours of nightly study often leads him to catch a glimpse of Fenway Park lights or the ever present Citgo sign in Kenmore Square.

Lewis Trott was introduced to baseball by his grandfather in the early 1970s, attending Baltimore Orioles games at Memorial Stadium. Lewis has been a member of SABR since 2001 and is presently a librarian at Fayetteville State University in North Carolina. He still cheers for the Orioles and makes a few trips back home to see them play in Camden Yards each year. His other passion is books and reading.

Scott Turner, a native Texan, grew up rooting for the Astros and Rangers. He currently resides in Tucson and has switched allegiances to the D-backs. A member of SABR's Deadball Era Committee since 2000, Scott loathes the DH, interleague play and shorter fences; prefers triples to home runs; and yearns for a return to rainbow orange in Houston. He attended both Nolan Ryan's 7th no-hitter and Game 7 of the 2001 World Series.

Jeff Twiss heard the name "Johnny Unitas" at the age of seven and has been a fan of all things Baltimore from that moment. He learned the difference between induction and deduction at his first Orioles game, in which Boog Powell bunted for a base hit and Brooks Robinson short-hopped a throw to the plate. It was Friday, July 26, 1968, a crucial game with the Tigers.

A native New Englander, Jay Walker currently resides in San Diego, a mere 3 or 4 homerun shots from Teddy Ballgame's boyhood home.

Angela Jane Weisl was in the stands for both David Wells' and David Cone's perfect games and has seen an unassisted triple play. She is still waiting for someone to hit four home runs in a game she attends. In the off season, she is an associate professor of English at Seton Hall University, and the author of *The Persistence of Medievalism: Narrative Adventures in Contemporary Culture* (Palgrave/MacMillan, 2003), which combines her baseball fandom with her medieval scholarship. She lives in Brooklyn with her husband, Robert Squillace, who got her started on this whole baseball business.

Peter Winske grew up listening to and watching the Cubs, keeping score and typing out the games so his father could read them after work. "As my father taught me, I taught my children how to watch and appreciate baseball. SABR member since 1983, a Florida Marlins season ticket holder, but still a Cubs fan."

Saul Wisnia is the author of several books, including *Prime Time Baseball Stars*, *Wit and Wisdom of Baseball*, and *The Jimmy Fund of Dana-Farber Cancer Institute*. A former sports and feature correspondent for *The Washington Post*, he is now a publications editor-writer at Dana-Farber. His latest book, *From Yawkey to Milwaukee: Boston's Bloom and Demise as a Two-Team Baseball Town*, is nearing completion and slated for release in 2004.

John Zajc learned a little about baseball history by playing "Superstar Baseball" as a teen. He started working for SABR in 1990 while in graduate school and was named Executive Director in January 2003. He lives in the Tremont neighborhood of Cleveland with his wife Catherine and dog Zoe.

Andrew Zinner writes: "I am 46 and a native of Chicago. I graduated from Southern Illinois University School of Law and practice law in Phoenix. I am a life-long baseball fan. I have seen games at Wrigley Field and Old Comiskey Park, Busch Stadium, Ewing Kauffman Field, Bank One Ballpark, Qualcomm Park, Dodger Stadium, the Kingdome, Safeco Field, Pro Player Stadium, Shea Stadium and Fenway Park."

INDEX

Ruth, Babe, 18, 22, 23, 24, 35, 36, 38, 39, 54, 58, 72, 81, 98, 102, 111, 129, 130, 143
Ryan, Bob, 146
Sain, Johnny, 22, 24
San Diego Padres, 7, 84, 157
San Francisco Giants, 9, 26, 79, 103, 105
Sanchez, Rey, 115
Santiago, Benito, 26
Sarmiento, Domingo F., 42
Schourek, Pete, 28, 29
Schuerholtz, John, 77, 95
Schwartz, Glenn, 143
Scott, George, 133
Seanez, Rudy, 28
Seattle Mariners, 26
Seaver, Tom, 84
Sele, Aaron, 15, 26
Selig, Bud, 25, 52, 143
Shaughnessy, Dan, 36, 146
Sheffield, Gary, 9, 31, 37, 38, 39, 50, 52, 55, 58, 59, 60, 61, 77, 94, 95, 96, 116, 117, 120, 132, 138, 146, 152, 157
Sherman, Joel, 108
Shore, Ernie, 54
Silverman, Michael, 108, 111, 114
Silverstein, Josh, 142
Simon, Tom, 118
Simpson, Joe, 52, 53, 93, 94, 95, 96, 120
Sisti, Sibby, 19, 21, 24, 51, 55, 88
Smith, Reggie, 35
Smoltz, John, 9, 15, 26, 30, 31, 38, 50, 53, 55, 61, 76, 77, 95, 96, 119, 132, 151, 153
Snider, Duke, 79
Snipes, Wesley, 53
Somers, Charles, 10
Soriano, Alfonso, 36
Sosa, Sammy, 64
Southworth, Billy, 16, 23
Spahn, Warren, 10, 17, 18, 22, 24, 55
Speaker, Tris, 16, 54
Speier, Alex, 110
Spina, Guy, 112
Spooneybarger, Tim, 51, 151
Springsteen, Bruce, 82

St. Louis Cardinals, 129
Stanley, Bob, 35, 114
Stanley, Mike, 28
Stengel, Casey, 24, 85
Stephenson, Larry, 89
Subrizio, Rick, 68, 69, 70, 71, 72, 74
Sullivan, Billy, 23
"Take Me Out to the Ballgame", 90, 119, 130, 142
Tampa Bay Devil Rays, 30
Taylor, Nikki, 79
Teitel, Ellen, 141, 142
Thomas, Clarence, 82
Thomas, Frank, 36
Thome, Jim, 52, 59
Thompson, Rich, 77
Thorpe, Jim, 64
Tiant, Luis, 133
Tiger Stadium, 62, 65, 100, 123, 129
Timmons, Tim, 52, 58, 88
Tinker, Joe, 143
Tobin, Jim, 55
Toby, Amy, 142
Tomase, John, 110, 114, 115
Torgeson, Earl, 17
Toronto Blue Jays, 9, 129
Torre, Joe, 108
Tost, Lou, 19
Totaro, Ray, 88, 142
Trupiano, Jerry, 57, 58, 59, 60, 61
Turner, Ted, 51, 95
Uecker, Bob, 36, 51
Urbina, Ugueth, 121, 152
Unglaub, Bob, 16
Valentin, John, 27
Valentine, Bobby, 136
VanWieren, Pete, 52, 53, 119, 120, 121
Varitek, Jason, 9, 59, 60, 61, 91, 117, 119, 127, 146, 151
Vaughan, Stevie Ray, 126
Vaughn, Mo, 27, 70
Ventura, Robin, 36, 136
Veterans Stadium, 36, 65
Vincent, Fay, 25
Village People, The, 82
Villamon, J. P., 101, 102
Vincent, Stephanie, 143
Von Der Ahe, Chris, 81

Von Poppel, Todd, 75
Wakefield, Tim, 9, 26, 29, 30, 31, 47, 50, 55, 57, 61, 85, 92, 95, 108, 114, 120, 125, 132, 146, 152
Walker, Larry, 125
Wally the Green Monster, 93, 138
Waner, Lloyd, 24
Waner, Paul, 24
Wasdin, John, 26, 28
Wayne, John, 37, 53
Wells, David, 126
Wengert, Don, 28
White, Rondell, 150
White, Sammy, 18, 100
Whitman, Walt, 64
Who, The, 122, 123, 142
Williams, Billy, 133
Williams, Jimy, 26, 30
Williams, Ted, 16, 17, 18, 19, 22, 23, 24, 36, 37, 40, 41, 54, 56, 64, 70, 74, 85, 86, 100, 111, 115, 129, 146
Willoughby, Jim, 35
Wohlers, Mark, 55, 61
Wood, Smoky Joe, 74, 85
Wrigley Field, 43, 48, 62, 99, 100, 129, 133, 134
Wychorski, Christine, 143
Yankee Stadium, 65, 76, 79, 82, 104, 105, 109, 137
Yankees, see "New York Yankees"
"Yankees Suck," 38, 61, 83, 116, 117, 118, 123, 129, 143
Yastrzemski, Carl, 40, 54, 58, 98, 130, 133, 146
Yawkey, Tom and Jean, 22, 40, 43, 111
Yawkey Way, 39, 44, 46, 71, 93, 123
Young, Cy, 16, 24, 114
Young, Irv, 16
Zajc, John, 49, 65
Zauchin, Norm, 99
Zimmer, Don, 30
Zito, Barry, 150
Zocco, Tom, 57

ACKNOWLEDGMENTS

Thanks to the following SABR members for their encouragement in this project. Even though they did not contribute an actual piece, their support and assistance is greatly appreciated:

Seamus Kearney and the entire local convention staff for the Boston convention in June 2002: Roland Bassett, Barbara Flanagan, Jeff Foust, Chris Fry, Lynne Glickman, Mark Kanter, Len Levin, Tom Nahigian, Guy St. Andre, Neal Traven and Paul Wendt. Without Seamus' support and encouragement, this project might never have become a reality. Some other SABRBoston members contributed with suggestions and enthusiasm, including Harvey Soolman, Dan Desrochers, and other chapter members who offered moral support at meetings and in email.

Mat Olkin and Skip McAfee were among the SABR members who offered advice and assistance, and of course we must thank Tom Larwin, Andy Strasberg and Bill Swank and all the others from San Diego who worked on *Facets of the Diamond*.

Many thanks as well to the Boston Red Sox, in particular Dick Bresciani, Steve Conley, Jim Healey, Danny Kischel, Kevin Shea, Rick Subrizio and Marcita Thompson. Their support and aid has made this project much richer.

SOCIETY ⬥FOR⬥ AMERICAN BASEBALL RESEARCH

Since August 1971, when sixteen "statistorians" gathered in Cooperstown to form the Society for American Baseball Research, SABR has been committed to helping people produce and publish baseball research.

Today, SABR has nearly 7,000 members worldwide. They come from all walks of life—the one thing they all have in common? A love for the game and its history.

Members receive the latest editions of SABR's research annuals, *The Baseball Research Journal* and *The National Pastime*. Also included is a subscription to *The SABR Bulletin*, special access to online newsgroups and research forums, and other special publications.

SABR membership is open to all those interested in baseball research. Annual dues are $50 US, $60 Canada and Mexico, and $65 overseas (US funds only). Student and senior discounts are also available. For details about the benefits of SABR membership, call (800) 969-SABR or visit **www.sabr.org** today!

SOCIETY FOR AMERICAN BASEBALL RESEARCH
812 HURON ROAD, CLEVELAND, OH 44115 (800)969-SABR

Pictured publications have been previously issued. For information
about past SABR publications, call (800) 755-1105.